THE MAGIC OF THINKING BIG

DAVID J. SCHWARTZ, PH.D.

A FIRESIDE BOOK
Published by Simon & Schuster
New York London Toronto Sydney

FIRESIDE
Rockefeller Center
1230 Avenue of the Americas
New York, NY 10020

This Fireside Edition 2007

Fireside and colophon are registered trademarks
of Simon & Schuster, Inc.

For information regarding special discounts for bulk purchases,
please contact Simon & Schuster Special Sales at 1-800-456-6798
or business@simonandschuster.com.

Designed by Mary Austin Speaker

Manufactured in the United States of America

80   79   78   77   76

Library of Congress Cataloging-in-Publication Data
  Schwartz, David Joseph.
    The magic of thinking big / David Joseph Schwartz.
        p.   cm.
    "A Fireside book."
    Includes index.
    1. Success. I. Title.
    BF637.S86S36   1987
    158'.1—dc19   87-8516

ISBN-13: 978-0-671-64678-3
ISBN-10:   0-671-64678-8

For David III

Our six-year-old son, David, felt mighty big when he was graduated from kindergarten. I asked him what he plans to be when he finishes growing up. Davey looked at me intently for a moment and then answered, "Dad, I want to be a professor."

"A professor? A professor of what?" I asked.

"Well, Dad," he replied, "I think I want to be a professor of happiness."

"A professor of happiness! That's a pretty wonderful ambition, don't you think?"

To David, then, a fine boy with a grand goal, and to his mother, this book is dedicated.

CONTENTS

PREFACE

Why this big book? Why a full-scale discussion of *The Magic of Thinking Big*? Thousands of books will be published this year. Why one more?

Permit me to give you just a little background.

Several years ago I witnessed an exceptionally impressive sales meeting. The vice president in charge of marketing for this company was tremendously excited. He wanted to drive home a point. He had with him on the platform the leading representative in the organization, a very ordinary-looking fellow, who earned in the year just ended just a little under $60,000. The earnings of other representatives averaged $12,000.

The executive challenged the group. Here is what he said: "I want you to take a good look at Harry. Look at him! Now, what's Harry got that the rest of you haven't? Harry earned five times the average, but is Harry five times smarter? No, not according to our personnel tests. I checked. They show he's about average in that department.

"And did Harry work five times harder than you fellows? No—not according to the reports. In fact, he took more time off than most of you.

"Did Harry have a better territory? Again I've got to say no. The accounts averaged about the same. Did Harry have more education? Better health? Again, no. Harry is about as average as an average guy could be except for one thing.

"The difference between Harry and the rest of you," said the vice president, "the difference is that Harry thought five times bigger."

Then the executive proceeded to show that success is determined not so much by the size of one's brain as it is *by the size of one's thinking.*

This was an intriguing thought. And it stayed with me. The more I observed, the more people I talked with, the deeper I dug into what's really behind success, the clearer was the answer. Case history after case history proved that the size of bank accounts, the size of happiness accounts, and the size of one's general satisfaction account is dependent on *the size of one's thinking.* There *is* magic in thinking big.

"If Thinking Big accomplishes so much, why doesn't everyone think that way?" I've been asked that question many times. Here, I believe, is the answer. All of us, more than we recognize, are products of the thinking around us. And much of this thinking is little, not big. All around you is an environment that is trying to tug you, trying to pull you down Second Class Street. You are told almost daily that there are "too many chiefs and not enough Indians." In other words, that opportunities to lead no longer exist, that there is a surplus of chiefs, so be content to be a little guy.

But this "too many chiefs" idea simply doesn't square with the truth. Leading people in all occupations will tell you, as they've told me, that "the trouble is, there are too many Indians and not nearly enough chiefs."

This pettily petty environment says other things too. It tells you, "Whatever will be will be," that your destiny is outside your control, that "fate" is in complete control. So forget those dreams, forget that finer home, forget that special college for the children, forget the better life. Be resigned. Lie down and wait to die.

And who hasn't heard the statement that "Success isn't worth the price," as if you have to sell your soul, your family life, your conscience, your set of values to reach the top. But, in truth, success doesn't demand a price. Every step forward pays a dividend.

This environment also tells us there's too much competition for the top spots in life. But is there? A personnel selection executive told me that he receives 50 to 250 times as many applicants for jobs that pay $10,000 per year as for jobs that pay $50,000 a year. This is to say that there is at least 50 times as much competition for jobs on Second Class Street as for jobs on First Class Avenue. First Class Avenue, U.S.A., is a short, uncrowded street. There are countless vacancies waiting there for people like you who dare to think big.

The basic principles and concepts supporting *The Magic of Thinking Big* come from the highest-pedigree sources, the very finest and biggest-thinking minds yet to live on planet Earth. Minds like the prophet David, who wrote, "As one thinketh in his heart, so is he"; minds such as Emerson, who said, "Great men are those who see that thoughts rule the world"; minds like Milton, who in *Paradise Lost* wrote, "The mind is its own place and in itself can make a heaven of hell or a hell of heaven." Amazingly perceptive minds like Shakespeare, who observed, "There is nothing either good or bad except that thinking makes it so."

But where does the proof come from? How do we know the master thinkers were right? Fair questions. The proof comes from the lives of the select people around us who, through winning success, achievement, and happiness, prove that thinking big *does* work magic.

The simple steps we have set down here are not untested theories. They are not one man's guesses and opinions. They are proven approaches to life's situations, and they are universally applicable steps that work and work like magic.

That you're reading this page proves you are interested in larger success. You want to fulfill your desires. You want to enjoy a fine standard of living. You want this life to deliver to you all the good things you deserve. Being interested in success is a wonderful quality.

You have another admirable quality. The fact that you're holding this book in your hands shows you have the intelligence to look for tools that will help take you where you want to go. In building anything—automobiles, bridges, missiles—we need tools. Many people, in their attempt to build a successful life, forget there are tools to help them. You have not forgotten. You have, then, the two basic qualities needed to realize real profit from this book: a desire for greater success and the intelligence to select a tool to help you realize that desire.

Think Big and you'll live big. You'll live big in happiness. You'll live big in accomplishment. Big in income. Big in friends. Big in respect.

Enough for the promise.

Start now, right now, to discover how to make your thinking make magic for you. Start out with this thought of the great philosopher Disraeli: "Life is too short to be little."

WHAT THIS BOOK WILL DO FOR YOU

In every chapter of this book you will find dozens of hardheaded, practical ideas, techniques, and principles that will enable you to harness the tremendous power of thinking big, so as to gain for yourself the success, happiness, and satisfaction you want so much. Every technique is dramatically illustrated by a real-life case history. You discover not only what to do, but, what is even more important, you see exactly how to apply each principle to actual situations and problems. Here, then, is what this book will do for you; it will show you how you can . . .

1

BELIEVE YOU CAN SUCCEED AND YOU WILL

SUCCESS MEANS MANY WONDERFUL, positive things. Success means personal prosperity: a fine home, vacations, travel, new things, financial security, giving your children maximum advantages. Success means winning admiration, leadership, being looked up to by people in your business and social life. Success means freedom: freedom from worries, fears, frustrations, and failure. Success means self-respect, continually finding more real happiness and satisfaction from life, being able to do more for those who depend on you.

Success means winning.

Success—achievement—is the goal of life!

Every human being wants success. Everybody wants the best this life can deliver. Nobody enjoys crawling, living in mediocrity. No one likes feeling second-class and feeling forced to go that way.

Some of the most practical success-building wisdom is found in that biblical quotation stating that faith can move mountains.

Believe, really believe, you can move a mountain, and you can. Not many people believe that they can move mountains. So, as a result, not many people do.

On some occasion you've probably heard someone say something like "It's nonsense to think you can make a mountain move away just by saying 'Mountain, move away.' It's simply impossible."

People who think this way have belief confused with wishful thinking. And true enough, you can't *wish* away a mountain. You can't *wish* yourself into an executive suite. Nor can you wish yourself into a five-bedroom, three-bath house or the high-income brackets. You can't wish yourself into a position of leadership.

But you *can* move a mountain with belief. You *can* win success by believing you can succeed.

There is nothing magical or mystical about the power of belief.

Belief works this way. Belief, the "I'm-positive-I-can" attitude, generates the power, skill, and energy needed to do. When you believe I-can-do-it, the *how*-to-do-it develops.

Every day all over the nation young people start working in new jobs. Each of them "wishes" that someday he could enjoy the success that goes with reaching the top. But the majority of these young people simply don't have the belief that it takes to reach the top rungs. And they don't reach the top. Believing it's impossible to climb high, they do not discover the steps that lead to great heights. Their behavior remains that of the "average" person.

But a small number of these young people really believe they will succeed. They approach their work with the "I'm-going-to-the-top" attitude. And with substantial belief they reach the top. Believing they will succeed—and that it's not impossible—these folks study and observe the behavior of senior executives. They learn how successful people approach problems and make decisions. They observe the attitudes of successful people.

The how-to-do-it always comes to the person who believes he can do it.

A young woman I'm acquainted with decided two years ago that she was going to establish a sales agency to sell mobile homes. She was advised by many that she shouldn't—and couldn't—do it.

She had less than $3,000 in savings and was advised that the minimum capital investment required was many times that.

"Look how competitive it is," she was advised. "And besides, what practical experience have you had in selling mobile homes, let alone managing a business?" her advisors asked.

But this young lady had belief in herself and her ability to succeed. She quickly admitted that she lacked capital, that the business was very competitive, and that she lacked experience.

"But," she said, "all the evidence I can gather shows that the mobile home industry is going to expand. On top of that, I've studied my competition. I know I can do a better job of merchandising trailers than anybody else in this town. I expect to make some mistakes, but I'm going to be on top in a hurry."

And she was. She had little trouble getting capital. Her absolutely unquestioned belief that she could succeed with this business won her the confidence of two investors. And armed with complete belief, she did the "impossible"—she got a trailer manufacturer to advance her a limited inventory with no money down.

Last year she sold over $1,000,000 worth of trailers.

"Next year," she says, "I expect to gross over $2,000,000."

Belief, *strong belief,* triggers the mind to figure ways and means and how-to. And believing you can succeed makes others place confidence in you.

Most people do not put much stock in belief. But some, the residents of Successfulville, U.S.A., do! Just a few weeks ago a friend who is an official with a state highway department in a midwestern state related a "mountain-moving" experience to me.

"Last month," my friend began, "our department sent notices to a number of engineering companies that we were authorized to retain some firm to design eight bridges as part of our highway-building program. The bridges were to be built at a cost of $5,000,000. The engineering firm selected would get a 4 percent commission, or $200,000, for its design work.

"I talked with twenty-one engineering firms about this. The four largest decided right away to submit proposals. The other seventeen companies were small, having only three to seven engineers each. The size of the project scared off sixteen of these seventeen. They went over the project, shook their heads, and said, in effect, 'It's too big for us. I wish I thought we could handle it, but it's no use even trying.'

"But one of these small firms, a company with only three engineers, studied the plans and said, 'We can do it. We'll submit a proposal.' They did, and they got the job."

Those who believe they can move mountains, do. Those who believe they can't, cannot. Belief triggers the power to do.

Actually, in these modern times belief is doing much bigger things than moving mountains. The most essential element—in fact, *the* essential element—in our space explorations today is belief that space can be mastered. Without firm, unwavering belief that man *can* travel in space, our scientists would not have the courage, interest, and enthusiasm to proceed. Belief that cancer can be cured will ultimately produce cures for cancer. Currently, there is some talk of building a tunnel under the English Channel to connect England with the Continent. Whether this tunnel is ever built depends on whether responsible people believe it can be built.

Belief in great results is the driving force, the power behind all great books, plays, scientific discoveries. Belief in success is behind every successful business, church, and political organization. Belief in success is the one basic, absolutely essential ingredient of successful people.

Believe, really believe, you can succeed, and you will.

Over the years I've talked with many people who have failed in business ventures and in various careers. I've heard a lot of reasons and excuses for failure. Something especially significant unfolds as conversations with failures develop. In a casual sort of way the failure drops a remark like "To tell the truth, I didn't think it would work" or "I had my misgivings before I even started out" or "Actually, I wasn't too surprised that it didn't work out."

The "Okay-I'll-give-it-a-try-but-I-don't-think-it-will-work" attitude produces failures.

Disbelief is negative power. When the mind disbelieves or doubts, the mind attracts "reasons" to support the disbelief. Doubt, disbelief, the *subconscious will to fail*, the *not really wanting* to succeed, is responsible for most failures.

Think doubt and fail.

Think victory and succeed.

A young fiction writer talked with me recently about her writing ambitions. The name of one of the top writers in her field came up.

"Oh," she said, "Mr. X is a wonderful writer, but of course, I can't be nearly as successful as he is."

Her attitude disappointed me very much because I know the writer mentioned. He is not superintelligent nor super-perceptive, nor super–anything else except superconfident. He believes he is among the best, and so he acts and performs the best.

It is well to respect the leader. Learn from him. Observe him. Study him. But don't worship him. Believe you can surpass. Believe you can go beyond. Those who harbor the second-best attitude are invariably second-best doers.

Look at it this way. Belief is the thermostat that regulates what we accomplish in life. Study the fellow who is shuffling down there in mediocrity. He believes he is worth little, so he receives little. He believes he can't do big things, and he doesn't. He believes he is unimportant, so everything he does has an unimportant mark. As times goes by, lack of belief in himself shows through in the way the fellow talks, walks, acts. Unless he readjusts his thermostat forward, he shrinks, grows smaller and smaller, in his own estimation. And, since others see in us what we see in ourselves, he grows smaller in the estimation of the people around him.

Now look across the way at the person who is advancing forward. He believes he is worth much, and he receives much. He believes he can handle big, difficult assignments—and he does. Everything he does, the way he handles himself with people, his character, his thoughts, his viewpoints, all say, "Here is a professional. He is an important person."

A person is a product of his own thoughts. Believe Big. Adjust your thermostat forward. Launch your success offensive with honest, sincere belief that you can succeed. Believe big and grow big.

Several years ago after addressing a group of businessmen in Detroit, I talked with one of the gentlemen who approached me, introduced himself, and said, "I really enjoyed your talk. Can you spare a few minutes? I'd like very much to discuss a personal experience with you."

In a few minutes we were comfortably seated in a coffee shop, waiting for some refreshments.

"I have a personal experience," he began, "that ties in perfectly with what you said this evening about making your mind work for you instead of letting it work against you. I've never explained to anyone how I lifted myself out of the world of mediocrity, but I'd like to tell you about it."

"And I'd like to hear it," I said.

"Well, just five years ago I was plodding along, just another guy working in the tool-and-die trade. I made a decent living by average standards. But it was far from ideal. Our home was much too small, and there was no money for those many things we wanted. My wife, bless her, didn't complain much, but it was written all over her that she was more resigned to her fate than she was happy. Inside I grew more and more dissatisfied. When I let myself see how I was failing my good wife and two children, I really hurt inside.

"But today things are really different," my friend continued. "Today we have a beautiful new home on a two-acre lot and a year-round cabin a couple hundred miles north of here. There's no more worry about whether we can send the kids to a good college, and my wife no longer has to feel guilty every time she spends money for some new clothes. Next summer the whole family is flying to Europe to spend a month's holiday. We're really living."

"How did this all happen?" I asked.

"It all happened," he continued, "when, to use the phrase you used tonight, 'I harnessed the power of belief.' Five years ago I learned about a job with a tool-and-die company here in Detroit. We were living in Cleveland at the time. I decided to look into it, hoping I could make a little more money. I got here early on Sunday evening, but the interview was not until Monday.

"After dinner I sat down in my hotel room, and for some reason, I got really disgusted with myself. 'Why,' I asked myself, 'am I just a middle-class failure? Why am I trying to get a job that represents such a small step forward?'

"I don't know to this day what prompted me to do it, but I took a sheet of hotel stationery and wrote down the names of five people I've known well for several years who had far surpassed me in earning power and job responsibility. Two were former neighbors who had moved away to fine subdivisions. Two others were fellows I had worked for, and the third was a brother-in-law.

"Next—again I don't know what made me do this—I asked myself, what do my five friends have that I don't have, besides better jobs? I compared myself with them on intelligence, but I honestly couldn't see that they excelled in the brains department. Nor could I truthfully say they had me beat on education, integrity, or personal habits.

"Finally, I got down to another success quality one hears a lot about: initiative. Here I hated to admit it, but I had to. On this point my record showed I was far below that of my successful friends.

"It was now about 3 A.M., but my mind was astonishingly clear. I was seeing my weak point for the first time. I discovered that I had held back. I had always carried a little stick. I dug into myself deeper and deeper and found the reason I lacked initiative was because I didn't believe inside that I was worth very much.

"I sat there the rest of the night just reviewing how lack of faith in myself had dominated me ever since I could remember, how I had used my mind to work against myself. I found I had been preaching to myself why I couldn't get ahead instead of why I could. I had been selling myself short. I found this streak of self-depreciation showed through in everything I did. Then it dawned on me that no one else was going to believe in me until I believed in myself.

"Right then I decided, 'I'm through feeling second-class. From here on in I'm not going to sell myself short.'

"Next morning I still had that confidence. During the job interview I gave my newfound confidence its first test. Before coming for the interview I'd hoped I would have courage to ask for $750 or maybe even $1,000 more than my present job was paying. But now, after realizing I *was* a valuable man, I upped it to $3,500. And I got it. I sold myself because after that one long night of self-analysis I found things in myself that made me a lot more salable.

"Within two years after I took that job I had established a reputation as the fellow who can get business. Then we went into a recession. This made me still more valuable because I was one of the best business-getters in the industry. The company was reorganized and I was given a substantial amount of stock plus a lot more pay."

Believe in yourself, and good things *do* start happening.

*

Your mind is a "thought factory." It's a busy factory, producing countless thoughts in one day.

Production in your thought factory is under the charge of two foremen, one of whom we will call Mr. Triumph and the other Mr. Defeat. Mr. Triumph is in charge of manufacturing positive thoughts. He specializes in producing reasons why you can, why you're qualified, why you will.

The other foreman, Mr. Defeat, produces negative, deprecating thoughts. He is your expert in developing reasons why you can't, why you're weak, why you're inadequate. His specialty is the "why-you-will-fail" chain of thoughts.

Both Mr. Triumph and Mr. Defeat are intensely obedient. They snap to attention immediately. All you need do to signal either foreman is to give the slightest mental beck and call. If the signal is positive, Mr. Triumph will step forward and go to work. Likewise, a negative signal brings Mr. Defeat forward.

To see how these two foremen work for you, try this example. Tell yourself, "Today is a lousy day." This signals Mr. Defeat into action, and he manufactures some facts to prove you are right. He suggests to you that it's too hot or it's too cold, business will be bad today, sales will drop, other people will be on edge, you may get sick, your wife will be in a fussy mood. Mr. Defeat is tremendously efficient. In just a few moments he's got you sold. It *is* a bad day. Before you know it, it is a *heck* of a bad day.

But tell yourself, "Today is a fine day," and Mr. Triumph is signaled forward to act. He tells you, "This *is* a *wonderful* day. The weather is refreshing. It's good to be alive. Today you can catch up on some of your work." And then it is a good day.

In like fashion Mr. Defeat can show you why you can't sell

Mr. Smith; Mr. Triumph will show you that you can. Mr. Defeat will convince you that you will fail, while Mr. Triumph will demonstrate why you will succeed. Mr. Defeat will prepare a brilliant case against Tom, while Mr. Triumph will show you more reasons why you like Tom.

Now, the more work you give either of these two foremen, the stronger he becomes. If Mr. Defeat is given more work to do, he adds personnel and takes up more space in your mind. Eventually, he will take over the entire thought-manufacturing division, and virtually all thought will be of a negative nature.

The only wise thing to do is fire Mr. Defeat. You don't need him. You don't want him around telling you that you can't, you're not up to it, you'll fail, and so on. Mr. Defeat won't help you get where you want to go, so boot him out.

Use Mr. Triumph 100 percent of the time. When any thought enters your mind, ask Mr. Triumph to go to work for you. He'll show you how you can succeed.

Between now and tomorrow at this time another 11,500 new consumers will have made their grand entry into the U.S.A.

Population is growing at a record rate. In the next ten years the increase is conservatively estimated at 35 million. That's equal to the present combined metropolitan population of our five biggest cities: New York, Chicago, Los Angeles, Detroit, and Philadelphia. Imagine!

New industries, new scientific breakthroughs, expanding markets—all spell opportunity. This is good news. This is a most wonderful time to be alive!

All signs point to a record demand for top-level people in every field—people who have superior ability to influence others, to direct their work, to serve them in a leadership capacity.

And the people who will fill these leadership positions are all adults or near adults *right now.* One of them is you.

The guarantee of a boom is not, of course, a guarantee of personal success. Over the long pull, the United States has always been booming. But just a fast glance shows that millions and millions of people—in fact, a majority of them—struggle but don't really succeed. The majority of folks still plug along in mediocrity despite the record opportunity of the last two decades. And in the boom period ahead, most people will continue to worry, to be afraid, to crawl through life feeling unimportant, unappreciated, not able to do what they want to do. As a result, their performance will earn them petty rewards, petty happiness.

Those who convert opportunity into reward (and let me say, I sincerely believe you are one of those, else you'd rely on luck and not bother with this book) will be those wise people who learn how to think themselves to success.

Walk in. The door to success is open wider than ever before. Put yourself on record now that you are going to join that select group that is getting what it wants from life.

Here is the first step toward success. It's a basic step. It can't be avoided. Step One: Believe in yourself, believe you can succeed.

HOW TO DEVELOP THE POWER OF BELIEF

Here are the three guides to acquiring and strengthening the power of belief:

1. Think success, don't think failure. At work, in your home, substitute success thinking for failure thinking. When you face a difficult situation, think, "I'll win," not "I'll probably

lose." When you compete with someone else, think, "I'm equal to the best," not "I'm outclassed." When opportunity appears, think "I can do it," never "I can't." Let the master thought "I will succeed" dominate your thinking process. Thinking success conditions your mind to create plans that produce success. Thinking failure does the exact opposite. Failure thinking conditions the mind to think other thoughts that produce failure.

2. Remind yourself regularly that you are better than you think you are. Successful people are not supermen. Success does not require a superintellect. Nor is there anything mystical about success. And success isn't based on luck. Successful people are just ordinary folks who have developed belief in themselves and what they do. Never—yes, *never*—sell yourself short.

3. Believe Big. The size of your success is determined by the size of your belief. Think little goals and expect little achievements. Think big goals and win big success. Remember this, too! Big ideas and big plans are often easier—certainly no more difficult—than small ideas and small plans.

Mr. Ralph J. Cordiner, chairman of the board of the General Electric Company, said this to a leadership conference: "We need from every man who aspires to leadership—for himself and his company—a determination to undertake a personal program of self-development. Nobody is going to *order* a man to develop. . . . Whether a man lags behind or moves ahead in his specialty is a matter of his own personal application. This is something which takes time, work, and sacrifice. Nobody can do it for you."

Mr. Cordiner's advice is sound and practical. Live it. Persons who reach the top rungs in business management, selling, engineering, religious work, writing, acting, and in every other pursuit get there by following conscientiously and continuously a *plan for self-development and growth.*

Any training program—and that's exactly what this book is—must do three things. It must provide content, the what-to-do. Second, it must supply a method, the how-to-do-it. And third, it must meet the acid test; that is, get results.

The *what* of your personal training program for success is built on the attitudes and techniques of successful people. How do they manage themselves? How do they overcome obstacles? How do they earn the respect of others? What sets them apart from the ordinary? How do they think?

The *how* of your plan for development and growth is a series of concrete guides for action. These are found in each chapter. These guides work. Apply them and see for yourself.

What about the most important part of training: results? Wrapped up briefly, conscientious application of the program presented here will bring you success and on a scale that may now look impossible. Broken down into its components, your personal training program for success will bring you a series of rewards: the reward of deeper respect from your family, the reward of admiration from your friends and associates, the reward of feeling useful, of being someone, of having status, the reward of increased income and a higher standard of living.

Your training is self-administered. There will be no one standing over your shoulder telling you what to do and how to do it. This book will be your guide, but only you can understand yourself. Only *you* can command yourself to apply this training. Only *you* can evaluate your progress. Only *you* can bring about corrective action should you slip a little. In short, you are going to train yourself to achieve bigger and bigger success.

You already have a fully equipped laboratory in which you can work and study. Your laboratory is all around you. Your laboratory consists of human beings. This laboratory supplies you with every possible example of human action. And there is no limit to what you can learn once you see yourself as a scientist in your own lab. What's more, there is nothing to buy. There is no rent to pay. There are no fees of any kind. You can use this laboratory as much as you like for free.

As director of your own laboratory, you will want to do what every scientist does: observe and experiment.

Isn't it surprising to you that most people understand so little about why people act as they do even though they are surrounded by people all their lives? Most people are not trained observers. One important purpose of this book is to help you train yourself to observe, to develop deep insight into human action. You'll want to ask yourself questions like "Why is John so successful and Tom just getting by?" "Why do some people have many friends and other people have only few friends?" "Why will people gladly accept what one person tells them but ignore another person who tells them the same thing?"

Once trained, you will learn valuable lessons just through the very simple process of observing.

Here are two special suggestions to help you make yourself a trained observer. Select for special study the most successful and the most unsuccessful person you know. Then, as the book unfolds, observe how closely your successful friend adheres to the success principles. Notice also how studying the two extremes will help you see the unmistakable wisdom of following the truths outlined in this book.

Each contact you make with another person gives you a chance to see success development principles at work. Your objective is to make successful action habitual. The more we practice, the sooner it becomes second nature to act in the desired way.

Most of us have friends who grow things for a hobby. And we've all heard them say something like "It's exciting to watch those plants grow. Just look how they respond to plant food and water. See how much bigger they are today than they were last week."

To be sure, it is thrilling to watch what can happen when men cooperate carefully with nature. But it is not one-tenth as fascinating as watching yourself respond to your own carefully administered thought management program. It's fun to feel yourself growing more confident, more effective, more successful day by day, month by month. Nothing—absolutely nothing—in this life gives you more satisfaction than knowing you're on the road to success and achievement. And nothing stands as a bigger challenge than making the most of yourself.

2

CURE YOURSELF OF EXCUSITIS, THE FAILURE DISEASE

PEOPLE—AS YOU THINK YOURSELF to success, that's what you will study, people. You will study people very carefully to discover, then apply, success-rewarding principles to your life. And you want to begin right away.

Go deep into your study of people, and you'll discover unsuccessful people suffer a mind-deadening thought disease. We call this disease *excusitis*. Every failure has this disease in its advanced form. And most "average" persons have at least a mild case of it.

You will discover that excusitis explains the difference between the person who is going places and the fellow who is barely holding his own. You will find that the more successful the individual, the less inclined he is to make excuses.

But the fellow who has gone nowhere and has no plans for getting anywhere always has a bookful of reasons to explain why. Persons with mediocre accomplishments are quick to explain why they haven't, why they don't, why they can't, and why they aren't.

Study the lives of successful people and you'll discover this: all the excuses made by the mediocre fellow could be *but aren't* made by the successful person.

I have never met nor heard of a highly successful business executive, military officer, salesman, professional person, or leader in any field who could not have found one or more major excuses to hide behind. Roosevelt could have hidden behind his lifeless legs; Truman could have used "no college education"; Kennedy could have said, "I'm too young to be president"; Johnson and Eisenhower could have ducked behind heart attacks.

Like any disease, excusitis gets worse if it isn't treated properly. A victim of this thought disease goes through this mental process: "I'm not doing as well as I should. What can I use as an alibi that will help me save face? Let's see: poor health? lack of education? too old? too young? bad luck? personal misfortune? wife? the way my family brought me up?"

Once the victim of this failure disease has selected a "good" excuse, he sticks with it. Then he relies on the excuse to explain to himself and others why he is not going forward.

And each time the victim makes the excuse, the excuse becomes imbedded deeper within his subconsciousness. Thoughts, positive or negative, grow stronger when fertilized with constant repetition. At first the victim of excusitis knows his alibi is more or less a lie. But the more frequently he repeats it, the more convinced he becomes that it is completely true, that the alibi is the real reason for his not being the success he should be.

Procedure One, then, in your individual program of thinking yourself to success, must be to *vaccinate yourself against excusitis, the disease of the failures.*

THE FOUR MOST COMMON FORMS OF EXCUSITIS

Excusitis appears in a wide variety of forms, but the worst types of this disease are health excusitis, intelligence excusitis, age excusitis, and luck excusitis. Now let's see just how we can protect ourselves from these four common ailments.

1. "But My Health Isn't Good."

Health excusitis ranges all the way from the chronic "I don't feel good" to the more specific "I've got such-and-such wrong with me."

"Bad" health, in a thousand different forms, is used as an excuse for failing to do what a person wants to do, failing to accept greater responsibilities, failing to make more money, failing to achieve success.

Millions and millions of people suffer from health excusitis. But is it, in most cases, a legitimate excuse? Think for a moment of all the highly successful people you know who could—but who don't—use health as an excuse.

My physician and surgeon friends tell me the perfect specimen of adult life is nonexistent. There is something physically wrong with everybody. Many surrender in whole or in part to health excusitis, but success-thinking people do not.

Two experiences happened to me in one afternoon that illustrate the correct and incorrect attitudes toward health. I had just finished a talk in Cleveland. Afterwards, one fellow, about thirty, asked to speak to me privately for a few minutes. He complimented me on the meeting but then said, "I'm afraid your ideas can't do me much good."

"You see," he continued, "I've got a bad heart, and I've got to hold myself in check." He went on to explain that he'd seen four doctors but they couldn't find his trouble. He asked me what I would suggest he do.

"Well," I said, "I know nothing about the heart, but as one

layman to another, here are three things I'd do. First, I'd visit the finest heart specialist I could find and accept his diagnosis as final. You've already checked with four doctors, and none of them has found anything peculiar with your heart. Let the fifth doctor be your final check. It may very well be you've got a perfectly sound heart. But if you keep on worrying about it, eventually you may have a very serious heart ailment. Looking and looking and looking for an illness often actually produces illness.

"The second thing I'd recommend is that you read Dr. Schindler's great book, *How to Live 365 Days a Year.* Dr. Schindler shows in this book that three out of every four hospital beds are occupied by people who have EII—Emotionally Induced Illness. Imagine, three out of four people who are sick right now would be well if they had learned how to handle their emotions. Read Dr. Schindler's book and develop your program for 'emotions management.'

"Third, I'd resolve to live until I die." I went on to explain to this troubled fellow some sound advice I received many years ago from a lawyer friend who had an arrested case of tuberculosis. This friend knew he would have to live a regulated life but this hasn't stopped him from practicing law, rearing a fine family, and really enjoying life. My friend, who now is seventy-eight years old, expresses his philosophy in these words: "I'm going to live until I die and I'm not going to get life and death confused. While I'm on this earth I'm going to *live.* Why be only half alive? Every minute a person spends worrying about dying is just one minute that fellow might as well have been dead."

I had to leave at that point, because I had to be on a certain plane for Detroit. On the plane the second but much more pleasant experience occurred. After the noise of the takeoff, I heard a ticking sound. Rather startled, I glanced at the fellow sitting beside me, for the sound seemed to be coming from him.

He smiled a big smile and said, "Oh, it's not a bomb. It's just my heart."

I was obviously surprised, so he proceeded to tell me what had happened.

Just twenty-one days before, he had undergone an operation that involved putting a plastic valve into his heart. The ticking sound, he explained, would continue for several months, until new tissue had grown over the artificial valve. I asked him what he was going to do.

"Oh," he said, "I've got big plans. I'm going to study law when I get back to Minnesota. Someday I hope to be in government work. The doctors tell me I must take it easy for a few months, but after that I'll be like new."

There you have two ways of meeting health problems. The first fellow, not even sure he had anything organically wrong with him, was worried, depressed, on the road to defeat, wanting somebody to second his motion that he couldn't go forward. The second individual, after undergoing one of the most difficult of operations, was optimistic, eager to do something. The difference lay in how they thought toward health!

I've had some very direct experience with health excusitis. I'm a diabetic. Right after I discovered I had this ailment (about 5,000 hypodermics ago), I was warned, "Diabetes *is* a physical condition; but the biggest damage results from having a negative attitude toward it. Worry about it, and you may have real trouble."

Naturally, since the discovery of my own diabetes, I've gotten to know a great many other diabetics. Let me tell you about two extremes. One fellow who has a very mild case belongs to that fraternity of the living dead. Obsessed with a fear of the weather, he is usually ridiculously bundled up. He's afraid of infection, so he shuns anybody who has the slightest sniffle. He's afraid of overexertion, so he does almost nothing. He spends most of his mental energy worrying about what *might* happen. He bores other people telling them "how awful" his problem really is. His real ailment is not diabetes. Rather, he's a victim of health excusitis. He has pitied himself into being an invalid.

The other extreme is a division manager for a large publishing company. He has a severe case; he takes about thirty times as much insulin as the fellow mentioned above. But he is not living to be sick. He is living to enjoy his work and have fun. One day he said to me, "Sure it is an inconvenience, but so is shaving. But I'm *not* going to think myself to bed. When I take those shots, I just praise the guys who discovered insulin."

A good friend of mine, a widely known college educator, came home from Europe in 1945 minus one arm. Despite his handicap, John is always smiling, always helping others. He's about as optimistic as anyone I know. One day he and I had a long talk about his handicap.

"It's just an arm," he said, "Sure, two *are* better than one. But they just cut off my arm. My spirit is one hundred percent intact. I'm really grateful for that."

Another amputee friend is an excellent golfer. One day I asked him how he had been able to develop such a near-perfect style with just one arm. I mentioned that most golfers with two arms can't do nearly as well. His reply says a lot. "Well, it's my experience," he said, "that the right attitude and one arm will beat the wrong attitude and two arms every time." *The right attitude and one arm will beat the wrong attitude and two arms every time.* Think about that for a while. It holds true not only on the golf course but in every facet of life.

Four Things You Can Do to Lick Health Excusitis

The best vaccine against health excusitis consists of these four doses:

1. Refuse to talk about your health. The more you talk about an ailment, even the common cold, the worse it seems to get. Talking about bad health is like putting fertilizer on weeds. Besides, talking about your health is a bad habit. It bores people. It makes one appear self-centered and old-maidish. Success-minded people defeat the natural tendency to talk about their "bad" health. One may (and let me emphasize the word *may*) get a little sympathy, but one doesn't get respect and loyalty by being a chronic complainer.

2. Refuse to worry about your health. Dr. Walter Alvarez, emeritus consultant to the world-famous Mayo Clinic, wrote recently, "I always beg worriers to exercise some self-control. For instance, when I saw this man (a fellow who was convinced he had a diseased gallbladder although eight separate X-ray examinations showed that the organ was perfectly normal), I begged him to quit getting his gallbladder X-rayed. I have begged hundreds of heart-conscious men to quit getting electrocardiograms made."

3. Be genuinely grateful that your health is as good as it is. There's an old saying worth repeating often: "I felt sorry for myself because I had ragged shoes until I met a man who had no feet." Instead of complaining about "not feeling good," it's far better to be glad you are as healthy as you are. Just being grateful for the health you have is powerful vaccination against developing new aches and pains and real illness.

4. Remind yourself often, "It's better to wear out than rust out." Life is yours to enjoy. Don't waste it. Don't pass up living by thinking yourself into a hospital bed.

2. "But You've Got to Have Brains to Succeed."

Intelligence excusitis, or "I lack brains," is common. In fact, it's so common that perhaps as many as 95 percent of the people around us have it in varying degrees. Unlike most other types of excusitis, people suffering from this particular type of the malady suffer in silence. Not many people will admit openly that they think they lack adequate intelligence. Rather, they feel it deep down inside.

Most of us make two basic errors with respect to intelligence:

1. We underestimate our own brainpower.

2. We overestimate the other fellow's brainpower.

Because of these errors many people sell themselves short. They fail to tackle challenging situations because it "takes a brain." But along comes the fellow who isn't concerned about intelligence, and he gets the job.

What really matters is not how much intelligence you have but how you use what you do have. The thinking that guides your intelligence is much more important than the quantity of your brainpower. Let me repeat, for this is vitally important: *the thinking that guides your intelligence is much more important than how much intelligence you may have.*

In answering the question, "Should your child be a scientist?" Dr. Edward Teller, one of the nation's foremost physicists, said, "A child does not need a lightning-fast mind to be a scientist, nor does he need a miraculous memory, nor is it necessary that he get very high grades in school. The only point that counts is that the child have a high degree of interest in science."

Interest, enthusiasm, is the critical factor even in science!

With a positive, optimistic, and cooperative attitude a person with an IQ of 100 will earn more money, win more respect, and achieve more success than a negative, pessimistic, uncooperative individual with an IQ of 120.

Just enough sense to stick with something—a chore, task, project—until it's completed pays off much better than *idle* intelligence, even if idle intelligence be of genius caliber.

For *stickability* is 95 percent of *ability*.

At a homecoming celebration last year I met a college friend whom I had not seen for ten years. Chuck was a very bright student and was graduated with honors. His goal when I last saw him was to own his own business in western Nebraska.

I asked Chuck what kind of business he finally established.

"Well," he confessed, "I didn't go into business for myself. I wouldn't have said this to anyone five years ago or even one year ago, but now I'm ready to talk about it.

"As I look back at my college education now, I see that I became an expert in why a business idea won't work out. I learned every conceivable pitfall, every reason why a small business *will* fail: 'You've got to have ample capital;' 'Be sure the business cycle is right;' 'Is there a big demand for what you will offer?' 'Is local industry stabilized?'—a thousand and one things to check out.

"The thing that hurts most is that several of my old high school friends who never seemed to have much on the ball and didn't even go to college now are very well established in their own businesses. But me, I'm just plodding along, auditing freight shipments. Had I been drilled a little more in why a small business *can* succeed, I'd be better off in every way today."

The *thinking* that guided Chuck's intelligence was a lot more important than the *amount* of Chuck's intelligence.

Why some brilliant people are failures. I've been close for many years to a person who qualifies as a genius, has high abstract intelligence, and is Phi Beta Kappa. Despite this very high native intelligence, he is one of the most unsuccessful people I know. He has a very mediocre job (he's afraid of responsibility). He has never married (lots of marriages end in divorce). He has few friends (people bore him). He's never invested in property of any kind (he might lose his money). This man uses his great brainpower to prove why things won't work rather than directing his mental power to searching for ways to succeed.

Because of the negative thinking that guides his great reservoir of brains, this fellow contributes little and creates nothing. With a changed attitude, he could do great things indeed. He has the brains to be a tremendous success, but not the thought power.

CURE YOURSELF OF EXCUSITIS, THE FAILURE DISEASE 35

Another person I know well was inducted into the Army shortly after earning the Ph.D. degree from a leading New York university. How did he spend his three years in the Army? Not as an officer. Not as a staff specialist. Instead, for three years he drove a truck. Why? Because he was filled with negative attitudes toward fellow soldiers ("I'm superior to them"), toward army methods and procedures ("They are stupid"), toward discipline ("It's for others, not me"), toward everything, including himself ("I'm a fool for not figuring out a way to escape this rap").

This fellow earned no respect from anyone. All his vast store of knowledge lay buried. His negative attitudes turned him into a flunky.

Remember, the thinking that guides your intelligence is much more important than how much intelligence you have. Not even a Ph.D. degree can override this basic success principle!

Several years ago I became a close friend of Phil F., one of the senior officers of a major advertising agency. Phil was director of marketing research for the agency, and he was doing a bang-up job.

Was Phil a "brain"? Far from it. Phil knew next to nothing about research technique. He knew next to nothing about statistics. He was not a college graduate (though all the people working for him were). And Phil did not *pretend* to know the technical side of research. What, then, enabled Phil to command $30,000 a year while not one of his subordinates earned $10,000?

This: Phil was a "human" engineer. Phil was 100 percent positive. Phil could inspire others when they felt low. Phil was enthusiastic. He generated enthusiasm; Phil understood people, and, because he could really see what made them tick, he liked them.

Not Phil's brains, but how he managed those brains, made him three times more valuable to his company than men who rated higher on the IQ scale.

Out of every 100 persons who enroll in college, fewer than 50 will graduate. I was curious about this so I asked a director of admissions at a large university for his explanation.

"It's not insufficient intelligence," he said. "We don't admit them if they don't have sufficient ability. And it's not money. Anyone who wants to support himself in college today can do so. The real reason is attitudes. You would be surprised," he said, "how many young people leave because they don't like their professors, the subjects they must take, and their fellow students."

The same reason, negative thinking, explains why the door to top-flight executive positions is closed to many young junior executives. Sour, negative, pessimistic, depreciating attitudes rather than insufficient intelligence hold back thousands of young executives. As one executive told me, "It's a rare case when we pass up a young fellow because he lacks brains. Nearly always it's attitude."

Once I was retained by an insurance company to learn why the top 25 percent of the agents were selling over 75 percent of the insurance while the bottom 25 percent of the agents sold only 5 percent of total volume.

Thousands of personnel files were carefully checked. The search proved beyond any question that no significant difference existed in native intelligence. What's more, differences in education did not explain the difference in selling success. The difference in the very successful and the very unsuccessful finally reduced to differences in *attitudes,* or difference in thought management. The top group worried less, was more enthusiastic, had a sincere liking for people.

We can't do much to change the amount of native ability, but we can certainly change the way we use what we have.

Knowledge is power—when you use it constructively. Closely allied to intelligence excusitis is some incorrect thinking about knowledge. We often hear that knowledge is power. But this statement is only a half-truth. Knowledge is only potential power. Knowledge is power only when put to use—and then only when the use made of it is constructive.

The story is told that the great scientist Einstein was once asked how many feet are in a mile. Einstein's reply was "I don't know. Why should I fill my brain with facts I can find in two minutes in any standard reference book?"

Einstein taught us a big lesson. He felt it was more important to use your mind *to think* than to use it as a warehouse for facts.

One time Henry Ford was involved in a libel suit with the *Chicago Tribune.* The *Tribune* had called Ford an ignoramus, and Ford said, in effect, "Prove it."

The *Tribune* asked him scores of simple questions such as "Who was Benedict Arnold?" "When was the Revolutionary War fought?" and others, most of which Ford, who had little formal education, could not answer.

Finally he became quite exasperated and said, "I don't know the answers to those questions, but I could find a man in five minutes who does."

Henry Ford was never interested in miscellaneous information. He knew what every major executive knows: that the ability to know how to get information is more important than using the mind as a garage for facts.

How much is a fact man worth? I spent a very interesting evening recently with a friend who is the president of a young but rapidly growing manufacturing concern. The TV set happened to be turned to one of the most popular quiz programs. The fellow being quizzed had been on the show for several weeks. He could answer questions on all sorts of subjects, many of which seemed nonsensical.

After the fellow answered a particularly odd question, something about a mountain in Argentina, my host looked at me and said, "How much do you think I'd pay that guy to work for me?"

"How much?" I asked.

"Not a cent over $300—not per week, not per month, but for life. I've sized him up. That 'expert' can't think. He can only memorize. He's just a human encyclopedia, and I figure for $300 I can buy a pretty good set of encyclopedias. In fact, maybe that's too much. Ninety percent of what that guy knows I can find in a $2 almanac.

"What I want around me," he continued, "are people who can solve problems, who can think up ideas. People who can dream and then develop the dream into a practical application; an idea man can make money with me; a fact man can't."

Three Ways to Cure Intelligence Excusitis

Three easy ways to cure intelligence excusitis are:

1. Never underestimate your own intelligence, and never overestimate the intelligence of others. Don't sell yourself

short. Concentrate on your assets. Discover your superior talents. Remember, it's not how many brains you've got that matters. Rather, it's how you use your brains that counts. Manage your brains instead of worrying about how much IQ you've got.

2. Remind yourself several times daily, "My attitudes are more important than my intelligence." At work and at home practice positive attitudes. See the reasons why you can do it, not the reasons why you can't. Develop an "I'm winning" attitude. Put your intelligence to creative positive use. Use it to find ways to win, not to prove you will lose.

3. Remember that the ability to *think* is of much greater value than the ability to memorize facts. Use your mind to create and develop ideas, to find new and better ways to do things. Ask yourself, "Am I using my mental ability to make history, or am I using it merely to record history made by others?"

3. "It's No Use. I'm Too Old (or Too Young)."

Age excusitis, the failure disease of never being the right age, comes in two easily identifiable forms: the "I'm too old" variety and the "I'm too young" brand.

You've heard hundreds of people of all ages explain their mediocre performance in life something like this: "I'm too old (or too young) to break in now. I can't do what I want to do or am capable of doing because of my age handicap."

Really, it's surprising how few people feel they are "just right" age-wise. And it's unfortunate. This excuse has closed the door of real opportunity to thousands of individuals. They think their age is wrong, so they don't even bother to try.

The "I'm too old" variety is the most common form of age excusitis. This disease is spread in subtle ways. TV fiction is produced about the big executive who lost his job because of a merger and can't find another because he's too old. Mr. Executive looks for months to find another job, but he can't, and in the end, after contemplating suicide for a while, he decides to rationalize that it's nice to be on the shelf.

Plays and magazine articles on the topic "Why You Are Washed Up at 40" are popular, not because they represent true facts, but because they appeal to many worried minds looking for an excuse.

How to Handle Age Excusitis

Age excusitis can be cured. A few years ago, while I was conducting a sales training program, I discovered a good serum that both cures this disease and vaccinates you so you won't get it in the first place.

In that training program there was a trainee named Cecil. Cecil, who was forty, wanted to shift over to set himself up as a manufacturer's representative, but he thought he was too old. "After all," he explained, "I'd have to start from scratch. And I'm too old for that now. I'm forty."

I talked with Cecil several times about his "old age" problem. I used the old medicine, "You're only as old as you feel," but I found I was getting nowhere. (Too often people retort with "But I *do* feel old!")

Finally, I discovered a method that worked. One day after

a training session, I tried it on Cecil. I said, "Cecil, when does a man's productive life begin?"

He thought a couple of seconds and answered, "Oh, when he's about twenty, I guess."

"Okay," I said, "now, when does a man's productive life end?"

Cecil answered, "Well, if he stays in good shape and likes his work, I guess a man is still pretty useful when he's seventy or so."

"All right," I said, "a lot of folks are highly productive after they reach seventy, but let's agree with what you've just said, a man's productive years stretch from twenty to seventy. That's fifty years in between, or half a century. Cecil," I said, "you're forty. How many years of productive life have you spent?"

"Twenty," he answered.

"And how many have you left?"

"Thirty," he replied.

"In other words, Cecil, you haven't even reached the half-way point; you've used up only forty percent of your productive years."

I looked at Cecil and realized he'd gotten the point. He was cured of age excusitis. Cecil saw he still had many opportunity-filled years left. He switched from thinking "I'm already old" to "I'm still young." Cecil now realized that how old we are is not important. It's one's attitude toward age that makes it a blessing or a barricade.

Curing yourself of age excusitis often opens doors to opportunities that you thought were locked tight. A relative of mine spent years doing many different things—selling, operating his own business, working in a bank—but he never quite found what he really wanted to do most. Finally, he concluded that the one thing he wanted more than anything else was to be a minister. But when he thought about it, he found he was too old. After all, he was forty-five, had three young children and little money.

But fortunately he mustered all of his strength and told himself, "Forty-five or not, I'm going to be a minister."

With tons of faith but little else, he enrolled in a five-year ministerial training program in Wisconsin. Five years later he was ordained as a minister and settled down with a fine congregation in Illinois.

Old? Of course not. He still has twenty years of productive life ahead of him. I talked with this man not long ago, and he said to me, "You know, if I had not made that great decision when I was forty-five, I would have spent the rest of my life growing old and bitter. Now I feel every bit as young as I did twenty-five years ago."

And he almost looked it, too. When you lick age excusitis, the natural result is to gain the optimism of youth and feel of youth. When you beat down your fears of age limitations, you add years to your life as well as success.

A former university colleague of mine provides an interesting angle on how age excusitis was defeated. Bill was graduated from Harvard in the 1920s. After twenty-four years in the stockbrokerage business, during which time he made a modest fortune, Bill decided he wanted to become a college professor. Bill's friends warned him that he would overtax himself in the rugged learning program ahead. But Bill was determined to reach his goal and enrolled in the University of Illinois—at the age of fifty-one. At fifty-five he had earned his degree. Today Bill is chairman of the Department of Economics at a fine liberal arts college. He's happy, too. He smiles when he says, "I've got almost a third of my good years left."

Old age is a failure disease. Defeat it by refusing to let it hold you back.

When is a person too young? The "I'm too young" variety of age excusitis does much damage, too. About a year ago, a twenty-three-year-old fellow named Jerry came to me with a problem. Jerry was a fine young man. He had been a paratrooper in the service and then had gone to college. While going to college, Jerry supported his wife and son by selling for a large transfer-and-storage company. He had done a terrific job, both in college and for his company.

But today Jerry was worried. "Dr. Schwartz," he said, "I've got a problem. My company has offered me the job of sales manager. This would make me supervisor over eight salesmen."

"Congratulations, that's wonderful news!" I said. "But you seem worried."

"Well," he continued, "all eight men I'm to supervise are from seven to twenty-one years older than I. What do you think I should do? Can I handle it?"

"Jerry," I said, "the general manager of your company obviously thinks you're old enough or he wouldn't have offered you this job. Just remember these three points and everything will work out just fine: first, don't be age conscious. Back on the farm a boy became a man when he proved he could do the work of a man. His number of birthdays had nothing to do with it. And this applies to you. When you prove you are able to handle the job of sales manager, you're automatically old enough.

"Second, don't take advantage of your new 'gold bars.' Show respect for the salesmen. Ask them for their suggestions. Make them feel they are working for a team captain, not a dictator. Do this and the men will work with you, not against you.

"Third, get used to having older persons working for you. Leaders in all fields soon find they are younger than many of the people they supervise. So get used to having older men work for you. It will help you a lot in the coming years, when even bigger opportunities develop.

"And remember, Jerry, your age won't be a handicap unless you make it one."

Today Jerry's doing fine. He loves the transportation business, and now he's planning to organize his own company in a few years.

Youth is a liability only when the youth thinks it is. You often hear that certain jobs require "considerable" physical maturity, jobs like selling securities and insurance. That you've got to have either gray hair or no hair at all in order to gain an investor's confidence is plain nonsense. What really matters is how well you know your job. If you know your job and understand people, you're sufficiently mature to handle it. Age has no real relation to ability, unless you convince yourself that years alone will give you the stuff you need to make your mark.

Many young people feel that they are being held back because of their youth. Now, it is true that another person in an organization who is insecure and job-scared may try to block your way forward, using age or some other reason.

But the people who really count in the company will not.

They will give you as much responsibility as they feel you can handle well. Demonstrate that you have ability and positive attitudes and your youthfulness will be considered an advantage.

In quick recap, the cure for age excusitis is:

1. Look at your present age positively. Think, "I'm still young," not "I'm already old." Practice looking forward to new horizons and gain the enthusiasm and the feel of youth.

2. Compute how much productive time you have left. Remember, a person age thirty still has 80 percent of his productive life ahead of him. And the fifty-year-old still has a big 40 percent—the best 40 percent—of his opportunity years left. Life is actually longer than most people think!

3. Invest future time in doing what you really want to do. It's too late only when you let your mind go negative and think it's too late. Stop thinking "I should have started years ago." That's failure thinking. Instead think, "I'm going to start now, my best years are ahead of me." That's the way successful people think.

4. "But My Case Is Different; I Attract Bad Luck."

Recently, I heard a traffic engineer discuss highway safety. He pointed out that upward of 40,000 persons are killed each year in so-called traffic accidents. The main point of his talk was that there is no such thing as a true accident. What we call an accident is the result of human or mechanical failure, or a combination of both.

What this traffic expert was saying substantiates what wise men throughout the ages have said: *there is a cause for everything*. Nothing happens without a cause. There is nothing accidental about the weather outside today. It is the result of specific causes.

And there is no reason to believe that human affairs are an exception.

Yet hardly a day passes that you do not hear someone blame his problems on "bad" luck. And it's a rare day that you do not hear someone attribute *another* person's success to "good" luck.

Let me illustrate how people succumb to luck excusitis. I lunched recently with three young junior executives. The topic of conversation that day was George C., who just yesterday had been picked from among their group for a major promotion.

Why did George get the position? These three fellows dug up all sorts of reasons: luck, pull, bootlicking, George's wife and how she flattered the boss, everything but the truth. The facts were that George was simply better qualified. He had been doing a better job. He was working harder. He had a more effective personality.

I also knew that the senior officers in the company had spent much time considering which one of the four would be promoted. My three disillusioned friends should have realized that top executives don't select major executives by drawing names from a hat.

I was talking about the seriousness of luck excusitis not long ago with a sales executive of a machine tool–manufacturing company. He became excited about the problem and began to talk about his own experience with it.

"I've never heard it called that before," he said, "but it is one of the most difficult problems every sales executive has to wrestle with. Just yesterday a perfect example of what you're talking about happened in my company.

"One of the salesmen walked in about four o'clock with a $112,000 order for machine tools. Another salesman, whose volume is so low he's a problem, was in the office at the time. Hearing John tell the good news, he rather enviously congratulated him and then said, 'Well, John, you're lucky again!'

"Now, what the weak salesman won't accept is that luck had nothing to do with John's big order. John had been working on that customer for months. He had talked repeatedly to a half-dozen people out there. John had stayed up nights figuring out exactly what was best for them. Then he got our engineers to make preliminary designs of the equipment. John wasn't lucky, unless you can call carefully planned work and patiently executed plans *luck*."

Suppose luck were used to reorganize General Motors. If luck determined who does what and who goes where, every business in the nation would fall apart. Assume for a moment that General Motors were to be completely reorganized on the basis of luck. To carry out the reorganization, the names of all employees would be placed in a barrel. The first name drawn would be president; the second name, the executive vice president, and so on down the line.

Sounds stupid, doesn't it? Well, that's how luck would work.

People who rise to the top in any occupation—business management, selling, law, engineering, acting, or what have you—get there because they have superior attitudes and use their good sense in applied hard work.

Conquer Luck Excusitis in Two Ways
1. Accept the law of cause and effect. Take a second look at what appears to be someone's "good luck." You'll find that

not luck but preparation, planning, and success-producing thinking preceded his good fortune. Take a second look at what appears to be someone's "bad luck." Look, and you'll discover certain specific reasons. Mr. Success receives a setback; he learns and profits. But when Mr. Mediocre loses, he fails to learn.

2. Don't be a wishful thinker. Don't waste your mental muscles dreaming of an effortless way to win success. We don't become successful simply through luck. Success comes from doing those things and mastering those principles that produce success. Don't count on luck for promotions, victories, the good things in life. Luck simply isn't designed to deliver these good things. Instead, just concentrate on developing those qualities in yourself that will make you a winner.

3

BUILD CONFIDENCE AND DESTROY FEAR

FRIENDS MEAN WELL WHEN they say, "It's only your imagination. Don't worry. There's nothing to be afraid of."

But you and I know this kind of fear medicine never really works. Such soothing remarks may give us fear relief for a few minutes or maybe even a few hours. But the "it's-only-in-your-imagination" treatment doesn't really build confidence and cure fear.

Yes, fear is real. And we must recognize it exists before we can conquer it.

Most fear today is psychological. Worry, tension, embarrassment, panic all stem from mismanaged, negative imagination. But simply knowing the breeding ground of fear doesn't cure fear. If a physician discovers you have an infection in some part of your body, he doesn't stop there. He proceeds with treatment to cure the infection.

The old "it's-only-in-your-mind" treatment presumes fear doesn't really exist. But it *does*. Fear is *real*. Fear is success enemy number one. Fear stops people from capitalizing on opportunity; fear wears down physical vitality; fear actually makes people sick, causes organic difficulties, shortens life; fear closes your mouth when you want to speak.

Fear—uncertainty, lack of confidence—explains why we still have economic recessions. Fear explains why millions of people accomplish little and enjoy little.

Truly, fear is a powerful force. In one way or another fear prevents people from getting what they want from life.

Fear of all kinds and sizes is a form of psychological infection. We can cure a mental infection the same way we cure a body infection—with specific, proved treatments.

First, though, as part of your pretreatment preparation, condition yourself with this fact: all confidence is acquired, developed. No one is born with confidence. Those people you know who radiate confidence, who have conquered worry, who are at ease everywhere and all the time, acquired their confidence, every bit of it.

You can, too. This chapter shows how.

During World War II the Navy made sure that all of its new recruits either knew how to swim or learned how—the idea being, of course, that the ability to swim might someday save the sailor's life at sea.

Nonswimming recruits were put into swimming classes. I watched a number of these training experiences. In a superficial sort of way, it was amusing to see young, healthy men terrified by a few feet of water. One of the exercises I recall required the new sailor to jump—not dive—from a board six feet in the air into eight or more feet of water while a half-dozen expert swimmers stood by.

In a deeper sense, it was a sad sight. The fear those young

men displayed was *real*. Yet all that stood between them and the defeat of that fear was one drop into the water below. On more than one occasion I saw young men "accidentally" pushed off the board. The result: fear defeated.

This incident, familiar to thousands of former Navy men, illustrates just one point: action cures fear. Indecision, postponement, on the other hand, fertilize fear.

Jot that down in your success rule book right now. *Action cures fear.*

Action *does* cure fear. Several months ago a very troubled executive in his early forties came to see me. He had a responsible job as a buyer for a large retailing organization.

Worriedly, he explained, "I'm afraid of losing my job. I've got that feeling that my days are numbered."

"Why?" I asked.

"Well, the pattern is against me. Sales figures in my department are off seven percent from a year ago. This is pretty bad, especially since the store's total sales are up six percent. I've made a couple of unwise decisions recently, and I've been singled out several times by the merchandise manager for not keeping pace with the company's progress.

"I've never felt quite like this before," he continued. "I've lost my grip, and it shows. My assistant buyer senses it. The salespeople see it, too. Other executives, of course, are aware that I'm slipping. One buyer even suggested at a meeting of all head buyers the other day that part of my line should be put in his department, where, he said, 'It could make money for the store.' It's like drowning and having a crowd of spectators just standing there waiting for me to sink away."

The executive talked on, elaborating further on his predicament. Finally I cut in and asked, "What are you doing about it? What are you trying to do to correct the situation?"

"Well," he answered, "there isn't much I can do, I guess, but hope for the best."

To this comment I asked, "Honestly, now, is hope enough?" Pausing, but not giving him a chance to answer, I put another question to him: "Why not take action to support your hope?"

"Go on," he said.

"Well, there are two kinds of action that seem to fit your case. First, start this afternoon to move those sales figures upward. We've got to face it. There's a reason your sales are slipping. Find it. Maybe you need a special sale to clear out your slow-moving merchandise, so you'll be in a position to buy some fresh stock. Perhaps you can rearrange your display counters. Maybe your salespeople need more enthusiasm. I can't pinpoint what will turn your sales volume upward, but something will. And it would probably be wise to talk privately with your merchandise manager. He may be on the verge of putting you out, but when you talk it over with him and ask his advice, he'll certainly give you more time to work things out. It's too expensive for the store to replace you as long as top management feels there's a chance you'll find a solution."

I went on, "Then get your assistant buyers on the ball. Quit acting like a drowning man. Let people around you know that you're still alive."

Courage was again in his eyes. Then he asked, "You said there are two kinds of action I should take. What's the second?"

"The second type of action, which you might say is an insurance policy, is to let two or three of your closest business friends in the trade know you might consider an offer from another store, assuming, of course, it is substantially better than your present job.

"I don't believe your job will be insecure after you take some affirmative action to get those sales figures on the rise. But just in case, it's good to have an offer or two. Remember, it's ten times easier for a man with a job to get another job than it is for someone unemployed to connect."

Two days ago this once-troubled executive called me.

"After our talk I buckled down. I made a number of changes, but the most basic one was with my salespeople. I used to hold sales meetings once a week, but now I'm holding one every morning. I've got those people really enthusiastic. I guess once they saw some life in me they were ready to push harder too. They were just waiting for me to start things moving again.

"Things sure are working out okay. Last week my sales were well ahead of a year ago and much better than the store's average.

"Oh, by the way," he continued, "I want to tell you some other good news. I got two job offers since we talked. Naturally I'm glad, but I've turned them both down since everything is looking good here again."

When we face tough problems, we stay mired in the mud until we take action. Hope is a start. But hope needs action to win victories.

Put the action principle to work. Next time you experience big fear or little fear, steady yourself. Then search for an answer to this question: What kind of action can I take to conquer my fear?

Isolate your fear. Then take appropriate action.

Below are some examples of fear and some possible action cures.

TYPE OF FEAR	ACTION
1. Embarrassment because of personal appearance.	Improve it. Go to a barbershop or beauty salon. Shine your shoes. Get your clothes cleaned and pressed. In general, practice better grooming. It doesn't always take *new* clothes.
2. Fear of losing an important customer.	Work doubly hard to give better service. Correct anything that may have caused customers to lose confidence in you.
3. Fear of failing an examination.	Convert worry time into study time.
4. Fear of things totally beyond your control.	Turn your attention to helping to relieve the fear of others. Pray.
5. Fear of being physically hurt by something you can't control, such as a tornado or an airplane out of control.	Switch your attention to something totally different. Go out into your yard and pull up weeds. Play with your children. Go to a movie.
6. Fear of what other people may think and say.	Make sure that what you plan to do is right. Then do it. No one ever does anything worthwhile for which he is not criticized.
7. Fear of making an investment or purchasing a home.	Analyze all factors. Then be decisive. Make a decision and stick with it. Trust your own judgment.
8. Fear of people.	Put them in proper perspective. Remember, the other person is just another human being pretty much like yourself

Use this two-step procedure to cure fear and win confidence:

1. Isolate your fear. Pin it down. Determine exactly what you are afraid of.

2. Then take action. There is some kind of action for any kind of fear.

And remember, hesitation only enlarges, magnifies the fear. Take action promptly. Be decisive.

Much lack of self-confidence can be traced directly to a mismanaged memory.

Your brain is very much like a bank. Every day you make thought deposits in your "mind bank." These thought deposits grow and become your memory. When you settle down to think or when you face a problem, in effect you say to your memory bank, "What do I already know about this?"

Your memory bank automatically answers and supplies you with bits of information relating to this situation that you deposited on previous occasions. Your memory, then, is the basic supplier of raw material for your new thought.

The teller in your memory bank is tremendously reliable. He never crosses you up. If you approach him and say, "Mr. Teller, let me withdraw some thoughts I deposited in the past proving I'm inferior to just about everybody else," he'll say, "Certainly, sir. Recall how you failed two times previously when you tried this? Recall what your sixth-grade teacher told you about your inability to accomplish things . . . Recall what you overheard some fellow workers saying about you . . . Recall . . ."

And on and on Mr. Teller goes, digging out of your brain thought after thought that proves you are inadequate.

But suppose you visit your memory teller with this request: "Mr. Teller, I face a difficult decision. Can you supply me with any thoughts which will give me reassurance?"

And again Mr. Teller says, "Certainly, sir," but this time he delivers thoughts you deposited earlier that say you can succeed. "Recall the excellent job you did in a similar situation before. . . . Recall how much confidence Mr. Smith placed in you. . . . Recall what your good friends said about you. . . . Recall . . ."

Mr. Teller, perfectly responsive, lets you withdraw the thought deposits you want to withdraw. After all, it is your bank.

Here are two specific things to do to build confidence through efficient management of your memory bank.

1. Deposit only positive thoughts in your memory bank. Let's face it squarely: everyone encounters plenty of unpleasant, embarrassing, and discouraging situations. But unsuccessful and successful people deal with these situations in directly opposite ways. Unsuccessful people take them to heart, so to speak. They dwell on the unpleasant situations, thereby giving them a good start in their memory. They don't take their minds away from them. At night the unpleasant situation is the last thing they think about.

Confident, successful people, on the other hand, "don't give it another thought." Successful people specialize in putting positive thoughts into their memory bank.

What kind of performance would your car deliver if every morning before you left for work you scooped up a double handful of dirt and put it into your crankcase? That fine engine would soon be a mess, unable to do what you want it to do. Negative, unpleasant thoughts deposited in your mind affect your mind the same way. Negative thoughts produce needless wear and tear on your mental motor. They create worry, frustration, and feelings of inferiority. They put you beside the road while others drive ahead.

Do this: in these moments when you're alone with your thoughts—when you're driving your car or eating alone—recall pleasant, positive experiences. Put good thoughts in your memory bank. This boosts confidence. It gives you that "I-sure-feel-good" feeling. It helps keep your body functioning right, too.

Here is an excellent plan. Just before you go to sleep, deposit good thoughts in your memory bank. Count your blessings. Recall the many good things you have to be thankful for: your wife or husband, your children, your friends, your health. Recall the good things you saw people do today. Recall your little victories and accomplishments. Go over the reasons why you are glad to be alive.

2. Withdraw only positive thoughts from your memory bank. I was closely associated several years ago in Chicago with a firm of psychological consultants. They handled many types of cases, but mostly marriage problems and psychological adjustment situations, all dealing with mind matters.

One afternoon as I was talking with the head of the firm about his profession and his techniques for helping the seriously maladjusted person, he made this remark: "You know, there would be no need for my services if people would do just one thing."

"What's that?" I asked eagerly.

"Simply this: destroy their negative thoughts before those thoughts become mental monsters."

"Most individuals I try to help," he continued, "are operating their own private museum of mental horror. Many marriage difficulties, for example, involve the 'honeymoon monster.' The honeymoon wasn't as satisfactory as one or both of the marriage partners had hoped, but instead of burying the memory, they reflected on it hundreds of times until it was a giant obstacle to successful marital relationships. They come to me as much as five or ten years later.

"Usually, of course, my clients don't see where their trouble lies. It's my job to uncover and explain the source of their difficulty to them and help them to see what a triviality it really is.

"A person can make a mental monster out of almost any unpleasant happening," my psychologist friend went on. "A job failure, a jilted romance, a bad investment, disappointment in the behavior of a teenage child—these are common monsters I have to help troubled people destroy."

It is clear that any negative thought, if fertilized with repeated recall, can develop into a real mind monster, breaking down confidence and paving the way to serious psychological difficulties.

In an article in *Cosmopolitan* magazine, "The Drive Toward Self-Destruction," Alice Mulcahey pointed out that upward of 30,000 Americans commit suicide each year and another 100,000 attempt to take their own lives. She went on to say, "There is shocking evidence that millions of other people are killing themselves by slower, less obvious methods. Still others are committing spiritual rather than physical suicide, constantly seeking out ways to humiliate, punish, and generally diminish themselves."

The psychologist friend mentioned before told me how he helped one of his patients to stop committing "mental and spiritual suicide." "This patient," he explained, "was in her late thirties and had two children. In lay terminology she suffered from severe depression. She looked back on every incident of her life as being an unhappy experience. Her school days, her marriage, the bearing of her children, the places she had lived all were thought of negatively. She volunteered that she couldn't remember ever having been truly happy. And since what one remembers from the past colors what one sees in the present, she saw nothing but pessimism and darkness.

"When I asked her what she saw in a picture which I showed her, she said, 'It looks like there will be a terrible thunderstorm tonight.' That was the gloomiest interpretation of the picture I've yet heard." (The picture was a large oil painting of the sun low in the sky and a jagged, rocky coastline. The painting was very cleverly done and could be construed to be either a sunrise or a sunset. The psychologist commented to me that what a person sees in the picture is a clue to his personality. Most people say it is a sunrise. But the depressed, mentally disturbed person nearly always says it's a sunset.)

"As a psychologist, I can't change what already is in a person's memory. But I can, with the patient's cooperation, help the individual to see his past in a different light. That's the general treatment I used on this woman. I worked with her to help her to see joy and pleasure in her past instead of total disappointment. After six months she began to show improvement. At that point, I gave her a special assignment. Each day I asked her to think of and write down three specific reasons she has to be happy. Then at her next appointment with me on Thursdays I'd go over her list with her. I continued this sort of treatment for three months. Her improvement was very satisfactory. Today that woman is very well adjusted to her situation. She's positive and certainly as happy as most people."

When this woman quit drawing negatives from her memory bank, she was headed toward recovery.

Whether the psychological problem is big or little, the cure comes when one learns to quit drawing negatives from one's memory bank and withdraws positives instead.

Don't build mental monsters. Refuse to withdraw the unpleasant thoughts from your memory bank. When you remember situations of any kind, concentrate on the good part of the experience; forget the bad. Bury it. If you find yourself thinking about the negative side, turn your mind off completely.

And here is something very significant and very encouraging. Your mind wants you to forget the unpleasant. If you will just cooperate, unpleasant memories will gradually shrivel and the teller in your memory bank will cancel them out.

Dr. Melvin S. Hattwick, noted advertising psychologist, in commenting on our ability to remember, says, "When the feeling aroused is pleasant, the advertisement has a better chance to be remembered. When the feeling aroused is unpleasant, the reader or listener tends to forget the advertisement message. The unpleasant runs counter to what we want, we don't want to remember it."

In brief, it really is easy to forget the unpleasant if we simply refuse to recall it. Withdraw only positive thoughts from your memory bank. Let the others fade away. And your confidence, that feeling of being on top of the world, will zoom upward. You take a big step forward toward conquering fear when you refuse to remember negative, self-deprecating thoughts.

Why do people fear other people? Why do many folks feel self-conscious around others? What's behind shyness? What can we do about it?

Fear of other people is a big fear. But there is a way to conquer it. You can conquer fear of people if you will learn to put them into proper perspective.

A business friend, who is doing exceptionally well operating his own wood-novelty plant, explained to me how he got the proper perspective of people. His example is interesting.

"Before I went into the army in World War II, I was scared of just about everybody. You just wouldn't believe how shy and timid I was. I felt everyone else was a lot smarter. I worried about my physical and mental inadequacies. I thought I was born to fail.

"Then by some fortunate quirk of fate I lost my fear of people in the Army. During part of 1942 and 1943, when the Army was inducting men at a terrific clip, I was stationed as a medic at one of the big induction centers. Day after day I assisted in examining those men. The more I looked at these recruits, the less afraid of people I became.

"All those men lined up by the hundreds, naked as jaybirds, looked so much alike. Oh sure, there were fat ones and skinny ones, tall ones and short ones, but they all were confused, all were lonesome. Just a few days before some of these were rising young executives. Some were farmers, some were salesmen, drifters, blue-collar workers. A few days before they had been many things. But at the induction center they were all alike.

"I figured out something pretty basic back then. I discovered people are alike in many, many more ways than they are different. I discovered the other fellow is pretty much like me. He likes good food, he misses his family and friends, he wants to get ahead, he has problems, he likes to relax. So if the other fellow is basically like me, there's no point in being afraid of him."

Now, doesn't that make sense? If the other fellow is basically like me, there's no reason to be afraid of him.

Here are two ways to put people in proper perspective:

1. *Get a balanced view of the other fellow.* Keep these two points in mind when dealing with people: first, the other fellow is important. Emphatically, he is important. Every human being is. But remember this, also: *You are important, too.* So when you meet another person, make it a policy to think, "We're just two important people sitting down to discuss something of mutual interest and benefit."

A couple of months ago, a business executive phoned to tell me he had just employed a young man whom I had recommended to him shortly before. "Do you know what really sold me on that fellow?" asked my friend. "What?" I asked. "Well, it was the way he handled himself. Most job applicants when they walk in here are half scared. They give me all the answers they think I want to hear. In a way, most job applicants are a little like beggars—they'll accept anything, and they aren't particular.

"But G. handled himself differently. He respected me, but what's just as important, he respects himself. What's more, he asked me as many questions as I asked him. He's no mouse. He's a real man, and he's going to do all right."

This mutually important attitude helps you keep the situation balanced. The other fellow does not become too important relative to you in your thinking.

The other fellow might look frightfully big, frightfully important. But remember, he is still a human being with essentially the same interests, desires, and problems as you.

2. Develop an understanding attitude. People who want figuratively to bite you, growl at you, pick on you, and otherwise chop you down are not rare. If you're not prepared for people like that, they can punch big holes in your confidence and make you feel completely defeated. You need a defense against the adult bully, the fellow who likes to throw his meager weight around.

A few months ago, at the reservations desk of a Memphis hotel, I saw an excellent demonstration of the right way to handle folks like this.

It was shortly after 5 P.M., and the hotel was busy registering new guests. The fellow ahead of me gave his name to the clerk in a commanding way. The clerk said, "Yes sir, Mr. R., we have a fine single for you."

"Single?" shouted the fellow. "I ordered a double."

The clerk said, very politely, "Let me check, sir." He pulled the guest's reservation from the file and said, "I'm sorry, sir. Your telegram specified a single. I'd be happy to put you in a double room, sir, if we had any available. But we simply do not."

Then the irate customer said, "I don't care what the h—— that piece of paper says, I want a double."

Then he started in with that "do-you-know-who-I-am?" bit, followed with "I'll have you fired. You'll see, I'll have you fired."

As best he could, under the verbal tornado, the young clerk injected, "Sir, we're terribly sorry, but we acted on your instructions."

Finally the customer, really furious now, said, "I wouldn't stay in the best suite in this — — hotel now that I know how badly managed it is," and stormed out.

I stepped up to the desk, thinking the clerk, who had taken one of the worst public tongue-lashings I'd seen in some time, would be upset. Instead he greeted me with one of the finest "Good evening, sir"s I'd ever heard. As he went through the routine of processing my room, I said to him, "I certainly admire the way you handled yourself just a moment ago. You have tremendous temper control."

"Well, sir," he said, "I really can't get mad at a fellow like that. You see, he really isn't mad at me. I was just the scapegoat. The poor fellow may be in bad trouble with his wife, or his business may be off, or maybe he feels inferior and this was his golden chance to feel like a wheel. I'm just the guy who gave him a chance to get something out of his system."

The clerk added, "Underneath he's probably a very nice guy. Most folks are."

Walking toward the elevators, I caught myself repeating aloud, "Underneath he's probably a very nice guy. Most folks are."

Remember those two short sentences next time someone declares war on you. Hold your fire. The way to win in situations like this is to let the other fellow blow his stack and then forget it.

Several years ago, while checking student examination papers, I came across one that especially disturbed me. The student who wrote the examination had demonstrated in class discussions and previous tests that he was far better qualified than his paper indicated. He was, in fact, the fellow who I thought would finish at the top of the class. Instead his paper put him at the bottom. As was my custom in such cases, I had my secretary call the student and ask him to come by my office on an urgent matter.

Paul W. appeared shortly. He looked as though he had been through a terrible experience. After he was comfortably seated, I said to him, "What happened, Paul? This just isn't the quality paper I expected you to write."

Paul struggled with himself, looked in the direction of his feet and replied, "Sir, after I saw that you had spotted me cheating, I just went to pieces. I couldn't concentrate on anything. Honest, this is the first time I've ever cheated at the university. I desperately wanted an A, so I worked up a little pony to use."

He was terribly upset. But now that he was talking, he wouldn't stop. "I suppose you'll have to recommend me for dismissal. The university rule says any student found cheating in any manner is subject to permanent dismissal."

Here Paul started bringing up the shame this incident would bring to his family, how it would wreck his life, and all sorts of repercussions. Finally I said, "Hold it, now. Slow down. Let me explain something. I didn't see you cheat. Until you walked in and told me, I hadn't the faintest idea that was the trouble. I am sorry, Paul, that you did."

Then I continued, "Paul, tell me, just what do you want to gain from your university experience?"

He was a little calmer now, and after a short pause he said, "Well, Doctor, I think my overall aim is to learn how to live, but I guess I'm failing pretty badly."

"We learn in different ways," I said. "I think you can learn a real success lesson from this experience.

"When you used your pony in there, your conscience bothered you terribly. This gave you a guilt complex that in turn broke your confidence. As you expressed it, you went to pieces.

"Most of the time, Paul, this matter of right and wrong is approached from a moral or religious standpoint. Now, understand, I'm not here to preach to you, give you a sermon about right and wrong. But let's look at the practical side. When you do anything that goes contrary to your conscience, you feel guilty, and this guilty feeling jams your thought processes. You can't think straight because your mind is asking 'Will I get caught? Will I get caught?'

"Paul," I continued, "you wanted an A so badly you did something you knew was wrong. There are many times in life when you'll want to make an A so badly you'll be tempted to do something that is contrary to your conscience. For example, someday you may want to make a sale so badly you'll think of deliberately misleading the customer to buy. And you may succeed. But here's what will happen. Your guilty feeling will grab hold of you and the next time you see your customer, you'll be self-conscious, ill at ease. You'll be wondering 'Has he discovered that I put something over?' Your presentation will be ineffective because you can't concentrate. Chances are you'll never make the second, third, fourth, and the many repeat sales. In the long run, making that sale using tactics that hurt your conscience will cost you a lot of income."

I went on and pointed out to Paul how an occasional business or professional man loses his grip because of an intense fear that his wife will learn about a secret love affair he is having with another woman. "Will she find out? Will she find out?" eats away the man's confidence until he can't do a good job at work or in the home.

I reminded Paul that many criminals are captured not because any clues point to them but because they act guilty and self-conscious. Their guilt feeling puts them on the suspect list.

There is within each of us a desire to be right, think right, and act right. When we go against that desire, we put a cancer in our conscience. This cancer grows and grows by eating away at our confidence. Avoid doing anything that will cause you to ask yourself, "Will I get caught? Will they find out? Will I get away with it?"

Don't try to make an A if it means violating your confidence.

Paul, I'm pleased to say, got the point. He learned the practical value of doing what's right. I then proposed he sit down and retake the examination. In answer to his question "But what about my dismissal?" I said, "I know what the regulations say about cheating. But, you know, if we dismissed all students who have cheated in any way, half the professors would have to leave. And if we dismissed all students who thought about cheating, the university would have to shut down.

"So I'm forgetting this whole incident if you'll do me a favor."

"Gladly," he said.

I walked over to my bookshelf, took down my personal copy of *Fifty Years with the Golden Rule*, and said, "Paul, read this book and return it. See how, in J. C. Penney's own words, just doing what's right made him one of America's richest men."

Doing what's right keeps your conscience satisfied. And this builds self-confidence. When we do what is known to be wrong, two negative things happen. First, we feel guilt and this guilt eats away confidence. Second, other people sooner or later find out and lose confidence in us.

Do what's right and keep your confidence. That's *thinking yourself to success.*

Here is a psychological principle that is worth reading over twenty-five times. Read it until it absolutely saturates you: *To think confidently, act confidently.*

The great psychologist Dr. George W. Crane said in his famous book *Applied Psychology,* "Remember, motions are the precursors of emotions. You can't control the latter directly but only through your choice of motions or actions. . . . To avoid this all too common tragedy (marital difficulties and misunderstandings) become aware of the true psychological facts. Go through the proper motions each day and you'll soon begin to feel the corresponding emotions! Just be sure you and your mate go through those motions of dates and kisses, the phrasing of sincere daily compliments, plus the many other little courtesies, and you need not worry about the emotion of love. You can't act devoted for very long without feeling devoted."

Psychologists tell us we can change our attitudes by changing our physical actions. For example, you actually feel more like smiling if you make yourself smile. You feel more superior when you make yourself stand tall than when you slouch. On the negative side, frown a really bitter frown and see if you don't feel more like frowning.

It is easy to prove that managed motions can change emotions. People who are shy in introducing themselves can replace this timidity with confidence just by taking three simple actions simultaneously: First, reach for the other person's hand and clasp it warmly. Second, look directly at the other person. And third, say, "I'm very glad to know you."

These three simple actions automatically and instantaneously banish shyness. Confident action produces confident thinking.

So, to think confidently, act confidently. Act the way you want to feel. Below are five confidence-building exercises. Read these guides carefully. Then make a conscious effort to practice them and build your confidence.

1. Be a front seater. Ever notice in meetings—in church, classrooms, and other kinds of assemblies—how the back seats fill up first? Most folks scramble to sit in the back rows so they won't be "too conspicuous." And the reason they are afraid to be conspicuous is that they lack confidence.

Sitting up front builds confidence. Practice it. From now on make it a rule to sit as close to the front as you can. Sure, you may be a little more conspicuous in the front, but remember, there is nothing inconspicuous about success.

2. Practice making eye contact. How a person uses his eyes tells us a lot about him. Instinctively, you ask yourself questions about the fellow who doesn't look you in the eye. "What's he trying to hide? What's he afraid of? Is he trying to put something over on me? Is he holding something back?"

Usually, failure to make eye contact says one of two things. It may say, "I feel weak beside you. I feel inferior to you. I'm afraid of you." Or avoiding another person's eyes may say, "I feel guilty. I've done something or I've thought something that I don't want you to know. I'm afraid if I let my eyes connect with yours, you'll see through me."

You say nothing good about yourself when you avoid making eye contact. You say, "I'm afraid. I lack confidence." Conquer this fear by *making* yourself look the other person in the eyes.

Looking the other person in the eye tells him, "I'm honest and aboveboard. I believe in what I'm telling you. I'm not afraid. I'm confident."

Make your eyes work for you. Aim them right at the other person's eyes. It not only *gives* you confidence, it *wins* you confidence, too.

3. Walk 25 percent faster. When I was a youngster, just going to the county seat was a big treat. After all the errands were accomplished and we were back in the car, my mother would often say, "Davey, let's just sit here a while and watch the people walk by."

Mother was an excellent game player. She'd say, "See that fellow. What do you suppose is troubling him?" Or "What do you think that lady there is going to do?" or "Look at that person. He just seems to be in a fog."

Watching people walk and move about became real fun. It was a lot cheaper than the movies (which was one of the reasons, I learned later, that Mother developed the game), and it was a lot more instructive.

I still am a walk watcher. In corridors, lobbies, on sidewalks I still occasionally find myself studying human behavior simply by watching people move about.

Psychologists link slovenly posture and sluggish walking to unpleasant attitudes towards oneself, work, and the people around us. But psychologists also tell us you can actually change your attitudes by changing your posture and speed of movement. Watch, and you discover that body action is the result of mind action. The extremely beaten people, the real down-and-outers, just shuffle and stumble along. They have zero self-confidence.

Average people have the "average" walk. Their pace is "average." They have the look of "I really don't have very much pride in myself."

Then there's a third group. Persons in this group show superconfidence. They walk faster than the average. There seems to be a slight sprint in the way they walk. Their walk tells the world, "I've got someplace important to go, something important to do. What's more, I will succeed at what I will do fifteen minutes from now."

Use the walk-25-percent-faster technique to help build self-confidence. Throw your shoulders back, lift up your head, move ahead just a little faster, and feel self-confidence grow.

Just try and see.

4. *Practice speaking up.* In working with many kinds of groups of all sizes, I've watched many persons with keen perception and much native ability freeze and fail to participate in discussions. It isn't that these folks don't want to get in and wade with the rest. Rather, it's a simple lack of confidence.

The conference clam thinks to himself, "My opinion is probably worthless. If I say something, I'll probably look foolish. I'll just say nothing. Besides, the others in the group probably know more than I. I don't want the others to know how ignorant I am."

Each time the conference clam fails to speak, he feels even more inadequate, more inferior. Often he makes a faint promise to himself (that down deep he knows he won't keep) to speak "next time."

This is very important: each time our clam fails to speak, he takes one more dose of confidence poison. He becomes less and less confident of himself.

But on the positive side, the more you speak up, the more you add to your confidence, and the easier it is to speak up the next time. Speak up. It's a confidence-building vitamin.

Put this confidence builder to use. Make it a rule to speak up at every open meeting you attend. Speak up, say something *voluntarily* at *every* business conference, committee meeting, community forum you attend. Make no exception. Comment, make a suggestion, ask a question. And don't be the last to speak. Try to be the icebreaker, the first one in with a comment.

And never worry about looking foolish. You won't. For each person who doesn't agree with you, odds are another person will. Quit asking yourself, "I wonder if I dare speak?"

Instead, concentrate on getting the discussion leader's attention so you *can* speak.

For special training and experience in speaking, consider joining your local toastmaster's club. Thousands of conscientious people have developed confidence through a planned program to feel at ease talking *with* people and *to* people.

5. *Smile big.* Most folks have heard at one time or another that a smile will give them a real boost. They've been told that a smile is excellent medicine for confidence deficiency. But lots of people still don't really believe this because they've never tried smiling when they feel fear.

Make this little test. Try to feel defeated and smile big at the same time. You can't. A big smile gives you confidence. A big smile beats fear, rolls away worry, defeats despondency.

And a real smile does more than cure just your ill feeling. A real smile melts away the opposition of others—and instantly, too. Another person simply can't be angry with you if you give him a big, sincere smile. Just the other day, a little incident happened to me that illustrates this. I was parked at an intersection waiting for the light to change when BAM! The driver behind me had let his foot slip the brake and put my rear bumper to a test. I looked back through my mirror and saw him getting out. I got out, too, and, forgetting the rule book, started preparing myself for verbal combat. I confess I was ready verbally to bite him to pieces.

But fortunately, before I got the chance, he walked up to me, smiled, and said in the most earnest voice, "Friend, I really didn't mean to do that." That smile, matched with his sincere comment, melted me. I mumbled something about "That's O.K. Happens all the time." Almost in less time than it takes to wink an eye, my opposition turned into friendship.

Smile big and you feel like "happy days are here again." But smile *big*. A half-developed smile is not fully guaranteed. Smile until your teeth show. That large-size smile is fully guaranteed.

I've heard many times, "Yes, but when I fear something, or when I'm angry, I don't feel like smiling."

Of course you don't. No one does. The trick is to tell yourself forcefully, "I'm going to smile."

Then smile.

Harness the power of smiling.

PUT THESE FIVE PROCEDURES TO WORK FOR YOU

1. Action cures fear. Isolate your fear and then take constructive action. Inaction—doing nothing about a situation—strengthens fear and destroys confidence.

2. Make a supreme effort to put only positive thoughts in your memory bank. Don't let negative, self-deprecatory thoughts grow into mental monsters. Simply refuse to recall unpleasant events or situations.

3. Put people in proper perspective. Remember, people are more alike, much more alike, than they are different. Get a balanced view of the other fellow. He is just another human being. And develop an understanding attitude. Many people will bark, but it's a rare one who bites.

4. Practice doing what your conscience tells you is right. This prevents a poisonous guilt complex from developing. Doing what's right is a very practical rule for success.

5. Make everything about you say, "I'm confident, really confident." Practice these little techniques in your day-to-day activities:

    Be a front seater.
    Make eye contact.
    Walk 25 percent faster.
    Speak up.
    Smile big.

4

HOW TO THINK BIG

RECENTLY I CHATTED WITH a recruitment specialist for one of the nation's largest industrial organizations. Four months each year she visits college campuses to recruit graduating seniors for her company's junior executive training program. The tenor of her remarks indicated that she was discouraged about the attitudes of many people she talked with.

"Most days I interview between eight and twelve college seniors, all in the upper third of their class, all at least mildly interested in coming with us. One of the main things we want to determine in the screening interview is the individual's motivation. We want to find out if he or she is the kind of person who can, in a few years, direct major projects, manage a branch office or plant, or in some other way make a really substantial contribution to the company.

"I must say I'm not too pleased with the personal objectives of most of those I talk with. You'd be surprised," she went on, "how many twenty-two-year-olds are more interested in our retirement plan than in anything else we have to offer. A second favorite question is 'Will I move around a lot?' Most of them seem to define the word *success* as synonymous with *security*. Can we risk turning our company over to people like that?

"The thing I can't understand is why should young people these days be so ultraconservative, so narrow in their view of the future? Every day there are more signs of expanding opportunity. This country is making record progress in scientific and industrial development. Our population is gaining rapidly. If there ever was a time to be bullish about America, it's now."

The tendency for so many people to think small means there is much less competition than you think for a very rewarding career.

Where success is concerned, people are not measured in inches or pounds or college degrees, or family background; they are measured by the size of their thinking. How big we think determines the size of our accomplishments. Now let's see how we can enlarge our thinking.

Ever ask yourself, "What is my greatest weakness?" Probably the greatest human weakness is self-deprecation—that is, selling oneself short. Self-deprecation shows through in countless ways. John sees a job advertisement in the paper; it's exactly what he would like. But he does nothing about it because he thinks, "I'm not good enough for that job, so why bother?" Or Jim wants a date with Joan, but he doesn't call her because he thinks he wouldn't rate with her.

Tom feels Mr. Richards would be a very good prospect for his product, but Tom doesn't call. He feels Mr. Richards is too big to see him. Pete is filling out a job application form. One question asks, "What beginning salary do you expect?" Pete puts down a modest figure because he feels he really isn't worth the bigger sum that he would like to earn.

Philosophers for thousands of years have issued good

advice: *Know thyself.* But most people, it seems, interpret this suggestion to mean *Know only thy negative self.* Most self-evaluation consists of making long mental lists of one's faults, shortcomings, inadequacies.

It's well to know our inabilities, for this shows us areas in which we can improve. But if we know only our negative characteristics, we're in a mess. Our value is small.

Here is an exercise to help you measure your true size. I've used it in training programs for executives and sales personnel. It works.

1. Determine your five chief assets. Invite some objective friend to help—possibly your wife, your superior, a professor—some intelligent person who will give you an honest opinion. (Examples of assets frequently listed are education, experience, technical skills, appearance, well-adjusted home life, attitudes, personality, initiative.)

2. Next, under each asset, write the names of three persons you know who have achieved large success but who do *not* have this asset to as great a degree as you.

When you've completed this exercise, you will find you outrank many successful people on at least one asset.

There is only one conclusion you can honestly reach: You're bigger than you think. So fit your thinking to your true size. Think as big as you really are! Never, never, never sell yourself short!

The person who says "adamantine" when in plain talk he means "immovable" or says "coquette" when we would understand him better if he said "flirt" may have a big vocabulary. But does he have a big thinker's vocabulary? Probably not. People who use difficult, high-sounding words and phrases that most folks have to strain themselves to understand are inclined to be overbearing and stuffed shirts. And stuffed shirts are usually small thinkers.

The important measure of a person's vocabulary is not the size or the number of words he uses. Rather, the thing that counts, the *only* thing that counts about one's vocabulary, is the effect his words and phrases have on his own and others' thinking.

Here is something very basic: *We do not think in words and phrases. We think only in pictures and/or images.* Words are the raw materials of thought. When spoken or read, that amazing instrument, the mind, automatically converts words and phrases into mind pictures. Each word, each phrase, creates a slightly different mind picture. If someone tells you, "Jim bought a new split-level," you see one picture. But if you're told, "Jim bought a new ranch house," you see another picture. The mind pictures we see are modified by the kinds of words we use to name things and describe things.

Look at it this way. When you speak or write, you are, in a sense, a projector showing movies in the minds of others. And the pictures you create determine how you and others react.

Suppose you tell a group of people, "I'm sorry to report we've failed." What do these people see? They see defeat and all the disappointment and grief the word "failed" conveys. Now suppose you said instead, "Here's a new approach that I think will work." They would feel encouraged, ready to try again.

Suppose you say, "We face a problem." You have created a picture in the minds of others of something difficult, unpleasant to solve. Instead say, "We face a challenge," and you create a mind picture of fun, sport, something pleasant to do.

Or tell a group, "We incurred a big expense," and people see money spent that will never return. Indeed, this is unpleasant. Instead say, "We made a big investment," and people see a picture of something that will return profits later on, a very pleasant sight.

The point is this: Big thinkers are specialists in creating positive, forward-looking, optimistic pictures in their own minds and in the minds of others. *To think big, we must use words and phrases that produce big, positive mental images.*

In the left-hand column below are examples of phrases that create small, negative, depressing thoughts. In the right-hand column the same situation is discussed but in a big, positive way.

As you read these, ask yourself: "What mind pictures do I see?"

PHRASES THAT CREATE SMALL, NEGATIVE MIND IMAGES	PHRASES THAT CREATE BIG, POSITIVE MIND IMAGES
1. It's no use, we're whipped.	We're not whipped yet. Let's keep trying. Here's a new angle.
2. I was in that business once and failed. Never again.	I went broke but it was my own fault. I'm going to try again.
3. I've tried but the product won't sell. People don't want it.	So far I've not been able to sell this product. But I know it is good and I'm going to find the formula that will put it over.

PHRASES THAT CREATE SMALL, NEGATIVE MIND IMAGES	PHRASES THAT CREATE BIG, POSITIVE MIND IMAGES
4. The market is saturated. Imagine, 75 percent of the potential has already been sold. Better get out.	Imagine, 25 percent of the market is still not sold. Count me in. This looks big!
5. Their orders have been small. Cut them off.	Their orders have been small. Let's map out a plan for selling them more of their needs.
6. Five years is too long a time to spend before I'll get into the top ranks in your company. Count me out.	Five years is not really a long time. Just think, that leaves me thirty years to serve at a high level.
7. The competition has all the advantage. How do you expect me to sell against them?	Competition is strong. There's no denying that, but no one ever has *all* the advantages. Let's put our heads together and figure out a way to beat them at their own game.
8. Nobody will ever want that product.	In its present form, it may not be salable, but let's consider some modifications.
9. Let's wait until a recession comes along, then buy stocks.	Let's invest now. Bet on prosperity, not depression.
10. I'm too young (old) for the job.	Being young (old) is a distinct advantage.
11. It won't work, let me prove it. The image: dark, gloom, disappointment, grief, failure.	It will work, let me prove it. The image: bright, hope, success, fun, victory.

FOUR WAYS TO DEVELOP THE BIG THINKER'S VOCABULARY

Here are four ways to help you develop a big thinker's vocabulary.

1. Use big, positive, cheerful words and phrases to describe how you feel. When someone asks, "How do you feel today?" and you respond with an "I'm tired (I have a headache, I wish it were Saturday, I don't feel so good)," you actually make yourself feel worse. Practice this: it's a very simple point, but it has tremendous power. Every time someone asks you, "How are you?" or "How are you feeling today?" respond with a "Just *wonderful*! thanks, and *you*?" or say "Great" or "Fine." Say you feel wonderful at every possible opportunity, and you will begin to feel wonderful—and bigger, too. Become known as a person who always feels great. It wins friends.

2. Use bright, cheerful, favorable words and phrases to describe other people. Make it a rule to have a big, positive word for all your friends and associates. When you and someone else are discussing an absent third party, be sure you compliment him with big words and phrases like "He's really a *fine* fellow." "They tell me he's working out *wonderfully* well." Be extremely careful to avoid the petty cut-him-down language. Sooner or later third parties hear what's been said, and then such talk only cuts *you* down.

3. Use positive language to encourage others. Compliment people personally at every opportunity. Everyone you know

craves praise. Have a special good word for your wife or husband every day. Notice and compliment the people who work with you. Praise, sincerely administered, is a success tool. Use it! Use it again and again and again. Compliment people on their appearance, their work, their achievements, their families.

4. Use positive words to outline plans to others. When people hear something like this: "Here is some *good* news. We face a genuine opportunity . . ." their minds start to sparkle. But when they hear something like "Whether we like it or not, we've got a job to do," the mind movie is dull and boring, and they react accordingly. Promise victory and watch eyes light up. Promise victory and win support. Build castles, don't dig graves!

SEE WHAT CAN BE, NOT JUST WHAT IS

Big thinkers train themselves to see not just what is but what can be. Here are four examples to illustrate this point.

1. What gives real estate value? A highly successful Realtor who specializes in rural property shows what can be done if we train ourselves to see something where little or nothing presently exists.

"Most of the rural property around here," my friend began, "is run-down and not very attractive. I'm successful because I don't try to sell my prospects a farm as it *is*.

"I develop my entire sales plan around what the farm *can* be. Simply telling the prospect, 'The farm has XX acres of bottom land and XX acres of woods and is XX miles from town,' doesn't stir him up and make him want to buy it. But when you show him a concrete plan for doing something with the farm, he's just about sold. Here, let me show you what I mean."

He opened his briefcase and pulled out a file. "This farm," he said, "is a new listing with us. It's like a lot of them. It's forty-three miles from the center of the metropolitan area, the house is run-down, and the place hasn't been farmed in five years. Now, here's what I've done. I spent two full days on the place last week, just studying it. I walked over the place several times. I looked at neighboring farms. I studied the location of the farm with respect to existing and planned highways. I asked myself, 'What's this farm good for?'

"I came up with three possibilities. Here they are." He showed them to me. Each plan was neatly typed and looked quite comprehensive. One plan suggested converting the farm into a riding stable. The plan showed why the idea was sound: a growing city, more love for the outdoors, more money for recreation, good roads. The plan also showed how the farm could support a sizable number of horses so that the revenue from the rides would be largely clear. The whole riding stable idea was very thorough, very convincing. The plan was so clear and convincing, I could "see" a dozen couples riding horseback through the trees.

In similar fashion this enterprising salesman developed a second thorough plan for a tree farm and a third plan for a combination tree and poultry farm.

"Now when I talk with my prospects, I won't have to convince them that the farm is a good buy as it is. I help them to see a picture of the farm changed into a moneymaking proposition.

"Besides selling more farms and selling them faster, my

method of selling the property for what it can be pays off in another way: I can sell a farm at a higher price than my competitors. People naturally pay more for acreage *and* an idea than they do for just acreage. Because of this, more people want to list their farms with me and my commission on each sale is larger.

The moral is this: *Look at things not as they are, but as they can be. Visualization adds value to everything. A big thinker always visualizes what can be done in the future. He isn't stuck with the present.*

2. How much is a customer worth? A department store executive was addressing a conference of merchandise managers. She was saying, "I may be a little old-fashioned, but I belong to the school that believes the best way to get customers to come back is to give them friendly, courteous service. One day I was walking through our store when I overheard a salesperson arguing with a customer. The customer left in quite a huff.

"Afterwards, the salesperson said to another, 'I'm not going to let a $1.98 customer take up all my time and make me take the store apart trying to find him what he wants. He's simply not worth it.'

"I walked away," the executive continued, "but I couldn't get that remark out of my mind. It is pretty serious, I thought, when our salespeople think of customers as being in the $1.98 category. I decided right then that this concept must be changed. When I got back to my office, I called our research director and asked him to find out how much the average customer spent in our store last year. The figure he came up with surprised even me. According to our research director's careful calculation, the typical customer spent $362 in our establishment.

"The next thing I did was call a meeting of all supervisory personnel and explain the incident to them. Then I showed them what a customer is really worth. Once I got these people to see that a customer is not to be valued on a single sale but rather on an annual basis, customer service definitely improved."

The point made by the retailing executive applies to any kind of business. It's repeat business that makes the profit. Often, there's no profit at all on the first several sales. Look at the potential expenditures of the customers, not just what they buy today.

Putting a big value on customers is what converts them into big, regular patrons. Attaching little value to customers sends them elsewhere. A student related this pertinent incident to me, explaining why he'll never again eat in a certain cafeteria.

"For lunch one day," the student began, "I decided to try a new cafeteria that had just opened a couple of weeks before. Nickels and dimes are pretty important to me right now, so I watch what I buy pretty closely. Walking past the meat section I saw some turkey and dressing that looked pretty good, and it was plainly marked 39 cents.

"When I got to the cash register, the checker looked at my tray and said, '1.09.' I politely asked her to check it again because my tally was 99 cents. After giving me a mean glare, she recounted. The difference turned out to be the turkey. She had charged me 49 cents instead of 39 cents. Then I called her attention to the sign, which read 39 cents.

"This really set her off! 'I don't care what that sign says. It's supposed to be 49 cents. See. Here's my price list for today. Somebody back there made a mistake. You'll have to pay the 49 cents.'

"Then I tried to explain to her the only reason I selected the turkey was because it *was* 39 cents. If it had been marked 49 cents I'd have taken something else.

"To this, her answer was 'You'll just have to pay the 49 cents.' I did, because I didn't want to stand there and create a scene. But I decided on the spot that I'd never eat there again. I spend about $250 a year for lunches, and you can be sure they'll not get one penny of it."

There's an example of the little view. The checker saw one thin dime, not the potential $250.

3. The case of the blind milkman. It's surprising how people sometimes are blind to potential. A few years ago a young milkman came to our door to solicit our dairy business. I explained to him that we already had milk delivery service and we were quite satisfied. Then I suggested that he stop next door and talk to the lady there.

To this he replied, "I've already talked to the lady next door, but they use only one quart of milk every two days, and that's not enough to make it worthwhile for me to stop."

"That may be," I said, "but when you talked to our neighbor, did you not observe that the demand for milk in that household will increase considerably in a month or so? There will be a new addition over there that will consume lots of milk."

The young man looked for a moment like he had been struck, and then he said, "How blind can a guy be?"

Today that same one-quart-every-two-days family buys seven quarts every two days from a milkman who had some foresight. That first youngster, a boy, now has two brothers and one sister. And I'm told there'll be another young one soon.

How blind can we be? See what can be, not just what is.

The schoolteacher who thinks of Jimmy only as he is—an ill-mannered, backward, uncouth brat—certainly will not aid Jimmy's development. But the teacher who sees Jimmy not as he is now but as he can be, she'll get results.

Most folks driving through skid row see only broken-down stumblebums hopelessly lost to the bottle. A few devoted people see something else in the skid row–ite; they see a reconstructed citizen. And because they see this, they succeed in many cases in doing an excellent rehabilitation job.

4. *What determines how much you're worth?* After a training session a few weeks ago, a young man came to see me and asked if he could talk with me for a few minutes. I knew that this young fellow, now about twenty-six, had been a very underprivileged child. On top of this, he had experienced a mountain of misfortune in his early adult years. I also knew that he was making a real effort to prepare himself for a solid future.

Over coffee, we quickly worked out his technical problem, and our discussion turned to how people who have few physical possessions should look toward the future. His comments provide a straightforward, sound answer.

"I've got less than $200 in the bank. My job as a rate clerk doesn't pay much, and it doesn't carry much responsibility. My car is four years old, and my wife and I live in a cramped second-floor apartment.

"But, Professor," he continued, "I'm determined not to let what I haven't got stop me."

That was an intriguing statement, so I urged him to explain.

"It's this way," he went on, "I've been analyzing people a lot lately, and I've noticed this. People who don't have much look at themselves as they are now. That's all they see. They don't see a future, they just see a miserable present.

"My neighbor is a good example. He's continually complaining about having a low-pay job, the plumbing that's always getting fouled up, the lucky breaks somebody else just got, the doctor bills that are piling up. He reminds himself so often that he's poor that now he just assumes that he's always going to be poor. He acts as if he were sentenced to living in that broken-down apartment all the rest of his life."

My friend was really speaking from the heart, and after a moment's pause he added, "If I looked at myself strictly as I am—old car, low income, cheap apartment, and hamburger diet—I couldn't help but be discouraged. I'd see a nobody and I'd *be* a nobody for the rest of my life.

"I've made up my mind to look at myself as the person I'm going to be in a few short years. I see myself not as a rate clerk but as an executive. I don't see a crummy apartment, I see a fine new suburban home. And when I look at myself that way, I feel bigger and think bigger. And I've got plenty of personal experiences to prove it's paying off."

Isn't that a splendid plan for adding value to oneself? This young fellow is on the expressway to really fine living. He's mastered this basic success principle: It isn't what one has that's important. Rather, it's how much one is planning to get that counts.

The price tag the world puts on us is just about identical to the one we put on ourselves.

Here is how you can develop your power to see what can be, not just what is. I call these the "practice adding value" exercises.

1. Practice adding value to things. Remember the real estate example. Ask yourself, "What can I do to 'add value' to this room or this house or this business?" Look for ideas to make things worth more. A thing—whether it be a vacant lot, a house, or a business—has value in proportion to the ideas for using it.

2. Practice adding value to people. As you move higher and higher in the world of success, more and more of your job becomes "people development." Ask, "What can I do to 'add value' to my subordinates? What can I do to help them to become more effective?" Remember, to bring out the best in a person, you must first visualize his best.

3. Practice adding value to yourself. Conduct a daily interview with yourself. Ask, "What can I do to make myself more valuable today?" Visualize yourself not as you are but as you can be. Then specific ways for attaining your potential value will suggest themselves. Just try and see.

A retired owner-manager of a medium-size printing company (sixty employees) explained to me how his successor was picked.

"Five years ago," my friend began, "I needed an accountant to head up our accounting and office routine. The fellow I hired was named Harry and was only twenty-six. He knew nothing about the printing business, but his record showed he was a good accountant. Yet a year and a half ago, when I retired, we made him president and general manager of the company.

"Looking back on it, Harry had one trait that put him out in front of everyone else. Harry was sincerely and actively interested in the whole company, not just writing checks and keeping records. Whenever he saw how he could help other employees, he jumped right in.

"The first year Harry was with me, we lost a few men. Harry came to me with a fringe benefit program which he promised would cut down turnover at low cost. And it worked.

"Harry did many other things, too, which helped the whole company, not just this department. He made a detailed cost study of our production department and showed me how a $30,000 investment in new machinery would pay off. Once we experienced a pretty bad sales slump. Harry went to our sales manager and said, in effect, 'I don't know much about the sales end of the business, but let me try to help.' And he did. Harry came up with several good ideas which helped us sell more jobs.

"When a new employee joined us, Harry was right there to help the fellow get comfortable. Harry took a real interest in the entire operation.

"When I retired, Harry was the only logical person to take over.

"But don't misunderstand," my friend continued, "Harry didn't try to put himself over on me. He wasn't a mere meddler. He wasn't aggressive in a negative way. He didn't stab people in the back, and he didn't go around giving orders. He just went around helping. Harry simply acted as if everything in the company affected him. He made company business his business."

We can all learn a lesson from Harry. The "I'm doing my job and that's enough" attitude is small, negative thinking. Big thinkers see themselves as members of a team effort, as winning or losing with the team, not by themselves. They help in every way they can, even when there is no direct and immediate compensation or other reward. The fellow who shrugs off a problem outside his own department with the comment "Well, that's no concern of mine, let them worry with it" hasn't got the attitude it takes for top leadership.

Practice this. Practice being a big thinker. See the company's interest as identical with your own. Probably only a very few persons working in large companies have a sincere, unselfish interest in their company. But after all, only a relatively few persons qualify as big thinkers. And these few are the ones eventually rewarded with the most responsible, best-paying jobs.

Many, many potentially powerful people let petty, small, insignificant things block their way to achievement. Let's look at four examples.

1. WHAT DOES IT TAKE TO MAKE A GOOD SPEECH?

Just about everyone wishes he had the "ability" to do a first-class job of speaking in public. But most people don't get their wish. Most folks are lousy public speakers.

Why? The reason is simple: most people concentrate on the small, trivial things of speaking at the expense of the big, important things. In preparing to give a talk, most people give themselves a host of mental instructions, like "I've got to remember to stand straight," "Don't move around and don't use your hands," "Don't let the audience see you use your notes," "Remember, don't make mistakes in grammar, especially don't say 'for he and I,' say 'for him and me,'" "Be sure your tie is straight," "Speak loud, but not too loud," and so on and on.

Now, what happens when the speaker gets up to speak? He's scared because he's given himself a terrific list of things not to do. He gets confused in his talk and finds himself silently asking, "Have I made a mistake?" He is, in brief, a flop. He's a flop because he concentrated on the petty, trivial, relatively unimportant qualities of a good speaker and failed to concentrate on the big things that make a good speaker: *knowledge of what he's going to talk about and an intense desire to tell it to other people.*

The real test of a speaker is not did he stand straight or did he make any mistakes in grammar, but rather did the audience get the points he wanted to put across. Most of our top speakers have petty defects; some of them even have unpleasant voices. Some of the most sought-after speakers in America would flunk a speech course taught by the old negative, "don't do this and don't do that," method.

Yet all these successful public speakers have one thing in common: *They have something to say and they feel a burning desire for other people to hear it.*

Don't let concern with trivia keep you from speaking successfully in public.

2. WHAT CAUSES QUARRELS?

Ever stop to ask yourself just what causes quarrels? At least 99 percent of the time, quarrels start over petty, unimportant matters like this: John comes home a little tired, a little on edge. Dinner doesn't exactly please him, so he turns up his nose and complains. Joan's day wasn't perfect either, so she rallies to her own defense with "Well, what do you expect on my food budget?" or "Maybe I could cook better if I had a new stove like everybody else." This insults John's pride, so he attacks with "Now, Joan, it's not lack of money; it's simply that you don't know how to manage."

And away they go! Before a truce is finally declared, all sorts of accusations are made by each party. In-laws, sex, money, pre-marital and postmarital promises, and other issues will be introduced. Both parties leave the battle nervous, tense. Nothing has been settled, and both parties have new ammunition to make the next quarrel more vicious. Little things, petty thinking, causes arguments. So, to eliminate quarrels, eliminate petty thinking.

Here's a technique that works: before complaining or accusing or reprimanding someone or launching a counterattack in self-defense, ask yourself, "Is it really important?" In most cases, it isn't and you avoid conflict.

Ask yourself, "Is it really important if he (or she) is messy with cigarettes or forgets to put the cap on the toothpaste or is late coming home?"

"Is it really important if he (or she) squandered a little money or invited some people in I don't like?"

When you feel like taking negative action, ask yourself, "Is it really important?" That question works magic in building a finer home situation. It works at the office, too. It works in home-going traffic when another driver cuts in ahead of you. It works in any situation in life that is apt to produce quarrels.

3. JOHN GOT THE SMALLEST OFFICE AND FIZZLED OUT

Several years ago, I observed small thinking about an office assignment destroy a young fellow's chances for a profitable career in advertising.

Four young executives, all on the same status level, were moved into new offices. Three of the offices were identical in size and decoration. The fourth was smaller and less elaborate.

J. M. was assigned the fourth office. This turned out to be a real blow to his pride. Immediately he felt discriminated against. Negative thinking, resentment, bitterness, jealousy built up. J. M. began to feel inadequate. The result was that J. M. grew hostile toward his fellow executives. Rather than cooperate, he did his best to undermine their efforts. Things got worse. Three months later J. M. slipped so badly that management had no choice but to issue him a pink slip.

Small thinking over a very small matter stopped J. M. In his haste to feel he was discriminated against, J. M. failed to observe that the company was expanding rapidly and office space was at a premium. He didn't stop to consider the possibility that the executive who made the office assignments didn't even know which one was the smallest! No one in the organization, except J. M., regarded his office as an index of his value.

Small thinking about unimportant things like seeing your name last on the department route sheet or getting the fourth carbon of an office memo can hurt you. Think big, and none of these little things can hold you back.

4. EVEN STUTTERING IS A DETAIL

A sales executive told me how even stuttering is a mere detail in salesmanship if the fellow has the really important qualities.

"I have a friend, also a sales executive, who loves to play practical jokes, though sometimes these jokes aren't jokes at all. A few months ago a young fellow called on my practical-joking friend and asked for a sales job. The fellow had a terrible stutter, though, and my friend decided right here was a chance to play a joke on me. So the friend told the stammering applicant that he wasn't in the market for a salesman right now but one of his friends (me) had a spot to fill. Then he phoned me, and, boy, did he give this fellow a buildup. Not suspecting anything, I said, 'Send him right over!'

"Thirty minutes later, in he walked. The young fellow hadn't said three words before I knew why my friend was so eager to send him over. 'I-I-I'm J-J-Jack R.,' he said, 'Mr. X sent me over t-t-to talk t-t-to you about a j-j-job.' Almost every word was a struggle. I thought to myself, 'This guy couldn't sell a dollar bill for 90 cents on Wall Street.' I was sore at my friend, but I really felt sorry for this fellow, so I thought the least I could do was to ask him some polite questions while I thought up a good excuse as to why I couldn't use him.

"As we talked on, however, I discovered this fellow was no stupe. He was intelligent. He handled himself very nicely, but I just couldn't overlook the fact that he stuttered. Finally, I decided I'd wind up the interview by asking one last question. 'What makes you think you can sell?'

"'Well,' he said, 'I learn f-f-fast, I-I-I like people, I-I-I think you've got a good company, and I-I-I want t-t-to make m-m-money. Now, I-I-I do have a speech im-im-pairment, b-b-but that doesn't b-b-bother me, so why should it b-b-bother anybody else?'

"His answer showed me he had all the really important qualifications for a salesman. I decided right then to give him a chance. And you know, he's working out very well."

Even a speech impairment in a talker's profession is a triviality if the person has the big qualities.

Practice these three procedures to help yourself think about trivialities:

1. Keep your eyes focused on the big objective. Many times we're like the salesman who, failing to make the sale, reports to his manager, "Yes, but I sure convinced the customer he was wrong." In selling, the big objective is winning sales, not arguments.

   In marriage the big objective is peace, happiness, tranquillity—not winning quarrels or saying "I could have told you so."

   In working with employees, the big objective is developing their full potential, not making issues out of their minor errors.

   In living with neighbors, the big objective is mutual respect and friendship—not seeing if you can have their dog impounded because once in a while it barks at night.

   Paraphrasing some military lingo, it is much better to lose a battle and win the war than to win a battle and lose the war.

   Resolve to keep your eyes on the big ball.

2. Ask "Is it really important?" Before becoming negatively excited, just ask yourself, "Is it important enough for me to get all worked up about?" There is no better way to avoid frustration over petty matters than to use this medicine. At least 90 percent of quarrels and feuds would never take place if we just faced troublesome situations with "Is this really important?"

3. Don't fall into the triviality trap. In making speeches, solving problems, counseling employees, think of those things that really matter, things that make the difference. Don't become submerged under surface issues. Concentrate on important things.

TAKE THIS TEST TO MEASURE THE SIZE OF YOUR THINKING

In the left-hand column below are listed several common situations. In the middle and right-hand columns are comparisons of how petty thinkers and big thinkers see the same situation. Check yourself. Then decide, which will get me where I want to go? Petty thinking or big thinking?

The same situation handled in two entirely different ways. The choice is yours.

SITUATION	THE PETTY THINKER'S APPROACH	THE BIG THINKER'S APPROACH
Expense accounts	1. Figures out ways to increase income through chiseling on expense accounts.	1. Figures out ways to increase income by selling more merchandise.
Conversation	2. Talks about the negative qualities of his friends, the economy, his company, the competition.	2. Talks about the positive qualities of his friends, his company, the competition.

SITUATION	THE PETTY THINKER'S APPROACH	THE BIG THINKER'S APPROACH
Progress	3. Believes in retrenchment or at best the status quo.	3. Believes in expansion.
Future	4. Views the future as limited.	4. Sees the future as very promising.
Work	5. Looks for ways to avoid work.	5. Looks for more ways and things to do, especially helping others.
Competition	6. Competes with the average.	6. Competes with the best.
Budget problems	7. Figures out ways to save money by cutting down on necessary items.	7. Figures out ways to increase income and buy more of the necessary items.
Goals	8. Sets goals low.	8. Sets goals high.
Goals vision	9. Sees only the short run.	9. Is preoccupied with the long run.
Security	10. Is preoccupied with security problems.	10. Regards security as a natural companion of success.
Companionship	11. Surrounds himself with petty thinkers.	11. Surrounds himself with persons with large, progressive ideas.
Mistakes	12. Magnifies minor errors. Turns them into big issues.	12. Ignores errors of little consequence.

REMEMBER, IT PAYS IN EVERY WAY TO THINK BIG!

1. Don't sell yourself short. Conquer the crime of self-depre-cation. Concentrate on your assets. You're better than you think you are.

2. Use the big thinker's vocabulary. Use big, bright, cheerful words. Use words that promise victory, hope, happiness, pleasure; avoid words that create unpleasant images of fail-ure, defeat, grief.

3. Stretch your vision. See what can be, not just what is. Practice adding value to things, to people, and to yourself.

4. Get the big view of your job. Think, really think your pres-ent job is important. That next promotion depends mostly on how you think toward your *present* job.

5. Think above trivial things. Focus your attention on big objectives. Before getting involved in a petty matter, ask yourself, "Is it really important?"

Grow big by thinking big!

5

HOW TO THINK AND DREAM CREATIVELY

FIRST, LET'S CLEAR UP a common fallacy about the meaning of *creative thinking*. For some illogical reason, science, engineering, art, and writing got tabbed as about the only truly creative pursuits. Most people associate creative thinking with things like the discovery of electricity or polio vaccine, or the writing of a novel or the development of color television.

Certainly, accomplishments like these are evidence of creative thinking. Each forward step made in the conquest of space is the result of creative thinking, lots of it. But creative thinking is not reserved for certain occupations, nor is it restricted to superintelligent people.

Well, then, what is creative thinking?

A low-income family devises a plan to send their son to a leading university. That's creative thinking.

A family turns the street's most undesirable lot into the neighborhood beauty spot. That's creative thinking.

A minister develops a plan that doubles his Sunday evening attendance. That's creative thinking.

Figuring out ways to simplify record keeping, selling the "impossible" customer, keeping the children occupied constructively, making employees really like their work, or preventing a "certain" quarrel—all of these are examples of practical, everyday creative thinking.

Creative thinking is simply finding new, improved ways to do anything. The rewards of all types of success—success in the home, at work, in the community—hinge on finding ways to do things better. Now let's see what we can do to develop and strengthen our creative thinking ability.

Step one: Believe it can be done. Here is a basic truth: To do *anything*, we must first believe it can be done. Believing something can be done sets the mind in motion to find a way to do it.

To illustrate this point of creative thinking in training sessions, I often use this example: I ask the group, "How many of you feel it is possible to eliminate jails within the next thirty years?"

Invariably the group looks bewildered, not quite sure they heard right and thinking they are listening to a real fuzzy-wuzzy. So after a pause I repeat, "How many of you feel it is possible to eliminate jails within the next thirty years?"

Once they're sure I'm not joking, someone always blasts me with something like "You mean to say you want to turn all those murderers, thieves, and rapists loose? Don't you realize what this would mean? Why, none of us would be safe. We *have* to have jails."

Then the others cut loose:

"All order would break down if we didn't have jails."

"Some people are born criminals."

"If anything, we need more jails."

"Did you read in this morning's paper about that murder?"

And the group goes on, telling me all sorts of *good* reasons why we must have jails. One fellow even suggested we've got to have jails so the police and prison guards can have jobs.

After about ten minutes of letting the group "prove" why we can't eliminate the need for jails, I say to them, "Now let me mention here that this question of eliminating jails is used to make a point.

"Each of you has come up with reasons why we can't eliminate the need for jails. Will you do me a favor? Will you try extra hard for a few minutes to believe we *can* eliminate jails?"

Joining in the spirit of the experiment, the group says, in effect, "Oh, well, but just for kicks." Then I ask, "Now, assuming we can eliminate jails, how could we begin?"

Suggestions come slowly at first. Someone hesitantly says something like, "Well, you might cut down crime if you established more youth centers."

Before long, the group, which ten minutes ago was solidly against the idea, now begins to work up real enthusiasm.

"Work to eliminate poverty. Most crime stems from the low income levels."

"Conduct research to spot potential criminals before they commit a crime."

"Develop surgical procedures to cure some kinds of criminals."

"Educate law enforcement personnel in positive methods of reform."

These are just samples of the seventy-eight specific ideas I've tabulated that could help accomplish the goal of eliminating jails. WHEN YOU *BELIEVE*, YOUR MIND FINDS WAYS TO *DO*.

This experiment has just one point: *When you believe some-*

thing is impossible, your mind goes to work for you to prove why. But when you believe, really believe, something can be done, your mind goes to work for you and helps you find the ways to do it.

Believing something can be done paves the way for creative solutions. Believing something can't be done is destructive thinking. This point applies to all situations, little and big. The political leaders who do not genuinely believe permanent world peace can be established will fail because their minds are closed to creative ways to bring about peace. The economists who believe business depressions are inevitable will not develop creative ways to beat the business cycle.

In a similar fashion, you *can* find ways to like a person if you believe you can.

You *can* discover solutions to personal problems if you believe you can.

You *can* find a way to purchase that new, larger home if you believe you can.

Belief releases creative powers. Disbelief puts the brakes on.

Believe, and you'll start thinking—constructively.

Your mind will create a way if you let it. A little over two years ago a young man asked me to help him find a job with more future. He was employed as a clerk in the credit department of a mail-order company and felt that he was getting nowhere. We talked about his past record and what he wanted to do. After knowing something about him, I said, "I admire you very much for wanting to move up the ladder to a better job and more responsibility. But getting a start in the kind of job you want requires a college degree these days. I notice you've finished three semesters.

May I suggest you finish college. Going summers, you can do it in two years. Then I'm sure you can land the job you want, with the company you want to work for."

"I realize," he answered, "that a college education would help. But it's impossible for me to go back to school."

"Impossible? Why?" I asked.

"Well, for one thing," he began, "I'm twenty-four. On top of that, my wife and I are expecting our second child in a couple of months. We barely get by now on what I make. I wouldn't have time to study since I'd have to keep my job. It's just impossible, that's all."

This young man really had himself convinced that finishing college was impossible.

Then I said to him, "If you believe it is impossible to finish school, then it is. But by the same token, if you'll just believe it is possible to return to the university, a solution will come.

"Now, here's what I would like you to do. Make up your mind you are going to go back to school. Let that one thought dominate your thinking. Then think, really think, about how you can do it and still support your family. Come back in a couple of weeks and let me know what ideas you've come up with."

My young friend returned two weeks later.

"I thought a lot about what you said," he began. "I've decided I must go back to school. I haven't figured out all the angles yet, but I'll find a solution."

And he did.

He managed to get a scholarship provided by a trade association, which paid his tuition, books, and incidentals. He rearranged his work schedule so he could attend classes. His enthusiasm and the promise of a better life won him his wife's full support. Together they creatively found ways to budget money and time more effectively.

Last month he received his degree one day and went to work the next as a management trainee for a large corporation.

Where there's a will, there *is* a way.

Believe it can be done. That's basic to creative thinking. Here are suggestions to help you develop creative power through belief:

1. Eliminate the word *impossible* from your thinking and speaking vocabularies. *Impossible* is a failure word. The thought "It's impossible" sets off a chain reaction of other thoughts to prove you're right.

2. Think of something special you've been wanting to do but felt you couldn't. Now make a list of reasons why you can do it. Many of us whip and defeat our desires simply because we concentrate on why we can't when the only thing worthy of our mental concentration is why we can.

Recently I read a newspaper item that said there are too many counties in most states. The article pointed out that most county boundaries were established decades before the first automobile was built and while the horse and buggy was the chief mode of travel. But today, with fast automobiles and good roads, there is no reason why three or four counties could not be combined. This would cut down greatly on duplicated services so that taxpayers would actually get better service for less money.

The writer of this article said he thought he had stumbled across a really live idea, so he interviewed thirty people at random to get their reactions. The result: not one person thought the idea had merit, even though it would provide them with better local government at less cost.

That's an example of traditional thinking. The traditional thinker's mind is paralyzed. He reasons, "It's been this way for a hundred years. Therefore, it must be good and must stay this way. Why risk a change?"

"Average" people have always resented progress. Many voiced a protest toward the automobile on the grounds that nature meant for us to walk or use horses. The airplane seemed drastic to many. Man had no "right" to enter the province "reserved" for birds. A lot of "status-quo-ers" still insist that man has no business in space.

One top missile expert recently gave an answer to this kind of thinking. "Man belongs," says Dr. von Braun, "where man wants to go."

Around 1900 a sales executive discovered a "scientific" principle of sales management. It received a lot of publicity and even found its way into textbooks. The principle was this: There is one best way to sell a product. Find the best way. Then never deviate from it.

Fortunately for this man's company, new leadership came in in time to save the organization from financial ruin.

Contrast that experience with the philosophy of Crawford H. Greenewalt, president of one of the nation's largest business organizations, E. I. du Pont de Nemours. In a talk at Columbia University, Mr. Greenewalt said, ". . . there are many ways in which a good job can be done—as many ways, in fact, as there are men to whom the task is given."

In truth, there is no one best way to do anything. There

is no one best way to decorate an apartment, landscape a lawn, make a sale, rear a child, or cook a steak. There are as many best ways as there are creative minds.

Nothing grows in ice. If we let tradition freeze our minds, new ideas can't sprout. Make this test sometime soon. Propose one of the ideas below to someone and then watch his behavior.

1. The postal system, long a government monopoly, should be turned over to private enterprise.

2. Presidential elections should be held every two or six years instead of four.

3. Regular hours for retail stores should be 1 P.M. to 8 P.M., instead of 9 A.M. to 5:30 P.M.

4. The retirement age should be raised to seventy.

Whether these ideas are sound or practical is not the point. What is significant is how a person handles propositions like these. If he laughs at the idea and doesn't give it a second thought (and probably 95 percent will laugh at it) chances are he suffers from tradition paralysis. But the one in twenty who says, "That's an interesting idea; tell me more about it," has a mind that's turned to creativity.

Traditional thinking is personal enemy number one for the person who is interested in a creative personal success program. Traditional thinking freezes your mind, blocks your progress, and prevents you from developing creative power. Here are three ways to fight it:

1. Become receptive to ideas. Welcome new ideas. Destroy these thought repellents: "Won't work," "Can't be done," "It's useless," and "It's stupid."

   A very successful friend of mine who holds a major position with an insurance company said to me, "I don't pretend to be the smartest guy in the business. But I think I am the best sponge in the insurance industry. I make it a point to soak up all the good ideas I can."

2. Be an experimental person. Break up fixed routines. Expose yourself to new restaurants, new books, new theaters, new friends; take a different route to work someday, take a different vacation this year, do something new and different this weekend.

   If your work is in distribution, develop an interest in production, accounting, finance, and the other elements of business. This gives you breadth and prepares you for larger responsibilities.

3. Be progressive, not regressive. Not "That's the way we did it where I used to work, so we ought to do it that way here" but "How can we do it better than we did it where I used to work?" Not backward, regressive thinking but forward, progressive thinking. Because you got up at 5:30 A.M. to deliver papers or milk the cows when you were a youngster doesn't necessarily mean it's a good idea for you to require your children to do the same.

Imagine what would happen to the Ford Motor Company if its management allowed itself to think, "This year we've built the ultimate in automobiles. Further improvement is impossible. Therefore, all experimental engineering and designing activities are hereby permanently terminated." Even the mammoth Ford Motor Company would shrivel fast with this attitude.

Successful people, like successful businesses, live with these questions: "How can I improve the quality of my performance? How can I do better?"

Absolute perfection in all human undertakings from building missiles to rearing children is unattainable. This means there is endless room for improvement. Successful people know this, and they are always searching for a better way. (Note: The successful person doesn't ask, "Can I do it better?" He *knows* he can. So he phrases the question: "*How* can I do it better?")

A few months ago, a former student of mine, in business for just four years, opened her fourth hardware store. This was quite a feat, considering the young lady's small initial capital investment of only $3,500, strong competition from other stores, and the relatively short time she had been in business.

I visited her new store shortly after it opened to congratulate her on the fine progress she had made.

In an indirect way I asked her how she was able to make a success of three stores and open a fourth one when most merchants had to struggle to make a success of just one store.

"Naturally," she answered, "I worked hard, but just getting up early and working late isn't responsible for the four stores. Most people in my business work hard. The main thing I attribute my success to is my self-styled 'weekly improvement program.'"

"A weekly improvement program? Sounds impressive. How does it work?" I asked.

"Well, it really isn't anything elaborate," she continued, "it's just a plan to help me do a better job as each week rolls around.

"To keep my forward thinking on the track, I've divided my job into four elements: customers, employees, merchandise, and promotion. All during the week I make notes and jot down ideas as to how I can improve my business.

"Then, every Monday evening, I set aside four hours to review the ideas I've jotted down and figure out how to put the solid ones to use in the business.

"In this four-hour period I force myself to take a hard look at my operation. I don't simply wish more customers would shop in my store. Instead I ask myself, 'What can I do to attract more customers?' 'How can I develop regular, loyal customers?'"

She went on describing numerous little innovations that made her first three stores so successful: things like the way she arranged the merchandise within her stores, her suggestion-selling technique that sold two out of three customers merchandise they had not planned to buy when they entered her stores, the credit plan she devised when many of her customers were out of work because of a strike, the contest she developed that boosted sales during a slack season.

"I ask myself, 'What can I do to improve my merchandise offerings?' and I get ideas. Let me cite just one case. Four weeks ago, it occurred to me that I should do something to get more youngsters into the store. I reasoned, if I had something here to draw the kids to the store, I'd also draw more of the parents. I kept thinking about it, and then this idea came: Put in a line of small carded toys for children in the four-to-eight age bracket. It's working! The toys take little space and I make a nice profit on them. But, most important, the toys have increased store traffic.

"Believe me," she went on, "my weekly improvement plan works. Just by conscientiously asking myself, 'How can I do a better job?' I find the answers. It's a rare Monday night that I don't come up with some plan or technique that makes that profit and loss statement look better.

"And I've learned something else too about successful merchandising, something that I think every person going into business for himself should know."

"What's that?" I asked.

"Just this: It isn't so much what you know when you start that matters. It's what you learn and put to use after you open your doors that counts most."

Big success calls for persons who continually set higher standards for themselves and others, persons who are searching for ways to increase efficiency, to get more output at lower cost, do more with less effort. Top success is reserved for the I-can-do-it-better kind of person.

General Electric uses the slogan "Progress is our most important product."

Why not make progress your most important product?

The I-can-do-better philosophy works magic. When you ask yourself, "How can I do better?" your creative power is switched on and ways for doing things better suggest themselves.

Here is a daily exercise that will help you discover and develop the power of the I-can-do-better attitude.

Each day before you begin work, devote ten minutes to thinking "How can I do a better job today?" Ask, "What can I do today to encourage my employees?" "What special favor can I do for my customers?" "How can I increase my personal efficiency?"

This exercise is simple. But it works. Try it, and you'll find unlimited creative ways to win greater success.

Just about every time my wife and I would get together with a certain couple, the conversation would turn to "working wives." Mrs. S. had worked several years before her marriage, and she had genuinely liked it.

"But now," she'd say, "I've got two youngsters in school, a home to manage, and meals to prepare. I simply haven't got time."

Then, one Sunday evening, Mr. and Mrs. S. and their children were in an automobile accident. Mrs. S. and the youngsters escaped serious injury, but Mr. S. received a back injury that left him permanently disabled. Now Mrs. S. had no choice but to go to work.

When we saw her several months after the accident, we were amazed to find how well she had adjusted to her new responsibilities.

"You know," she said, "six months ago I never dreamed I could possibly manage the house and work full-time. But after the accident, I just made up my mind that I had to find the time. Believe me, my efficiency has gone up 100 percent. I discovered a lot of things I was doing didn't need to be done at all. Then I discovered that the children could and wanted to help. I found dozens of ways to conserve time—fewer trips to the store, less TV, less telephoning, less of those time killers."

This experience teaches us a lesson: *Capacity is a state of mind.* How much we can do depends on how much we think we can do. When you really believe you can do more, your mind thinks creatively and shows you the way.

A young bank executive related this personal experience about "work capacity."

"One of the other executives in our bank left us with very short notice. This put our department on the spot. The fellow leaving had filled an important job, and his work couldn't be postponed or left undone.

"The day after he left, the vice president in charge of my department called me in. He explained to me that he had already talked individually to the two others in my group, asking them if they could divide the work of the man who had just left until a replacement could be found. 'Neither of them flatly refused,' said the vice president, 'but each stated that he is up to his neck now with his own pressing work. I'm wondering if you could handle some of the overload temporarily?'

"Throughout my working career, I've learned that it never pays to turn down what looks like an opportunity. So I agreed and promised to do my very best to handle all the vacated job as well as keep up with my own work. The vice president was pleased at this.

"I walked out of his office knowing I had taken on a big job. I was just as busy as the two others in my department who had wiggled out of this extra duty. But I was determined to find a way to handle both jobs. I finished up my work that afternoon, and when the offices were closed, I sat down to figure out how I could increase my personal efficiency. I got a pencil and started writing down every idea I could think of.

"And you know, I came up with some good ones: like working out an arrangement with my secretary to channel all routine telephone calls to me during a certain hour each day, placing all outgoing calls during a certain hour, cutting my usual conference periods from fifteen minutes to ten, giving all my dictation at one time each day. I also discovered my secretary could—and was eager to—take over a number of little time-consuming details for me.

"I had been handling my present job for over two years, and frankly, I was amazed to discover how much inefficiency I had let creep in.

"Within a week's time, I was dictating twice as many letters, handling 50 percent more phone calls, attending half again as many meetings—all with no strain.

"A couple more weeks passed. The vice president called me in. He complimented me on doing a fine job. He went on to say that he had looked over a number of people from both inside and outside the bank but he had not yet found the right man. Then he confessed that he had already cleared with the bank's executive committee, and they had authorized him to combine the two jobs, put them both in my charge, and give me a substantial increase in salary.

"I proved to myself that how much I can do depends on how much I think I can do."

Capacity *is* indeed a state of mind.

Every day, it seems, this takes place in the fast-moving world of business. The boss calls in an employee and explains that a special task must be accomplished. Then he says, "I know you've got a lot of work to do, but can you handle this?" Too often the employee replies, "I'm awfully sorry, but I'm all loaded down now. I wish I could take it on, but I'm just too busy."

Under the circumstances, the boss doesn't hold it against the employee, because it is "extra duty," so to speak. But the boss realizes the task must be done, and he'll keep looking until he finds an employee who is just as busy as the rest but who feels he can take on more. And this employee is the fellow who will forge ahead.

In business, in the home, in the community, the success combination is *do what you do better* (improve the quality of your output) and *do more of what you do* (increase the quantity of your output).

Convinced it pays to do more and better? Then try this two-step procedure:

1. Eagerly accept the opportunity to do more. It's a compliment to be asked to take on a new responsibility. Accepting greater responsibility on the job makes you stand out and shows that you're more valuable. When your neighbors ask you to represent them on a civic matter, accept. It helps you to become a community leader.

2. Next, concentrate on "How can I do more?" Creative answers will come. Some of these answers may be better planning and organization of your present work or taking intelligent shortcuts in your routine activities, or possibly dropping nonessential activities altogether. But, let me repeat, the solution for doing more will appear.

As a personal policy I have accepted fully the concept: If you want it done, give it to a busy man. I refuse to work on important projects with persons who have lots of free time. I have learned from painful, expensive experience that the fellow who has plenty of time makes an ineffective work partner.

All the successful, competent people I know are busy. When I start something, some project, with them, I know it will be satisfactorily completed.

I have learned in dozens of instances that I can count on a busy man to deliver. But I have often been disappointed in working with people who have "all the time in the world."

Progressive business management constantly asks, "What can we do to expand output?" Why not ask yourself, "What can I do to expand my output?" Your mind will creatively show you how.

In hundreds of interviews with people at all levels I've made this discovery: The bigger the person, the more apt he is to encourage *you* to talk; the smaller the person, the more apt he is to preach to you.

Big people monopolize the *listening*.

Small people monopolize the *talking*.

Note this also: Top-level leaders in all walks of life spend much more time requesting advice than they do in giving it. Before a top man makes a decision, he asks, "How do you feel about it?" "What do you recommend?" "What would you do under these circumstances?" "How does this sound to you?"

Look at it this way: A leader is a decision-making human machine. Now, to manufacture anything, you've got to have raw material. In reaching creative decisions, the raw materials are the ideas and suggestions of others. Don't, of course, expect other people to give you ready-made solutions. That's not the primary reason for asking and listening. Ideas of others help to spark your own ideas so your mind is more creative.

Recently I participated as a staff instructor in an executive management seminar. The seminar consisted of twelve sessions. One of the highlights of each meeting was a fifteen-minute discussion by one of the executives on the topic "How I solved my most pressing management problem."

At the ninth session, the executive whose turn it was, a vice president of a large milk-processing company, did something different. Instead of telling how he had solved his problem, he announced his topic as "Needed: Help on solving my most pressing management problem." He quickly outlined his problem and then asked the group for ideas on solving it. To be sure he got a record of each idea suggested, he had a stenographer in the room taking down everything that was said.

Later I talked with this man and complimented him on his unique approach. His comment was "There are some very sharp men in this group. I just figured I'd harvest some ideas. There's a good possibility something someone said during that session may give me the clue I need to solve the problem."

Note: this executive presented his problem, then *listened*. In so doing, he got some decision-making raw material, and, as a side benefit, the other executives in the audience enjoyed the discussion because it gave them the opportunity to take part.

Successful businesses invest large sums in consumer research. They ask people about the taste, quality, size, and appearance of a product. Listening to people provides definite ideas for making the product more salable. It also suggests to the manufacturer what he should tell consumers about the product in his advertising. The procedure for developing successful products is to get as much opinion as you can, listen to the people who will buy the product, and then design the product and its promotion to please these people.

In an office recently I noticed a sign that said, "To sell John Brown what John Brown buys, you've got to see things through John Brown's eyes." And the way to get John Brown's vision is to listen to what John Brown has to say.

Your ears are your intake valves. They feed your mind raw materials that can be converted into creative power. We learn nothing from telling. But there is no limit to what we can learn by asking and listening.

Try this three-stage program to strengthen your creativity through asking and listening:

1. Encourage others to talk. In personal conversation or in group meetings, draw out people with little urges, such as "Tell me about your experience . . ." or "What do you think should be done about . . . ?" or "What do you think is the key point?" Encourage others to talk, and you win a double-barreled victory: your mind soaks up raw material that you can use to produce creative thought, and you win friends. There is no surer way to get people to like you than to encourage them to talk to you.

2. Test your own views in the form of questions. Let other people help you smooth and polish your ideas. Use the what-do-you-think-of-this-suggestion? approach. Don't be dogmatic. Don't announce a fresh idea as if it were handed down on a gold tablet. Do a little informal research first. See how your associates react to it. If you do, chances are you'll end up with a better idea.

3. Concentrate on what the other person says. Listening is more than just keeping your own mouth shut. Listening means letting what's said penetrate your mind. So often people pretend to listen when they aren't listening at all. They're just waiting for the other person to pause so they can take over with the talking. Concentrate on what the other person says. Evaluate it. That's how you collect mind food.

More and more leading universities are offering advanced management training programs for senior business executives. According to the sponsors, the big benefit of these programs is not that the executives get ready-made formulae that they can use to operate their business more efficiently. Rather, they benefit most from the opportunity to exchange and discuss new ideas. Many of these programs require the executives to live together in college dormitories, thus encouraging bull sessions. Boiled down to one word, the executives benefit most from the *stimulation* received.

A year ago I directed two sessions in a one-week sales management school in Atlanta sponsored by the National Sales Executives, Inc. A few weeks later I met a salesman friend who worked for one of the sales executives who'd attended the school.

"You people at the school sure gave my sales manager a lot of things to do to run our company better," my young friend said. Curious, I asked him specifically what changes he'd noticed. He reeled off a number of things—a revision in the compensation plan, sales meetings twice a month instead of once a month, new business cards and stationery, a revision in sales territories—not one of which was specifically recommended in the training program. The sales manager didn't get a bunch of canned techniques. Instead, he got something much more valuable, the stimulation to think of ideas directly beneficial to his own particular organization.

A young accountant for a paint manufacturer told me about a very successful venture of his that was sparked by ideas of others.

"I never had had more than a casual interest in real estate," he told me. "I've been a professional accountant for several years now, and I've stuck pretty close to my profession. One day a Realtor friend invited me to be his guest at a luncheon of one of the city's real estate groups.

"The speaker that day was an older man who had seen the city grow. His talk was about 'The Next Twenty Years.' He predicted that the metropolitan area would continue to grow far out into the surrounding farmland. He also predicted that there would be a record demand for what he called gentlemen-size farms, two to five acres, big enough so the businessman or professional person could have a pool, horses, a garden, and other hobbies that require space.

"This man's talk really stimulated me. What he described was exactly what I wanted. The next few days I asked several friends what they thought about the idea of someday owning a five-acre estate. Everyone I talked to said, in effect, 'I'd love that.'

"I continued to think about it and to figure how I could turn the idea into profit. Then one day as I was driving to work the answer came out of nowhere. Why not buy a farm and divide it into estates? I figured the land might be worth more in relatively small pieces than in one big piece.

"Twenty-two miles from the center of the city, I found a worn-out fifty-acre farm priced at $8,500. I bought it, paying only one-third down and working out a mortgage with the owner for the balance.

"Next, I planted pine seedlings where there were no trees. I did this because a real estate man whom I feel knows his business told me, 'People want trees these days, lots of trees!'

"I wanted my prospective buyers to see that in a few years their estate would be covered with beautiful pine trees.

"Then I got a surveyor to divide the fifty acres into ten five-acre plots.

"Now I was ready to start selling. I got several mailing lists of young executives in the city and put on a small-scale direct-mail campaign. I pointed out how, for only $3,000, the price of a small city lot, they could buy an estate. I also described the potentials for recreation and wholesome living.

"In six weeks' time, working only evenings and on weekends, I sold all ten plots. Total income: $30,000. Total costs, including the land, advertising, surveying and legal expenses: $10,400. Profit: $19,600.

"I made a nice profit because I let myself be exposed to ideas of other intelligent people. Had I not accepted that invitation to attend a luncheon with a group completely foreign to my occupational interests, my brain would have never worked out this successful plan for making a profit."

There are many ways to get mental stimulation, but here are two that you can incorporate into your pattern of life.

First, join and meet regularly with at least one professional group that provides stimulation in your own occupational area. Rub shoulders—and minds—with other success-oriented people.

So often I hear someone say, "I picked up a great idea this noon at the —— meeting" or "During the meeting yesterday I got to thinking . . ." Remember, a mind that feeds only on itself soon is undernourished, becoming weak and incapable of creative progressive thought. Stimulation from others is excellent mind food.

Second, join and participate in at least one group outside your occupational interests. Association with people who have different job interests broadens your thinking and helps you to see the big picture. You'll be surprised how mixing regularly with people outside your occupational area will stimulate your on-the-job thinking.

Ideas are fruits of your thinking. But they've got to be harnessed and put to work to have value.

Each year an oak tree produces enough acorns to populate a good-sized forest. Yet from these bushels of seeds perhaps only one or two acorns will become a tree. The squirrels destroy most of them, and the hard ground beneath the tree doesn't give the few remaining seeds much chance for a start.

So it is with ideas. Very few bear fruit. Ideas are highly perishable. If we're not on guard, the squirrels (negative-thinking people) will destroy most of them. Ideas require special handling from the time they are born until they're transformed into practical ways for doing things better. Use these three ways to harness and develop your ideas:

1. Don't let ideas escape. Write them down. Every day lots of good ideas are born only to die quickly because they aren't nailed to paper. Memory is a weak slave when it comes to preserving and nurturing brand-new ideas. Carry a note-

book or some small cards with you. When you get an idea, write it down. A friend who travels a lot keeps a clipboard beside him so that he can write down an idea the instant it occurs to him. People with fertile, creative minds know a good idea may sprout any time, any place. Don't let ideas escape; else you destroy the fruits of your thinking. Fence them in.

2. Next, review your ideas. File these ideas in an active file. The file can be an elaborate cabinet, or it can be a desk drawer. A shoe box will do. But build a file and then examine your storehouse of ideas regularly. As you go over your ideas, some may, for very good reasons, have no value at all. Get rid of them. But so long as the idea has any promise, keep it.

3. Cultivate and fertilize your idea. Now make your idea grow. Think about it. Tie the idea to related ideas. Read anything you can find that is in any way akin to your idea. Investigate all angles. Then, when the time is ripe, put it to work for yourself, your job, your future.

When an architect gets an idea for a new building, he makes a preliminary drawing. When a creative advertising person gets an idea for a new TV commercial, he puts it into storyboard form, a series of drawings that suggest what the idea will look like in finished form. Writers with ideas prepare a first draft.

Note: Shape up the idea on paper. There are two excellent reasons for this. When the idea takes tangible form, you can literally look at it, see the loopholes, see what it needs in the way of polish. Then, too, ideas have to be "sold" to someone: customers, employees, the boss, friends, fellow club members, investors. Somebody must "buy" the idea; else it has no value.

One summer I was contacted by two life insurance salesmen. Both wanted to work on my insurance program. Both promised to return with a plan for making the needed changes. The first salesman gave me strictly an oral presentation. He told me in words what I needed. But I soon was confused. He brought in taxes, options, Social Security, all the technical details of insurance programming. Frankly, he lost me and I had to say no.

The second salesman used a different approach. He had charted his recommendations. All the details were shown in diagram form. I could grasp his proposal easily and quickly because I could literally see it. He sold me.

Resolve to put your ideas in salable form. An idea written or in some sort of picture or diagram form has many times more selling power than the idea presented only in oral form.

USE THESE TOOLS AND THINK CREATIVELY

1. Believe it can be done. When you believe something can be done, your mind will find the ways to do it. Believing a solution paves the way to solution.

   Eliminate "impossible," "won't work," "can't do," "no use trying" from your thinking and speaking vocabularies.

2. Don't let tradition paralyze your mind. Be receptive to new ideas. Be experimental. Try new approaches. Be progressive in everything you do.

3. Ask yourself daily, "How can I do better?" There is no limit to self-improvement. When you ask yourself, "How can I do better?" sound answers will appear. Try it and see.

4. Ask yourself, "How can I do more?" Capacity *is* a state of mind. Asking yourself this question puts your mind to work to find intelligent shortcuts. The success combination in business is: Do what you do better (improve the quality of your output), and: Do more of what you do (increase the quantity of your output).

5. Practice asking and listening. Ask and listen, and you'll obtain raw material for reaching sound decisions. Remember: Big people monopolize the *listening;* small people monopolize the *talking.*

6. Stretch your mind. Get stimulated. Associate with people who can help you think of new ideas, new ways of doing things. Mix with people of different occupational and social interests.

6

YOU ARE WHAT YOU THINK YOU ARE

IT'S OBVIOUS. MUCH HUMAN behavior is puzzling. Have you ever wondered why a salesperson will greet one customer with an alert "Yes sir, may I serve you?" but virtually ignore another? Or why a man will open a door for one woman but not for another? Or why an employee will consistently carry out the instructions of one superior but only grudgingly do what another superior requests? Or why we will pay close attention to what one person says but not to another?

Look around you. You'll observe some people receiving the "Hey, Mac" or "Hey, buddy" treatment while others receive the sincere and important "Yes, sir" treatment. Watch. You'll observe that some people command confidence, loyalty, and admiration while others do not.

Look closer still, and you'll also observe that those persons who command the most respect are also the most successful.

What is the explanation? It can be distilled into one word: *thinking*. Thinking *does* make it so. Others see in us what we see in ourselves. We receive the kind of treatment we *think* we deserve.

Thinking *does* make it so. The fellow who thinks he is inferior, regardless of what his real qualifications may be, is inferior.

For thinking regulates actions. If a man feels inferior, he acts that way, and no veneer of cover-up or bluff will hide this basic feeling for long. The person who feels he isn't important, *isn't*.

On the other side, a fellow who really thinks he is equal to the task, *is*.

To be important, we must *think* we are important, *really* think so; then others will think so too. Here again is the logic:

How you think determines how you act.
How you act in turn determines:
How others react to you.

Like other phases of your personal program for success, winning respect is fundamentally simple. To gain the respect of others, you must first think you deserve respect. And the more respect you have for yourself, the more respect others will have for you. Test this principle. Do you have much respect for the fellow on skid row? Of course not. Why? Because the poor fellow doesn't respect himself. He's letting himself rot away from lack of self-respect.

Self-respect shows through in everything we do. Let's focus our attention now on some of the specific ways we can increase self-respect and thereby earn more respect from others.

LOOK IMPORTANT—IT HELPS YOU THINK IMPORTANT

Rule: Remember, your appearance "talks." Be sure it says positive things about you. Never leave home without feeling certain you look like the kind of person you want to be.

The most honest advertisement ever appearing in print is the "Dress Right. You Can't Afford Not To!" slogan sponsored by the

American Institute of Men's and Boys' Wear. This slogan deserves to be framed in every office, restroom, bedroom, office, and schoolroom in America. In one ad a policeman speaks. He says:

> You can usually spot a wrong kid just by the way he looks. Sure it's unfair, but it's a fact: people today judge a youngster by appearance. And once they've tabbed a boy, it's tough to change their minds about him, their attitude toward him. Look at your boy. Look at him through his teacher's eyes, your neighbors' eyes. Could the way he looks, the clothes he wears, give them the wrong impression? Are you making sure he looks right, dresses right, everywhere he goes?

This advertisement, of course, refers primarily to children. But it can be applied to adults as well. In the sentence beginning with *look*, substitute the word *yourself* for *him*, *your* for *his*, *superior's* for *teacher's*, and *associates'* for *neighbors'*, and reread the sentence. *Look at yourself through your superior's eyes, your associates' eyes.*

It costs so little to be neat. Take the slogan literally. Interpret it to say: Dress right; it *always* pays. Remember: look important because it helps you to think important.

Use clothing as a tool to lift your spirits, build confidence. An old psychology professor of mine used to give this advice to students on last-minute preparations for final examinations: "Dress up for this important exam. Get a new tie. Have your suit pressed. Shine your shoes. Look sharp because it will help you think sharp."

The professor knew his psychology. Make no mistake about it. Your physical exterior affects your mental interior. How you look on the outside affects how you think and feel on the inside.

All boys, I'm told, go through the "hat stage." That is, they use hats to identify themselves with the person or character they want to be. I will always remember a hat incident with my own son, Davey. One day he was dead set on being the Lone Ranger, but he had no Lone Ranger hat.

I tried to persuade him to substitute another. His protest was "But, Dad, I can't *think* like the Lone Ranger without a Lone Ranger hat."

I gave in finally and bought him the hat he needed. Sure enough, donning the hat, he *was* the Lone Ranger.

I often recall that incident because it says so much about the effect of appearance on thinking. Anyone who has ever served in the Army knows a soldier feels and thinks like a soldier when he is in uniform. A woman feels more like going to a party when she is dressed for a party.

By the same token, an executive feels more like an executive when he is dressed like one. A salesman expressed it to me this way: "I can't feel prosperous—and I have to if I'm going to make big sales—unless I know I look that way."

Your appearance talks to you; but it also talks to others. It helps determine what others think of you. In theory, it's pleasant to hear that people should look at a man's intellect, not his clothes. But don't be misled. People do evaluate you on the basis of your appearance. Your appearance is the *first* basis for evaluation other people have. And *first* impressions last, out of all proportion to the time it takes to form them.

In a supermarket one day I noticed one table of seedless grapes marked 15 cents a pound. On another table were what appeared to be identical grapes, this time packaged in polyethylene bags and marked 2 pounds for 35 cents.

I asked the young fellow at the weighing station, "What's the difference between the grapes priced at 15 cents a pound and those priced at two pounds for 35 cents?"

"The difference," he answered, "is polyethylene. We sell about twice as many of the grapes in the polyethylene bags. They look better that way."

Think about the grape example the next time you're selling yourself. Properly "packaged," you have a better chance to make the sale—and at a higher price.

The point is: the better you are packaged, the more public acceptance you will receive.

Tomorrow watch who is shown the most respect and courtesy in restaurants, on buses, in crowded lobbies, in stores, and at work. People look at another person, make a quick and often subconscious appraisal, and then treat him accordingly.

We look at some people and respond with the "Hey, Mac" attitude. We look at others and respond with the "Yes, sir" feeling.

Yes, a person's appearance definitely talks. The well-dressed person's appearance says positive things. It tells people, "Here is an important person: intelligent, prosperous, and dependable. This man can be looked up to, admired, trusted. He respects himself, and I respect him."

The shabby-looking fellow's appearance says negative things. It says, "Here is a person who isn't doing well. He's careless, inefficient, unimportant. He's just an average person. He deserves no special consideration. He's used to being pushed around."

When I stress "Respect your appearance" in training programs, almost always I am asked the question "I'm sold. Appearance *is* important. But how do you expect me to afford the kind of clothing that really makes me feel right and that causes others to look up to me?"

• That question puzzles many people. It plagued me for a long time. But the answer is really a simple one: *Pay twice as much and buy half as many.* Commit this answer to memory. Then practice it. Apply it to hats, suits, shoes, socks, coats—everything you wear. Insofar as appearance is concerned, quality is far more important than quantity. When you practice this principle, you'll find that both your respect for yourself and the respect of others for you will zoom upward. And you'll find you're actually ahead money-wise when you pay twice as much and buy half as many because:

1. Your garments will last more than twice as long because they are more than twice as good, and as a rule they will show "quality" as long as they last.

2. What you buy will stay in style longer. Better clothing always does.

3. You'll get better advice. Merchants selling $200 suits are usually much more interested in helping you find the garment that is "just right" for you than are merchants selling $100 suits.

Remember: Your appearance talks to you and it talks to others. Make certain it says, "Here is a person who has self-respect. He's important. Treat him that way."

You owe it to others—*but, more important, you owe it to yourself*—to look your best.

You are what you think you are. If your appearance makes you think you're inferior, you *are* inferior. If it makes you think small, you are small. Look your best and you will think and act your best.

THINK YOUR WORK IS IMPORTANT

There's a story often told about the job attitudes of three bricklayers. It's a classic, so let's go over it again.

When asked, "What are you doing?" the first bricklayer replied, "Laying brick." The second answered, "Making $9.30 an hour." And the third said, "Me? Why, I'm building the world's greatest cathedral."

Now, the story doesn't tell us what happened to these bricklayers in later years, but what do you think happened? Chances are that the first two bricklayers remained just that: bricklayers. They lacked vision. They lacked job respect. There was nothing behind them to propel them forward to greater success.

But you can wager every cent you have the bricklayer who visualized himself as building a great cathedral did not remain a bricklayer. Perhaps he became a foreman, or perhaps a contractor, or possibly an architect. He moved forward and upward. Why? Because thinking *does* make it so. Bricklayer number three was tuned to thought channels that pointed the way to self-development in his work.

Job thinking tells a lot about a person and his potential for larger responsibility.

A friend who operates a personnel selection firm said this to me recently: "One thing we always look for in appraising a job applicant for a client is how the applicant thinks about his present job. We are always favorably impressed when we find that an applicant thinks his present job is important, even though there may be something about it he doesn't like.

"Why? Simply this: If the applicant feels his present job is important, odds are that he will take pride in his next job, too. We've found an amazingly close correlation between a person's job respect and his job performance."

Like your appearance, the way you think toward your work says things about you to your superiors, associates, and subordinates—in fact, to everyone with whom you come in contact.

A few months ago I spent several hours with a friend who is personnel director for an appliance manufacturer. We talked about "building men." He explained his "personnel audit system" and what he had learned from it.

"We have about eight hundred nonproduction people," he began. "Under our personnel audit system, an assistant and I interview each employee every six months. Our purpose is simple. We want to learn how we can help him in his job. We think this is a good practice because each person working with us is important, else he wouldn't be on the payroll.

"We are careful not to ask the employees any point-blank questions. Instead we encourage him to talk about whatever he wants to. We aim to get his honest impressions. After each interview we fill out a rating form on the employee's attitudes toward specific aspects of his job.

"Now, here's something I've learned," he went on. "Our employees fit into one of two categories, group A and group B, on the basis of how they think toward their jobs.

"The persons in group B talk mainly about security, company retirement plans, sick leave policy, extra time off, what we're doing to improve the insurance program, and if they will be asked to work overtime next March as they were last March. They also talk a lot about disagreeable features of their job, things they don't like in fellow workers, and so on. People in group B—and they include close to 80 percent of all nonproduction personnel—view their jobs as a sort of necessary evil.

"The group A fellow sees his job through different glasses. He is concerned about his future and wants concrete suggestions on what he can do to make faster progress. He doesn't expect us to give him anything except a chance. The group A people think on a broader scale. They make suggestions for improving the business. They regard these interviews in my office as constructive. But the group B people often feel our personnel audit system is just a brainwashing affair, and they're glad to get it over with.

"Now, there's a way I check attitudes and what they mean to job success. All recommendations for promotions, pay increases, and special privileges are channeled to me by the employee's immediate supervisor. Almost invariably, it's a group A person who was recommended. And again almost without exception, problems come from the group B category.

"The biggest challenge in my job," he said, "is to try and help people move from group B to group A. It's not easy, though, because until a person thinks his job is important and thinks positively about it, he can't be helped."

This is concrete evidence that you are what you think you are, what your thought power directs you to become. Think you're weak, think you lack what it takes, think you will lose, think you are second-class—think this way, and you are doomed to mediocrity.

But think instead, *I am important. I do have what it takes. I am a first-class performer. My work is important.* Think this way, and you're headed straight to success.

The key to winning what you want lies in thinking positively toward yourself. The only real basis other people have for judging your abilities is your actions. And your actions are controlled by your thoughts.

You *are* what you *think* you are.

Wear the shoes of a supervisor for a few moments and ask yourself which person you would recommend for a raise or a promotion:

1. The secretary who, when the executive is out of the office, spends her time reading magazines or the secretary who uses such time to do the many little things that help the executive to accomplish more when he returns?

2. The employee who says, "Oh well, I can always get another job. If they don't like the way I do my work, I'll just quit" or the employee who views criticism constructively and sincerely tries to do higher-quality work?

3. The salesman who tells a customer, "Oh, I just do what they tell me to do. They said come out and see if you need anything" or the salesman who says, "Mr. Brown, I'm here to help you"?

4. The foreman who says to an employee, "To tell you the truth, I don't like my job much. Those guys up top give me

a pain in the neck. I don't know what they're talking about half the time" or the supervisor who says, "You've got to expect some unpleasantness on any job. But let me assure you, the men in the front office are on the ball. They'll do right by us"?

Isn't it obvious why many people stay at one level all their lives? Their thinking alone keeps them there.

An advertising executive once told me about his agency's informal training to "break in" new, inexperienced men.

"As company policy," he said, "we feel the best initial training is to start the young fellow, who, incidentally, is usually a college graduate, as a mail boy. We don't do this, of course, because we feel a fellow needs four years of college to take mail from one office to another. Our purpose is to give the new fellow maximum exposure to the many varied things which must be done in agency work. After he knows his way around, we give him an assignment.

"Now, occasionally, even after we've carefully explained why we're starting him out in the mail room, a young fellow feels that carrying the mail is belittling and unimportant. When this is the case, we know we've picked the wrong man. If he doesn't have the vision to see that being a mail boy is a necessary, practical step to important assignments, then he has no future in the agency business."

Remember, executives answer the question *What would he do on that specific level?* by first answering the question *What kind of job is he doing where he is now?*

Here is some logic, sound, straight, and easy. Read it at least five times before you go on:

A person who thinks *his job is important*
Receives mental signals on how to do his job better;
And a better job means
More promotions, more money, more prestige, more hap-
    piness.

We've all noticed how children quickly pick up the attitudes, habits, fears, and preferences of their parents. Whether it be food preferences, mannerisms, religious and political views, or any other type of behavior, the child is a living reflection of how his parents or guardians think; for he learns through imitation.

And so do adults! People continue to imitate others throughout life. And they imitate their leaders and supervisors; their thoughts and actions are influenced by these people.

You can check this easily. Study one of your friends and the person he works for, and note the similarities in thinking and action.

Here are some of the ways your friend may imitate his boss or other associate: slang and word choice, the way he smokes cigarettes, some facial expressions and mannerisms, choice of clothing, and automobile preferences. There are many, many more, of course.

Another way to note the power of imitation is to observe the attitudes of employees and compare them with those of the "chief." When the chief is nervous, tense, worried, his close associates reflect similar attitudes. But when Mr. Chief is on top, feeling good, so are his employees.

The point is this: *The way we think toward our jobs determines how our subordinates think toward their jobs.*

The job attitudes of our subordinates are direct reflections of our own job attitudes. It's well to remember that our points of superiority—and weakness—show up in the behavior of those who report to us, just as a child reflects the attitudes of his parents.

Consider just one characteristic of successful people: enthusiasm. Ever notice how an enthusiastic salesperson in a department store gets you, the customer, more excited about the merchandise? Or have you observed how an enthusiastic minister or other speaker has a wide-awake, alert, enthusiastic audience? If you have enthusiasm, those around you will have it, too.

But how does one develop enthusiasm? The basic step is simple: Think enthusiastically. Build in yourself an optimistic, progressive glow, a feeling that "this is great and I'm 100 percent for it."

You are what you think. Think enthusiasm and you'll be enthusiastic. To get high-quality work, be enthusiastic about the job you want done. Others will catch the enthusiasm you generate and you'll get first-class performance.

But if, in negative fashion, you "cheat" that company on expense money, supplies, and time, and in other little ways, then what can you expect your subordinates to do? Habitually arrive late and leave early, and what do you think the "troops" will do?

And there is a major incentive for us to think right about our jobs so that our subordinates will think right about their jobs. Our superiors evaluate us by measuring the quality and quantity of output we get from those reporting to us.

Look at it this way: whom would you elevate to division

sales manager—the branch sales manager whose salesmen are doing superior work or the branch sales manager whose salesmen deliver only average performance? Or whom would you recommend for promotion to production manager—the supervisor whose department meets its quota or the supervisor whose department lags behind?

Here are two suggestions for getting others to do more for you:

1. Always show positive attitudes toward your job so that your subordinates will "pick up" right thinking.

2. As you approach your job each day, ask yourself, "Am I worthy in every respect of being imitated? Are all my habits such that I would be glad to see them in my subordinates?"

GIVE YOURSELF A PEP TALK SEVERAL TIMES DAILY

Several months ago an automobile salesman told me about the success-producing technique he's developed. It makes sense. Read it.

"A big part of my job, for two hours a day," the salesman explained, "is telephoning prospects to arrange demonstration appointments. When I first started selling cars three years ago, this was my big problem. I was shy and afraid, and I know my voice sounded that way on the phone. It was easy for people I called to say, 'I'm not interested,' and hang up.

"Every Monday morning back then our sales manager held a sales meeting. It was a pretty inspirational affair, and it made me feel good. And what's more, I always seemed to arrange more demonstrations on Monday than on any other day. But the trouble was that little of Monday's inspiration carried over to Tuesday and the rest of the week.

"Then I got an idea. If the sales manager can pep me up, why can't I pep myself up? Why not give myself a pep talk just before I start making those phone calls? That day I decided to try it. Without telling anyone I walked out on the lot and found a vacant car. Then for several minutes I talked to myself. I told myself, 'I'm a good car salesman and I'm going to be the best. I sell good cars and I give good deals. The people I'm phoning need those cars and I'm going to sell them.'

"Well, from the very beginning this self-supercharging paid off. I felt so good I didn't dread making those calls. I *wanted* to make them. I no longer go out on the lot and sit in a car to give myself a pep talk. But I still use the technique. Before I dial a number I silently remind myself that I'm a top-notch salesman and I'm going to get results, and I do."

That's a pretty good idea, isn't it? To be on top, you've got to feel like you're on top. Give yourself a pep talk and discover how much bigger and stronger you feel.

Recently, in a training program I conducted, each person was asked to give a ten-minute talk on "being a leader." One of the trainees gave a miserable presentation. His knees literally shook and his hands trembled. He forgot what he was going to say. After fumbling for five or six minutes, he sat down, thoroughly defeated.

After the session, I spoke to him just long enough to ask him to be there fifteen minutes early at the next session.

As promised, he was there fifteen minutes ahead of time for the next session. The two of us sat down to discuss his talk of the night before. I asked him to remember as clearly as he could exactly what he had thought about the five minutes just before he gave his talk.

"Well, I guess all I thought about was how scared I was. I knew I was going to make a fool of myself. I knew I was going to be a flop. I kept thinking, 'Who am I to be talking about being a leader?' I tried to remember what I was going to say, but all I could think about was failing."

"Right there," I injected, "is the answer to your problem. Before you got up to talk you gave yourself a terrible mental beating. You convinced yourself that you would fail. Is it any wonder your talk didn't come off well? Instead of developing courage, you developed fear.

"Now, this evening's session," I continued, "starts in just four minutes. Here's what I'd like you to do. Give yourself a pep talk for the next few minutes. Go in that vacant room across the hall and tell yourself, 'I'm going to give a great talk. I've got something those people need to hear and I want to say.' Keep repeating those sentences forcefully, with complete conviction. Then come into the conference room and give your talk again."

I wish you could have been there to hear the difference. That brief, self-administered, hard-hitting pep talk helped him to make a splendid speech.

The moral: Practice uplifting self-praise. Don't practice belittling self-punishment.

You are what you think you are. Think more of yourself and there is more of you.

Build your own "sell-yourself-to-yourself" commercial. Think for a moment about one of America's most popular products,

Coca-Cola. Every day your eyes or ears come in contact many times with the good news about Coke. The people who make Coca-Cola are continually reselling you on Coke, and for a good reason. If they stopped reselling you, chances are you'd grow lukewarm and eventually cold to Coke. Then sales would drop.

But the Coca-Cola Company isn't going to let this happen. They resell you and resell you and resell you on Coke.

Every day you and I see half-alive people who are no longer sold on themselves. They lack self-respect for their most important product—themselves. These folks are indifferent. They feel small. They feel like nobodies, and because they feel that way, that's what they are.

The half-alive person needs to be resold on himself. He needs to realize that he's a first-class person. He needs honest, sincere belief in himself.

Tom Staley is a young fellow who is going places—and fast. Tom regularly resells himself on himself three times every day with what he calls "Tom Staley's 60-Second Commercial." He carries his personalized commercial in his billfold at all times. Here is exactly what it says:

> Tom Staley, meet Tom Staley—an important, a really important person. Tom, you're a big thinker, so think big. Think Big about Everything. You've got plenty of ability to do a first-class job, so do a first-class job.
> Tom, you believe in Happiness, Progress, and Prosperity.
> So: talk only Happiness,
>   talk only Progress,
>   talk only Prosperity.
> You have lots of drive, Tom, lots of drive.

So put that drive to work. Nothing can stop you, Tom,
   nothing.
Tom, you're enthusiastic. Let your enthusiasm show
   through.
You look good, Tom, and you feel good. Stay that way.
Tom Staley, you were a great fellow yesterday and you're
   going to be an even greater fellow today. Now go to it,
   Tom. Go forward.

Tom credits his commercial with helping him become a more successful, dynamic person. "Before I started selling myself to myself," says Tom, "I thought I was inferior to just about anybody and everybody. Now I realize that I've got what it takes to win and I'm winning. And I'm always going to win."

Here's how to build your "sell-yourself-to-yourself" commercial. First, select your assets, your points of superiority. Ask yourself, "What are my best qualities?" Don't be shy in describing yourself.

Next, put these points down on paper in your own words. Write your commercial to you. Reread Tom Staley's commercial. Notice how he talks to Tom. Talk to yourself. Be very direct. Don't think of anyone but *you* as you say your commercial.

Third, practice your commercial *out loud* in private at least once a day. It helps a lot to do this before a mirror. Put your body into it. Repeat your commercial forcefully with determination. Make your blood travel faster through your body. Get yourself warmed up.

Fourth, read your commercial silently several times every day. Read it before you tackle anything that demands courage. Read it every time you feel let down. Keep your commercial handy at all times—then use it.

Just one thing more. A lot of people, maybe even a majority, may "ho ho" at this success-rewarding technique. That's because they refuse to believe that success comes from managed thinking. But please! Don't accept the judgment of average people. You are *not* average. If you have any doubts as to the basic soundness of the "sell-yourself-to-yourself" principle, ask the most successful person you know what he thinks about it. Ask him, and then start selling yourself to yourself.

UPGRADE YOUR THINKING. THINK LIKE IMPORTANT PEOPLE THINK

Upgrading your thinking upgrades your actions, and this produces success. Here is an easy way to help you make more of yourself by thinking like important people think. Use the form below as a guide.

HOW AM I THINKING? CHECKLIST

SITUATION	ASK YOURSELF
1. When I worry	Would an important person worry about this? Would the most successful person I know be disturbed about this?
2. An idea	What would an important person do if he had this idea?
3. My appearance	Do I look like someone who has maximum self-respect?
4. My language	Am I using the language of successful people?
5. What I read	Would an important person read this?
6. Conversation	Is this something successful people would discuss?

SITUATION	ASK YOURSELF
7. When I lose my temper	Would an important person get mad at what I'm mad at?
8. My jokes	Is this the kind of joke an important person would tell?
9. My job	How does an important person describe his job to others?

Cement in your mind the question "Is this the way an important person does it?" Use this question to make you a bigger, more successful person.

In a nutshell, remember:

1. Look important; it helps you think important. Your appearance talks to you. Be sure it lifts your spirits and builds your confidence. Your appearance talks to others. Make certain it says, "Here is an important person: intelligent, prosperous, and dependable."

2. Think your work is important. Think this way, and you will receive mental signals on how to do your job better. Think your work is important, and your subordinates will think their work is important too.

3. Give yourself a pep talk several times daily. Build a "sell-yourself-to-yourself" commercial. Remind yourself at every opportunity that you're a first-class person.

4. In all of life's situations, ask yourself, "Is this the way an important person thinks?" Then obey the answer.

7

MANAGE YOUR ENVIRONMENT: GO FIRST CLASS

YOUR MIND IS AN amazing mechanism. When your mind works one way, it can carry you forward to outstanding success. But the same mind operating in a different manner can produce a total failure.

The mind is the most delicate, most sensitive instrument in all creation. Let's look now and see what makes the mind think the way it does. Millions of people are diet conscious. We're a calorie-counting nation. We spend millions of dollars on vitamins, minerals, and other dietary supplements. And we all know why. Through nutritional research, we've learned that the body reflects the diet fed the body. Physical stamina, resistance to disease, body size, even how long we live are all closely related to what we eat.

The body is what the body is fed. By the same token, the mind is what the mind is fed. Mind food, of course, doesn't come in packages, and you can't buy it at the store. Mind food is your environment—all the countless things that influence your conscious and subconscious thought. The kind of mind food we consume determines our habits, attitudes, personality. Each of us inherited a certain capacity to develop. But how much of that capacity we have developed and the way we have developed that capacity depends on the kind of mind food we feed it.

The mind reflects what its environment feeds it just as surely as the body reflects the food you feed it.

Have you ever thought what kind of person you would be had you been reared in some foreign country instead of the United States? What kinds of foods would you prefer? Would your preferences for clothing be the same? What sort of entertainment would you like the most? What kind of work would you be doing? What would your religion be?

You can't, of course, be sure of the answers to these questions. But chances are you would be a materially different person had you grown up in a different country. Why? Because you would have been influenced by a different environment. As the saying goes, you are a product of your environment.

Mark it well. Environment shapes us, makes us think the way we do. Try to name just one habit or one mannerism you have that you did not pick up from other people. Relatively minor things, like the way we walk, cough, hold a cup; our preferences for music, literature, entertainment, clothing—all stem in very large part from environment.

More important, the size of your thinking, your goals, your attitudes, your very personality is formed by your environment.

Prolonged association with negative people makes us think negatively; close contact with petty individuals develops petty habits in us. On the bright side, companionship with people with big ideas raises the level of our thinking; close contact with ambitious people gives us ambition.

Experts agree that the person you are *today*, your personality, ambitions, present status in life, are largely the result of your psychological environment. And experts agree also that the person you *will be* one, five, ten, twenty years from now depends almost entirely on your future environment.

You will change over the months and years. This we know. But *how* you will change depends on your future environment, the mind food you feed yourself. Let's look now at what we can do to make our future environment pay off in satisfaction and prosperity.

RECONDITION YOURSELF FOR SUCCESS

The number one obstacle on the road to high-level success is the feeling that major accomplishment is beyond reach. This attitude stems from many, many suppressive forces that direct our thinking toward mediocre levels.

To understand these suppressive forces, let's go back to the time we were children. As children, all of us set high goals. At a surprisingly young age we made plans to conquer the unknown, to be leaders, to attain positions of high importance, to do exciting and stimulating things, to become wealthy and famous—in short, to be first, biggest, and best. And in our blessed ignorance we saw our way clear to accomplish these goals.

But what happened? Long before we reached the age when we could begin to work toward our great objectives, a multitude of suppressive influences went to work.

From all sides we heard "It's foolish to be a dreamer" and that our ideas were "impractical, stupid, naive, or foolish," that you have "got to have money to go places," that "luck determines who gets ahead or you've got to have important friends," or you're "too old or too young."

As a result of being bombarded with the "you-can't-get-ahead-so-don't-bother-to-try" propaganda, most people you know can be classified into three groups:

First group: Those who surrendered completely. The majority of people are convinced deep down inside that they haven't got what it takes, that real success, real accomplishment, is for others who are lucky or fortunate in some special respect. You can easily spot these people because they go to great lengths to rationalize their status and explain how "happy" they really are.

A very intelligent man, age thirty-two, who has dead-ended himself in a safe but mediocre position, recently spent hours telling me why he was so satisfied with his job. He did a good job of rationalizing, but he was only kidding himself and he knew it. What he really wanted was to work in a challenging situation where he could grow and develop. But that "multitude of suppressive influences" had convinced him that he was inadequate for big things.

This group is, in reality, just the other extreme of the discontented job switcher searching for opportunity. Rationalizing yourself into a rut, which incidentally has been described as a grave with both ends open, can be as bad as wandering aimlessly, hoping opportunity will somehow, someday hit you in the face.

Second group: Those who surrendered partially. A second but much smaller group enters adult life with considerable hope for success. These people prepare themselves. They work. They plan. But, after a decade or so, resistance begins to build up, competition for top-level jobs looks rugged. This group then decides that greater success is not worth the effort.

They rationalize, "We're earning more than the average and we live better than the average. Why should we knock ourselves out?"

Actually, this group has developed a set of fears: fear of failure, fear of social disapproval, fear of insecurity, fear of losing what they already have. These people aren't satisfied because deep down they know they have surrendered. This group includes many talented, intelligent people who elect to crawl through life because they are afraid to stand up and run.

Third group: Those who never surrender. This group, maybe 2 or 3 percent of the total, doesn't let pessimism dictate, doesn't believe in surrendering to suppressive forces, doesn't believe in crawling. Instead, these people live and breathe success. This group is the happiest because it accomplishes the most. These people become top salesmen, top executives, top leaders in their respective fields. These people find life stimulating, rewarding, worthwhile. These people look forward to each new day, each new encounter with other people, as adventures to be lived fully.

Let's be honest. All of us would like to be in the third group, the one that finds greater success each year, the one that does things and gets results.

To get—and stay—in this group, however, we must fight off the suppressive influences of our environment. To understand how persons in the first and second groups will unwittingly try to hold you back, study this example.

Suppose you tell several of your "average" friends, with the greatest sincerity: "Someday I'm going to be vice president of this company."

What will happen? Your friends will probably think you are joking. And if they should believe you mean it, chances are they will say, "You poor guy, you sure have a lot to learn."

Behind your back they may even question whether you have all your marbles.

Now, assume you repeat the same statement with equal sincerity to the president of your company. How will he react? One thing is certain: he will *not* laugh. He will look at you intently and ask himself: "Does this fellow really mean this?"

But he will not, we repeat, laugh.

Because big men do not laugh at big ideas.

Or suppose you tell some average people you plan to own an expensive home, and they may laugh at you because they think it's impossible. But tell your plan to a person already living in an expensive home, and he won't be surprised. He knows it isn't impossible, because he's already done it.

Remember: *People who tell you it cannot be done almost always are unsuccessful people, are strictly average or mediocre at best in terms of accomplishment.* The opinions of these people can be poison.

Develop a defense against people who want to convince you that you can't do it. Accept negative advice only as a challenge to prove that you *can* do it.

Be extra, extra cautious about this: don't let negative-thinking people—"negators"—destroy your plan to think yourself to success. Negators are everywhere, and they seem to delight in sabotaging the positive progress of others.

During college I buddied for a couple of semesters with W. W. He was a fine friend, the kind of fellow who would loan you a little money when you were short or help you in many little ways. Despite this fine loyalty, W. W. was just about 100 percent sour and bitter toward life, the future, opportunity. He was a real negator.

During that period I was an enthusiastic reader of a certain newspaper columnist who stressed hope, the positive approach, opportunity. When W. W. would find me reading this columnist, or when her column was mentioned, he'd swing verbally and say, "Oh, for Pete's sake, Dave. Read the front page. That's where you learn about life. You ought to know that columnist is just making a quick buck dishing out sweet sauce for the weak."

When our discussions turned to getting ahead in life, W. W. was right there with his moneymaking formula. In his own words, it went like this: "Dave, there are just three ways to make money these days. One, marry a rich woman: two, steal in a nice, clean, legal way; or three, get to know the right people, somebody with plenty of pull."

W. W. was always prepared to defend his formula with examples. Sticking to the front page, he was quick to cite that one labor leader in a thousand who had siphoned off a pile of money from the union till and got away with it. He kept his eyes open for that rare, rare marriage of the fruit picker to Miss Millionaire. And he knew a fellow who knew a fellow who knew a big man and got cut in on a big deal that made him rich.

W. W. was several years older than I, and he made excellent grades in his engineering classes. I looked up to him in a younger-brother sort of way. I came dangerously close to ditching my basic convictions about what it takes to be a success and accepting the negators' philosophy.

Fortunately, one evening after a long discussion with W. W. I grabbed hold of myself. It dawned on me that I was listening to the voice of failure. It seemed to me W. W. was talking more to convince himself than he was to convert me to his way of thinking. From then on I regarded W. W. as an object lesson, a sort of experimental guinea pig. Rather than buy what he said, I studied him, trying to figure out why he thought the way he did and where such thinking would take him. I turned my negator friend into a personal experiment.

I haven't seen W. W. in eleven years. But a mutual friend saw him just a few months ago. W. W. is working as a low-paid drafts-man in Washington. I asked my friend whether W. W. has changed.

"No, except if anything he's more negative than when we knew him. He's having a tough go of it. He has four children, and on his income it's rough. Old W. W. has the brains to be making five times what he is if he just knew how to use those brains."

Negators are everywhere. Some negators, like the one who almost tripped me, are well-meaning folks. But others are jealous people who, not moving ahead themselves, want you to stumble too. They feel inadequate themselves, so they want to make a mediocre person out of you.

Be extra careful. Study negators. Don't let them destroy your plans for success.

A young office worker recently explained to me why he had changed car pools. "One fellow," he said, "talked about nothing trip in and trip out except what an awful company we worked for. Regardless of what management did, he found fault. He was nega-tive about everyone from his supervisor on up. The products we sold were no good. Every policy had something wrong with it. As he saw it, absolutely everything had something wrong with it.

"Each morning I arrived at work tense and wound up tight. And each night, after hearing him preach and rant for forty-five minutes about all the things that went wrong that day, I got home discouraged and depressed. Finally, I got sense enough to get in another car pool. It's made a world of difference, for now I'm with a group of fellows who can see two sides to a question."

That young fellow changed his environment. Smart, wasn't he?

Make no mistake about it. You *are* judged by the company you keep. Birds of a feather *do* flock together. Fellow workers are not all alike. Some are negative, others positive. Some work because they "have to"; others are ambitious and work for advancement. Some associates belittle everything the boss says or does; others are much more objective and realize they must be good followers before they can be good leaders.

How we think is directly affected by the group we're in. *Be sure you're in the flock that thinks right.*

There are pitfalls to watch in your work environment. In every group there are persons who, secretly aware of their own inadequacies, want to stand in your way and prevent you from making progress. Many ambitious fellows have been laughed at, even threatened, because they tried to be more efficient and produce more. Let's face it. Some folks, being jealous, want to make you feel embarrassed because you want to move upward.

This often happens in factories, where fellow workers sometimes resent the fellow who wants to speed up production. It happens in the military service when a clique of negative-minded individuals poke fun at and try to humiliate the young soldier who wants to go to officers' school.

It happens in business, too, when a few individuals not qualified to advance try to block the way for someone else.

You've seen it happen time and again in high schools when a group of lunkheads deride a classmate who has the good sense to make the most of his educational opportunities and come out with high grades. Sometimes—and all too sadly often—the bright student is jeered at until he reaches the conclusion that it isn't smart to be intelligent.

Ignore such negative thinkers in your midst.

For often the remarks made in your direction aren't so personal as you might at first think. They are merely a projection of the speaker's own feeling of failure and discouragement.

Don't let negative thinkers pull you down to their level. Let them slide by, like the water from the proverbial duck's back. Cling to people who think progressively. Move upward with *them*.

You can do it, simply by thinking right!

A special word of caution: be careful about your source of advice. In most organizations you will encounter freelance advisors who "know the ropes" and are tremendously eager to clue you in. One time I overheard a freelance advisor explaining the facts of office life to a bright young man just starting in. Said the advisor: "The best way to get along here is just stay out of everybody's way. If they ever get to know you, all they'll do is pile more work on you. Be especially careful to stay away from Mr. Z. [the department manager]. If he thinks you haven't got enough to do, he'll really load you down . . ."

This freelance advisor had been with the company for almost thirty years and was still bottom man on the totem pole. What a consultant for a young fellow who wants to move upward in the business!

MAKE IT A RULE TO SEEK ADVICE FROM PEOPLE WHO KNOW

There's a lot of incorrect thinking that successful people are inaccessible. The plain truth is that they are *not*. As a rule, it's the more successful people who are the most humble and ready to help. Since they are sincerely interested in their work and success, they are eager to see that the work lives on and that somebody capable succeeds them when they retire. It's the "would-be-big" people who are most often the most abrupt and hard to get to know.

An executive made this clear: "I'm a busy woman, but there's no Do Not Disturb sign on my office door. Counseling people is one of my key functions. We give standardized training of one kind or another to everybody in the company. But personal counseling, or 'tutoring,' as I like to call it, is available for the asking.

"I stand ready to help the fellow who comes in here with either a company or a personal problem. The fellow who displays curiosity and exhibits a real desire to know more about his job and how it relates to other jobs is the individual I like most to help.

"But," she said, "for obvious reasons, I can't spend time offering advice to anybody who isn't sincere in seeking it."

Go first class when you have questions. Seeking advice from a failure is like consulting a quack on how to cure cancer.

Many executives today never employ persons for key jobs without first interviewing the fellow's wife. One sales executive explained to me, "I want to be sure the prospective salesman has his family behind him, a cooperative family that won't object to travel, irregular hours, and other inconveniences which are part of selling, a family that will help the salesman over those inevitable rough spots."

Executives today realize that what happens on weekends and between 6 P.M. and 9 A.M. directly affects a person's performance from 9 A.M. to 6 P.M. The person with a constructive off-the-job life nearly always is more successful than the person who lives in a dull, dreary home situation.

Let's look in on the traditional way two co-workers, John and Milton, spend their weekends. Let's look, too, at the ultimate results.

John's psychological diet on weekends is something like this: Usually, one evening is spent with some carefully selected, interesting friends. Another evening is generally spent out: perhaps at a movie, a civic or community project, or some friends' house. John devotes Saturday morning to Boy Scout work. Saturday afternoon he does errands and chores around the house. Often he works on some special project. Currently it's building a patio in the backyard. On Sundays John and his family do something special. One Sunday recently they climbed a mountain; another Sunday they visited a museum. Occasionally they drive into the nearby countryside, for John wants to buy some country property in the not-too-distant future.

Sunday evening is spent quietly. John usually reads a book and catches up on the news.

Wrapped up, John's weekends are planned. His many refreshing activities keep boredom locked out. John gets plenty of psychological sunshine.

Milton's psychological diet is much less well balanced than John's. His weekends are unplanned. Milton is usually pretty "tired" on Friday night, but he goes through the motions of asking his wife, "Want to do anything tonight?" but the plan dies there. Rarely do Milton and his wife entertain, and rarely are they invited out. Milton sleeps late on Saturday morning, and the rest of the day is taken up with chores of one kind or another. Saturday night Milton and his family usually go to a movie or watch TV ("What else is there to do?"). Milton spends most of Sunday morning in bed. Sunday afternoon they drive over to Bill and Mary's or Bill and Mary drive over to see them. (Bill and Mary are the only couple Milton and his wife visit regularly.)

Milton's entire weekend is marked by boredom. By the time Sunday evening rolls around, the whole family is on each other's nerves as a result of "cabin fever." There are no knock-down, drag-out fights, but there are hours of psychological warfare.

Milton's weekend is dull, dreary, boring. Milton gets no psychological sunshine.

Now, what's the effect of these two home environments on John and Milton? Over a period of a week or two there probably is no perceptible effect. But over a period of months and years the effect is tremendous.

John's environmental pattern leaves him refreshed, gives him ideas, tunes up his thinking. He's like an athlete being fed steak.

Milton's environmental pattern leaves him psychologically starved. His thinking mechanism is impaired. He's like an athlete being fed candy and beer.

John and Milton may be on the same level today, but there will gradually be a wide gap between them in the months ahead, with John in the lead position.

Casual observers will say, "Well, I guess John has more on the ball than Milton."

But those of us who know will explain that much of the difference in job performance is the result of the difference in the mind food consumed by the two fellows.

Every farmer in the corn belt knows that if he puts plenty of fertilizer with his corn, he's going to get a bigger yield. Thinking too must be given additional nourishment if we want to get better results.

My wife and I, along with five other couples, spent a wonderful evening last month as guests of a department store executive and his wife. My wife and I lingered just a little longer than the others, so I had a chance to ask our host, whom I know well, a question that had been in my mind all evening. "This was really a wonderful evening," I said, "but I'm puzzled about one thing. I'd expected to meet mainly other retailing executives here tonight. But your guests all represented different fields. There was a writer, a doctor, an engineer, an accountant, and a teacher."

He smiled and said, "Well, we often do entertain retailing people. But Helen and I find it's very refreshing to mix with people who do something else for a living. I'm afraid if we confined our entertaining to people who have only interests similar to our own, we'd find ourselves in the old, well-known rut.

"Besides," he went on, "people are my business. Every day thousands of people of every occupational group imaginable visit our store. The more I can learn about other people—their ideas, interests, viewpoints—the better job I can do in giving them the merchandise and service they want and will buy."

Here are a few simple "do's" to help make your social environment first class:

1. Do circulate in new groups. Restricting your social environment to the same small group produces boredom, dullness,
   dissatisfaction; equally important, remember that your
   success-building program requires that you become an
   expert in understanding people. Trying to learn all there is
   to know about people by studying one small group is like
   trying to master mathematics by reading one short book.

   Make new friends, join new organizations, enlarge your
   social orbit. Then too, variety in people, like variety in anything else, adds spice to life and gives it a broader dimen-
   sion. It's good mind food.

2. Do select friends who have views different from your own.
   In this modern age, the narrow individual hasn't much
   future. Responsibility and positions of importance gravi-
   tate to the person who is able to see both sides. If you're
   a Republican, make sure you have some friends who are
   Democrats, and vice versa. Get to know people of different
   religious faiths. Associate with opposites. But just be sure
   they are persons with real potential.

3. Do select friends who stand above petty, unimportant
   things. Folks who are more concerned with the square foot-
   age of your home or the appliances you have or don't have
   than with your ideas and your conversation are inclined
   to be petty. Guard your psychological environment. Select
   friends who are interested in positive things, friends who
   really *do* want to see you succeed. Find friends who breathe
   encouragement into your plans and ideals. If you don't, if

you select petty thinkers as your close friends, you'll gradually develop into a petty thinker yourself.

We're a poison-conscious nation—body poison, that is.

Every restaurateur is on guard against food poisoning. Just a couple of cases of it, and his patrons won't come near his place. We've got tons of laws to protect the public against hundreds of body poisons. We put—or should put—poisons on the top shelves so the kids can't reach them. We go to any extreme to avoid body poison. And it's good that we do.

But there's another type of poison perhaps a little more insidious—thought poison—commonly called "gossip." Thought poison differs from body poison in two ways. It affects the mind, not the body, and is more subtle. The person being poisoned usually doesn't know it.

Thought poison is subtle, but it accomplishes "big" things. It reduces the size of our thinking by forcing us to concentrate on petty, unimportant things. It warps and twists our thinking about people because it is based on a distortion of facts, and it creates a guilt feeling in us that shows through when we meet the person we've gossiped about. Thought poison is 0 percent *right* thinking: it is 100 percent *wrong* thinking.

And contrary to lots of opinion, women have no exclusive franchise on gossip. Every day many men, too, live in a partially poisoned environment. Every day thousands of gossip fests staged by men take place on such topics as "the boss's marital or financial problems"; "Bill's politicking to get ahead in business"; "the probability of John being transferred"; "the reasons for special favors being awarded Tom"; and "why they brought in that new man." Gossiping goes something like this: "Say, I just heard . . . no, why . . . well, it doesn't surprise me . . . he had it coming to him . . . of course, this is confidential . . ."

Conversation is a big part of our psychological environment. Some conversation is healthy. It encourages you. It make you feel like you're taking a walk in the warm sunshine of a spring day. Some conversation makes you feel like a winner.

But other conversation is more like walking through a poisonous, radioactive cloud. It chokes you. It makes you feel ill. It turns you into a loser.

Gossip is just negative conversation about people, and the victim of thought poison begins to think he enjoys it. He seems to get a form of poisoned joy from talking negatively about others, not knowing that to successful people he is becoming increasingly unlikable, and unreliable.

One of these thought-poison addicts walked into a conversation some friends and I were having about Benjamin Franklin. As soon as Mr. Killjoy learned the topic of our chat, he came through with choice bits about Franklin's personal life, in a negative way. Perhaps it's true that Franklin was a character in some ways and he might have made the scandal magazines had they been around in the eighteenth century. But the point is, Benjamin Franklin's personal life had no bearing on the discussion at hand, and I couldn't help being glad that we weren't discussing somebody whom we knew intimately.

Talk about people? *Yes,* but stay on the positive side.

Let's make one point clear: Not all conversation is gossip. Bull sessions, shop talk, and just "batting the breeze" are necessary at times. They serve a good purpose when they are constructive. You can test your proneness to be a gossiper by taking this test:

1. Do I spread rumors about other people?

2. Do I always have good things to say about others?

3. Do I like to hear reports of a scandal?

4. Do I judge others only on the basis of facts?

5. Do I encourage others to bring their rumors to me?

6. Do I precede my conversations with "Don't tell anybody"?

7. Do I keep confidential information confidential?

8. Do I feel guilty about what I say concerning other people?

The right answers are obvious.

Meditate on this thought for just a moment: Taking an ax and chopping your neighbor's furniture to pieces won't make your furniture look one bit better; and using verbal axes and grenades on another person doesn't do one thing to make you a better you or me a better me.

Go first class: that is an excellent rule to follow in everything you do, including the goods and services you buy. Once, to prove the unconditional truth of the go-first-class thinking, I asked a group of trainees to give one example of how they had been penny-wise and pound-foolish. Here are some sample replies:

"I bought a low-priced suit from an offbeat retailer. Thought I got a bargain, but the suit was simply no good."

"My car needed a new automatic transmission. Took it to an alley garage that agreed to do the job for $25 less than an authorized dealer. The 'new' transmission lasted 1,800 miles. And the garage wouldn't make it right."

"For months I ate at a real greasy spoon trying to save money. The place wasn't clean, the food wasn't good, the service—well, you couldn't call it that—and the clientele was a bunch of down-at-heel-ers. One day a friend persuaded me to join him for lunch at one of the best restaurants in town. He ordered the businessman's lunch, so I did too. I was amazed at what I got: good food, good service, good atmosphere, and for just a little more than I had been paying at the greasy spoon. I learned a big lesson."

There were many other replies. One fellow reported that he got in trouble with the Bureau of Internal Revenue because he used a "bargain" accountant; another went to a cut-rate doctor and later learned he had received a completely wrong diagnosis. Others related the costs of going second class in home repairs, hotels, and other goods and services.

Of course, I've heard the argument many times "but I can't afford to go first class." The simplest answer is: you cannot afford to go any other way. Certainly in the long run, going first class actually costs you less than going second class. Then, too, it's better to have fewer things and have quality than to have many things and have junk. It's better, for example, to have one really good pair of shoes than to have three pairs of second-class shoes.

People rate you for quality, often subconsciously perhaps. Develop an instinct for quality. It pays. And it costs no more, often costs less, than second class.

MAKE YOUR ENVIRONMENT MAKE YOU SUCCESSFUL

1. Be environment-conscious. Just as body diet makes the body, mind diet makes the mind.

2. Make your environment work for you, not against you. Don't let suppressive forces—the negative, you-can't-do-it people—make you think defeat.

3. Don't let small-thinking people hold you back. Jealous people want to see you stumble. Don't give them that satisfaction.

4. Get your advice from successful people. Your future is important. Never risk it with freelance advisors who are living failures.

5. Get plenty of psychological sunshine. Circulate in new groups. Discover new and stimulating things to do.

6. Throw thought poison out of your environment. Avoid gossip. Talk about people, but stay on the positive side.

7. Go first class in everything you do. You can't afford to go any other way.

8

MAKE YOUR ATTITUDES YOUR ALLIES

CAN YOU READ MINDS? Reading minds is easier than you think. Perhaps you've never thought of it, but you read the minds of other people, and they read your mind, every day.

How do we do it? We do it automatically, through attitude appraisals.

Remember the song "You Don't Need to Know the Language to Say You're in Love"? Bing Crosby made it famous some years ago. There's a whole bookful of applied psychology packed into those simple lyrics. You *don't* need to know the language to say you're in love. Anyone who's ever been in love knows that.

And you don't need to know any language to say "I like you" or "I despise you" or "I think you're important" or "unimportant" or "I envy you." You don't need to know words or to use words to say "I like my job" or "I'm bored" or "I'm hungry." People speak without a sound.

How we think shows through in how we act. Attitudes are mirrors of the mind. They reflect thinking.

You can read the mind of the fellow sitting at a desk. You sense, by observing his expressions and mannerisms, how he feels toward his job. You can read the minds of salesmen, students, husbands, and wives; you not only can—you *do*.

The expert actors—those in demand in movies and television year after year—in a sense are not actors at all. They don't play their roles. Instead they lose their own identity and actually think and feel like the character they are playing. They've *got* to. Else they'd look like phonies and their ratings would plunge.

Attitudes do more than show through. They "sound" through too. A secretary does more than identify an office when she says, "Good morning, Mr. Shoemaker's office." In just five words one secretary says, "I like you. I'm glad you're calling. I think you are important. I like my job."

But another secretary saying exactly the same words tells you, "You bothered me. I wish you hadn't called. I'm bored with my job, and I don't like people who bother me."

We read attitudes through expressions and voice tones and inflections. Here's why. In the long, long history of humankind, a speaking language even remotely resembling what we use today is a very recent invention. So recent, you might say, in terms of the great clock of time, that we developed a language only this morning. For millions and millions of years, people got by with little more than moans and groans and grunts and growls.

So for millions of years people communicated with other people by body and facial expressions and sounds, not words. And we still communicate our attitudes, our feelings toward people and things, the same way. Aside from direct body contact, body movements, facial expressions, and sound are the only ways we have to communicate with infants. And those young ones show an uncanny ability to spot the phony.

Professor Erwin H. Schell, one of America's most respected authorities on leadership, says, "Obviously, there is something more than facilities and competence that makes for accomplishment. I have come to believe that this linkage factor, this catalyst, if you will, can be defined in a single word—*attitude*. When our attitude is right, our abilities reach a maximum of effectiveness and good results inevitably follow."

Attitudes *do* make the difference. Salesmen with the right attitude beat their quotas; students with the right attitude make As; right attitudes pave the way to really happy married life. Right attitudes make you effective in dealing with people, enable you to develop as a leader. Right attitudes win for you in every situation.

Grow these three attitudes. Make them your allies in everything you do.

1. Grow the attitude of *I'm activated.*

2. Grow the attitude of *You are important.*

3. Grow the attitude of *Service first.*

Now let's see how.

Years ago, when I was a college sophomore, I enrolled in an American history class. I remember the class vividly, not because I learned much about American history but because in an unusual way I learned this basic principle of successful living: *To activate others, you must first activate yourself.*

The history class was very large, and it was held in a fanshaped auditorium. The professor, who was a middle-aged fellow and apparently well educated, was, nevertheless, pathetically dull. Rather than interpret history as an alive, fascinating subject, the professor merely cited one dead fact after another. It was a frightful wonder how he could possibly make such an interesting subject so terribly dull. But he did.

You can imagine the effect the professor's boredom had on the students. Talking and sleeping got so out of hand that the professor had two assistants patrol the aisles to break up student conversations and wake up those who had dozed off.

Occasionally, the professor would stop and, shaking his finger at the class, would say, "I'm warning you. You've got to pay attention to what I say. You've got to stop this talking, and that's all there is to it." This, of course, made little impression on his students, many of whom, as veterans, had gambled their lives only months before, had made history on islands and in bombers.

As I sat there watching this potentially great, wonderful experience turn into a disgusting farce, I found myself wrestling with the question "Why are the students ignoring what the professor has to say?"

The answer came.

The students had no interest in what the professor was saying because the professor himself had no interest. He was bored with history, and it showed through. *To activate others, to get them to be enthusiastic, you must first be enthusiastic yourself.*

Over the years I've tested this principle in hundreds of different situations. It always holds true. A man who lacks enthusiasm never develops it in another. But a person who is enthusiastic soon has enthusiastic followers.

The enthusiastic salesman need never worry about unenthusiastic buyers. The enthusiastic teacher need never worry about disinterested students. The activated minister need never be distressed by a sleepy congregation.

Enthusiasm can make things 1,100 percent better. Two years ago, employees in a business I'm acquainted with donated $94.35 to the Red Cross. This year the same employees, with just about the same payroll, donated almost $1,100, an increase of 1,100 percent.

The drive captain who collected only $94.35 was totally lacking in enthusiasm. He made remarks like "I suppose it's a worthwhile organization"; "I've never had any direct contact with it"; "It's a big organization and they collect a lot from the wealthy, so I suppose it's not too important if you contribute"; "If you can make a donation, see me." This fellow did nothing to inspire anyone to want to join the Red Cross and do it in a big way.

This year's drive captain was a different sort. He had enthusiasm. He gave examples of case histories that showed how the Red Cross pitches in when disaster strikes. He showed how the Red Cross depends on donations from everyone. He asked the employees to be guided in giving by how much they would be willing to give their neighbor if disaster should strike him. He said, "Look what the Red Cross has done!" Notice, he did not beg. He did not say, "Each of you is expected to donate XX dollars." All he did was to show enthusiasm about the importance of the Red Cross. Success just naturally followed.

Think for a moment about a club or civic organization you know that is fading away. Chances are, all it needs is enthusiasm to bring it back to life.

Results come in proportion to enthusiasm applied.

Enthusiasm is simply "This is great!" Here's why.

Here is a three-step procedure that will help you to develop the power of enthusiasm.

1. Dig into it deeper. Make this little test. Think of two things in which you have little or no interest—maybe cards, certain kinds of music, a sport. Now ask yourself, "How much do I really know about these things?" Odds are 100 to 1 that your answer is "Not much."

I confess that for years I had absolutely no interest in modern art. It was just so many botched-up lines—until I let a friend who knows and loves modern art explain it to me. Really, now that I've dug into it, I find it fascinating.

That exercise supplies one important key for building enthusiasm: To get enthusiastic, learn more about the thing you are not enthusiastic about.

Chances are you are quite unenthusiastic about bumble-bees. But if you study bumblebees, find out what good they do, how they relate to other bees, how they reproduce, where they live in winter—if you find out all you can about bumblebees, you will soon find yourself really interested in bumblebees.

To show trainees how enthusiasm can be developed through the dig-into-it-deeper technique, I sometimes use a greenhouse example. In a deliberately casual way I ask the group, "Are any of you interested in manufacturing and selling greenhouses?" Not once have I gotten an affirmative answer. Then I make a few points about greenhouses: I remind the group how, as our standard of living rises, people become more and more interested in nonnecessities. I suggest how much Mrs. America would enjoy growing her own orchids and orange blossoms. I point out that if tens of thousands of families can afford private swimming pools, millions could afford greenhouses because greenhouses are relatively inexpensive. I show them that if you could sell a $600 greenhouse to only one family in fifty, you'd develop a $600 million business in producing greenhouses, and perhaps a $250 million industry supplying plants and seeds.

The only difficulty with this exercise is that the group, ten minutes before completely cold about greenhouses, now is so enthusiastic they don't want to move on to the next subject!

Use the dig-into-it-deeper technique to develop enthusiasm toward other people. Find out all you can about another person—what he does, his family, his background, his ideas and ambitions—and you'll find your interest in and enthusiasm about him mounting. Keep digging, and you're certain to find some common interests. Keep digging, and you'll eventually discover a fascinating person.

The dig-into-it-deeper technique works also in developing enthusiasm toward new places. Several years ago some young friends of mine decided to move from Detroit to a small town in mid-Florida. They sold their home, closed out their business connections, said good-bye to their friends, and were gone.

Six weeks later they were back in Detroit. The reason had nothing to do with employment. Rather, as they put it, "We just couldn't stand living in a small town. Besides, all our friends are in Detroit. We just had to come back."

In later conversations with these people, I learned the real reason why they didn't like the small Florida city. During their short stay there, they had taken only a surface view of the community—its history, its plans for the future, its people. They moved their bodies to Florida but left their minds in Detroit.

I've talked with dozens of executives, engineers, and salesmen who have developed career trouble because their companies want to move them to another location but they don't want to go. "I just can't see moving to Chicago (or San Francisco or Atlanta or New York or Miami)" is a remark spoken many times a day.

There's one way to build enthusiasm toward a new location. Simply resolve to dig into the new community. Learn all you can about it. Mix with the people. Make yourself feel and think like a community citizen from the very first day. Do this, and you'll be enthusiastic about your new environment.

Today millions of Americans invest in corporate securities. But there are many millions more who have no interest at all in the stock market. That's because they are people who have not familiarized themselves with what the securities market is, how it operates, the day-to-day romance of American business.

To get enthusiasm about anything—people, places, things— dig into it deeper.

Dig into it deeper, and you'll develop enthusiasm. Put this principle to work next time you must do something you don't want to do. Put this principle to work next time you find yourself becoming bored. Just dig in deeper and you dig up interest.

2. *In everything you do, life it up.* Enthusiasm, or lack of it, shows through in everything you do and say. Life up your handshaking. When you shake hands, *shake*. Make your handclasp say, "I'm *glad* to know you." "I *am* glad to see you again." A conservative, mouse-like handshake is worse than no handshake at all. It makes people think, "This guy is more dead than alive." Try to find a highly successful person with a conservative handshake. You'll have to look a long, long time.

Life up your smiles. Smile with your eyes. Nobody likes an artificial, pasted-on, rubbery smile. When you smile, *smile*. Show a few teeth. Maybe your teeth aren't attractive, but that's really unimportant. For when you smile, people don't see your teeth. They see a warm, enthusiastic personality, someone they like.

Life up your "thank yous." A routine, automatic "thank you" is almost like saying "gleep, gleep." It's just an expression. It says nothing. It doesn't accomplish results. Make your "thank you" mean "thank you *very* much."

Life up your talk. Dr. James F. Bender, the noted speech authority, in his excellent book *How to Talk Well*, says, "Is your 'Good morning!' really good? Are your 'Congratulations!' enthusiastic? Does your 'How are you?' sound interested? When you make a habit of coloring your words with sincere feelings you'll notice a great uptake in your ability to hold attention."

People go along with the fellow who *believes* what he says. Say it with *life*. Put vitality into your speaking. Whether you are talking to a garden club, a prospect, or your children, put enthusiasm behind what you say. A sermon delivered enthusiastically may be remembered for months, even years. But a sermon delivered without enthusiasm will be mostly forgotten 167 hours before next Sunday rolls around.

And when you put life in your talk, you automatically put more life in you. Just try this right now. Say out loud with force and vigor: "I feel great today!" Now, don't you actually feel better than you did before you said it? Make yourself alive all over.

Life it up. Be sure everything you do and say tells people, "That fellow is alive." "He means it." "He's going places."

3. Broadcast good news. You and I have been in many situations when someone burst in and said: "I've got good news." Immediately this person gets 100 percent attention from everyone present. Good news does more than get attention; good news pleases people. Good news develops enthusiasm. Good news even promotes good digestion.

Just because there are more broadcasters of bad news than there are broadcasters of good news, don't be misled. No one ever won a friend, no one ever made money, no one ever accomplished anything by broadcasting bad news.

Transmit good news to your family. Tell them the good that happened today. Recall the amusing, pleasant things you experienced and let the unpleasant things stay buried. Spread good news. It's pointless to pass on the bad. It only makes your family worry, makes them nervous. Bring home some sunlight every day.

Ever notice how seldom children complain about the weather? They take hot weather in stride until the negative news corps educate them to be conscious of unpleasant temperatures. Make it a habit always to speak favorably about the weather regardless of what the weather actually is. Complaining about the weather makes you more miserable and it spreads misery to others.

Broadcast good news about how you feel. Be an "I-feel-great" person. Just say "I feel great" at every possible opportunity, and you *will* feel better. By the same token, tell people, "I feel awful, just awful," and you will feel worse. How we feel is, in large part, determined by how we think we feel. Remember, too, that other people want to be around alive, enthusiastic people. Being around complainers and half-dead people is uncomfortable.

Transmit good news to the people you work with. Give them encouragement, compliment them at every opportunity. Tell them about the positive things the company is doing. Listen to their problems. Be helpful. Encourage people and win their support. Pat them on the back for the job they're doing. Give them hope. Let them know you believe they can succeed, that you have faith in them. Practice relieving worriers.

Make this little test regularly to keep you on the right track. Whenever you leave a person, ask yourself, "Does that person honestly feel better because he has talked with me?" This self-training device works. Apply it when talking with employees, associates, your family, customers, even with casual acquaintances.

A salesman friend is a real good-news broadcaster. He calls on his customers every month and always makes it a rule to have some good news to pass along.

Examples: "I met one of your good friends last week. He said to tell you hello." "Since I was here last big things have happened. Over 350,000 new babies were born last month, and more babies mean more business for both of us."

Usually we think of bank presidents as overly reserved, unemotional people who never really warm up. Not so with one bank president. His favorite way to answer the phone is to say, "Good *morning,* it's a wonderful world. May I sell you some money?" Improper for a banker? Some might say so, but let me point out that the banker who uses this greeting is Mills Lane, Jr., president of the Citizens and Southern Bank, the largest in the entire Southeast.

Good news gets good results. Broadcast it.

The president of a brush-manufacturing company I visited

recently had this maxim neatly framed on his desk facing the visitor's chair: "Give me a Good Word or none at all." I complimented him, saying that I thought the maxim was a clever way to encourage people to be optimistic.

He smiled and said, "It is an effective reminder. But from where I sit this is even more important." He turned the frame around so I could see it from his side of the desk. It said, "Give them a Good Word or none at all."

Broadcasting good news activates you, makes you feel better. Broadcasting good news makes other people feel better too.

GROW THE "YOU-ARE-IMPORTANT" ATTITUDE

This is a fact of paramount significance: Each human being, whether he lives in India or Indianapolis, whether he's ignorant or brilliant, civilized or uncivilized, young or old, has this desire: *He wants to feel important.*

Ponder on that. Everyone, yes, everyone—your neighbor, you, your wife, your boss—has a natural desire to feel he is "somebody." The desire to be important is man's strongest, most compelling nonbiological hunger.

Successful advertisers know that people crave prestige, distinction, recognition. Headlines that produce sales read like this: "For Smart Young Homemakers"; "Persons with Distinctive Tastes Use —"; "You Want Only the Best"; "Be the Envy of Everyone"; "For Women Who Want to Be Envied by Women and Admired by Men." These headlines in effect tell people, "Buy this product, and you put yourself in the important class."

Satisfying the craving, the hunger, to be important carries you forward to success. It is basic equipment in your success tool chest. Yet (and read this sentence again before you go on) even though displaying the attitude "You are important" gets results, and even though it costs nothing, few persons use it. A little fill-in is needed here to show why.

On the philosophical side, our religions, our laws, our entire culture are based on the belief of the importance of the individual.

Suppose, for example, you were flying your own plane and were forced down in an isolated mountain region. As soon as your accident was known, a large-scale search for you would begin. No one would ask, "Is that fellow important?" Without knowing anything about you except that you are a human being, helicopters, other aircraft, and searching parties on foot would begin looking for you. And they would keep on looking for you, spending thousands of dollars in the process, until they found you or until not one trace of hope remained.

When a little child wanders off into a woods, falls into a well, or gets into some other dangerous predicament, no one is concerned with whether or not the child comes from an "important" family. Every effort is made to rescue the child because *every* child is important.

It's not too wild a guess that, of all living creatures, probably not more than one in ten million is a human being. A person is a biological rarity. He is important in God's scheme of things.

Now let's look at the practical side. When most people shift their thinking from philosophical discussions to everyday situations, they tend to forget, unfortunately, their ivory-tower concepts of the importance of individuals. Tomorrow, take a good look at how most people exhibit an attitude that seems to say, "You are a nobody; you count for nothing; you mean nothing, absolutely nothing to me."

There is a reason why the "you are unimportant" attitude prevails. Most folks look at another person and think, "He can't do anything for me. Therefore, he's not important."

But right there is where people make a basic blunder. The other person, *regardless* of his status or his income, is important to you and for two giant, dollars-and-cents reasons.

First, *people do more for you when you make them feel important.* Years ago, in Detroit, I rode a certain bus to work each morning. The driver was an old grump. Dozens—maybe hundreds—of times, I saw this driver pull away from the curb when a wildly waving, shouting, and running passenger was just a second or two from the door. Over a period of several months I saw this driver show special courtesy to only one passenger, and this passenger was shown special courtesy many times. The driver would wait for *this* passenger.

And why? Because this passenger went out of his way to make the driver feel important. Every morning he greeted the driver with a personalized, sincere "Good morning, sir." Sometimes this passenger would sit near the driver and make little comments like "You sure have a lot of responsibility"; "It must take nerves of steel to drive through traffic like this every day"; "You sure keep this thing on schedule." That passenger made the driver feel as important as if he were piloting a 180-passenger jet airliner. And the driver in return showed special courtesy to the passenger.

It pays to make "little" people feel like big people.

Today, in thousands of offices all over America, secretaries are helping salesmen make sales or lose sales depending on how the salesman has treated them. Make someone feel important, and he cares about you. And when he cares about you, he does more for you.

Customers will buy more from you, employees will work harder for you, associates will go out of their way to cooperate with you, your boss will do more to help you if you will only make these people feel important.

It pays to make "big" people feel even bigger. The big thinker always adds value to people by visualizing them at their best. Because he thinks big about people, he gets their best out of them.

Here's the second giant reason for making others feel important: *When you help others feel important, you help yourself feel important too.*

One of the elevator operators who carried me "up and down" for several months had the look of complete unimportance written all over. She was fiftyish, unattractive, and certainly uninspired in her work. It was obvious that her longing to be important was completely unfulfilled. She was one of the millions of people who live for months at a time without ever being given a reason to believe that someone notices them or cares about them.

One morning shortly after I became one of her regular "uppers and downers," I noticed that she had had her hair redone. It was nothing fancy. It was obviously a home-made job. But it had been cut and it did look better.

So I said, "Miss S. (Note: I had learned her name), I do like what you've done to your hair. It really looks fine." She blushed, said, "Thank you, sir," and nearly missed her next stop. She appreciated the compliment.

Next morning, lo and behold, when I stepped into the elevator I heard, "Good morning, Dr. Schwartz." Not one time before had I heard this operator address anyone by name. And in the remaining months that I had an office in the building I never heard anyone called by name except me. I had made the operator feel important. I had sincerely complimented her and called her by name.

I had made her feel important. Now she was repaying me by making me feel important.

Let's not kid ourselves. People who do not have a deep-down feeling of self-importance are slated for mediocrity. Again and again this point must be driven home: *You must feel important to succeed. Helping others to feel important rewards you because it makes you feel more important. Try it and see.* Here's how to do it:

1. *Practice appreciation.* Make it a rule to let others know you appreciate what they do for you. Never, never let anyone feel he is taken for granted. Practice appreciation with a warm, sincere smile. A smile lets others know you notice them and feel kindly toward them.

Practice appreciation by letting others know how you depend on them. An earnest "Jim, I don't know what we'd do without you" type of remark makes people feel necessary, and when they feel necessary they do increasingly better work.

Practice appreciation with honest, personalized compliments. People thrive on compliments—whether two or twenty, nine or ninety, a person craves praise. He wants to be assured that he's doing a good job, that he is important. Don't feel that you should hand out praise only for big accomplishments. Compliment people on little things: their appearance, the way they do their routine work, their ideas, their loyal efforts. Praise by writing personal notes complimenting people you know on their achievements. Make a special phone call or a special trip to see them.

Don't waste time or mental energy trying to classify people as "very important persons," "important persons," or "unimportant persons." Make no exceptions. A person, whether he is garbage collector or company vice president, is important to you. Treating someone as second-class never gets you first-class results.

2. *Practice calling people by their names.* Every year shrewd manufacturers sell more briefcases, pencils, Bibles, and hundreds of other items just by putting the buyer's name on the product. People like to be called by name. It gives everyone a boost to be addressed by name.

Two special things you must remember. Pronounce the name correctly, and spell it correctly. If you mispronounce or misspell someone's name, that person feels that you feel he is unimportant.

And here's one special reminder: When talking with people you don't know well, add the appropriate title—Miss, Mister, or Mrs. The office boy prefers Mr. Jones to just Jones. So does your junior assistant. So do people at every level. These little titles help tremendously to make people feel important.

3. *Don't hog glory, invest it instead.* Just recently I was a guest at an all-day sales convention. After dinner that evening the vice president in charge of sales for the company passed out awards to the two district managers, a man and a woman, whose sales organizations had attained the best records for the year just ended. Then the vice president asked those district managers to take fifteen minutes to tell the entire group how their organizations did so exceptionally well.

The first district manager (who, I later learned, had been appointed a manager only three months before and was therefore only partially responsible for his organization's record) got up and explained how *he* did it.

He conveyed the impression that *his* efforts and *his* efforts alone caused the sales increase. Remarks such as "When *I* took over, *I* did such-and-such"; "Things were in a mess but *I* cleared them up"; "It wasn't easy but *I* just grabbed hold of the situation and wouldn't let go" characterized his talk.

As he talked, I could see the increasing resentment gathering in the faces of his salesmen. They were being ignored for the sake of the district manager's personal glory. Their hard work, which was responsible for the sales increase, was completely unrecognized.

Then, the second district manger got up to make her short talk. But this lady used an entirely different approach. First, she explained that the reason for her organization's success was the wholehearted effort of her sales force. Then she asked each one to stand and paid a sincere personal compliment to each for his or her efforts.

Note this difference; the first manager squandered the vice president's praise entirely on himself. In doing so, he offended his own people. His sales force was demoralized. The second passed the praise on to her sales force, where it could do *more* good. This manager knew that praise, like money, can be invested to pay dividends. She knew that passing the credit on to her salespeople would make them work even harder next year.

Remember, praise is power. Invest the praise you receive from your superior. Pass praise on down to your subordinates, where it will encourage still greater performance. When you share praise, your subordinates know you sincerely appreciate their value.

Here's a daily exercise that pays off surprisingly well. Ask yourself every day, "What can I do today to make my wife and family happy?"

This may seem almost too simple, but it is amazingly effective. One evening, as part of a sales training program, I was discussing "Building the Home Environment for Selling Success." To illustrate a point, I asked the salesmen (who were all married), "When was the last time, aside from Christmas, your wedding anniversary, or her birthday, that you surprised your wife with a special gift?"

Even I was shocked at the answers. Of the thirty-five salesmen, only one had surprised his wife in the past month. Many of the group answered "between three and six months." And over a third said, "I can't remember."

Imagine! And some men wonder why their wives no longer treat them like Mr. King with a crown!

I wanted to impress these salesmen with the power of the thoughtful gift. The next evening I arranged to have a florist appear just before the close of the session. I introduced him and leveled with them: "I want each of you to discover what a little unexpected remembrance will do to build a better home environment. I've arranged with the florist for each of you to get a fine, long-stemmed red rose for just 50 cents. Now if you don't have 50 cents, or if you think your wife isn't worth that [they laughed], I'll buy the flower for her myself. All I ask is that you take the rose to your wife and then tomorrow evening tell us what happened.

"Don't, of course, tell her how you came to purchase this rose for her."

They understood.

Without exception, every fellow testified the next evening that the mere investment of 50 cents had made his wife happy.

Do something special for your family often. It doesn't have to be something expensive. It's thoughtfulness that counts. Anything that shows that you put your family's interests first will do the trick.

Get the family on your team. *Give them planned attention.*

In this busy age a lot of people never seem able to find time for their families. But if we plan, we can find it. One company vice president told me of this method, which he says works well for him:

"My job carries a lot of responsibility, and I have no choice but to bring quite a lot of work home every night. But I will not neglect my family because it's the most important thing in my life. It's the main reason I work as hard as I do. I've worked out a schedule that enables me to give attention to my family as well as to my work. From 7:30 to 8:30 every evening I devote my time to my two young children. I play games with them, read them stories, draw, answer questions—anything they want me to do. After an hour with those kids of mine, they're not only satisfied, but I'm 100 percent fresher. At 8:30 they trot off to bed, and I settle down to work for two hours.

"At 10:30 I quit working and spend the next hour with my wife. We talk about the kids, her various activities, our plans for the future. This hour, undisturbed by anything, is a wonderful way to cap off the day.

"I also reserve Sundays for my family. The whole day is theirs. I find my organized program for giving my family the attention it deserves is good not only for them, but also good for me. It gives me new energy."

WANT TO MAKE MONEY? THEN GET THE PUT-SERVICE-FIRST ATTITUDE

It's perfectly natural—in fact, it's highly desirable—to want to make money and accumulate wealth. Money is power to give your family and yourself the standard of living they deserve. Money is power to help the unfortunate. Money is one of the means to living life fully.

Once criticized for urging people to make money, the great minister Russel H. Conwell, author of *Acres of Diamonds,* said, "Money printed your Bible, money builds your churches, money sends your missionaries, and money pays your preachers, and you would not have many of them, either, if you did not pay them."

The person who says he wants to be poor usually suffers from a guilt complex or a feeling of inadequacy. He's like the youngster who feels he can't make As in school or make the football team, so he pretends he doesn't want to make As or play football.

Money, then, is a desirable objective. What's puzzling about money is the backward approach so many people use in trying to make it. Everywhere you see people with a "money-first" attitude. Yet these same people always have little money. Why? Simply this: People with a money-first attitude become so money conscious that they forget money can't be harvested unless they plant the seeds that grow the money.

And the seed of money is service. That's why "put service first" is an attitude that creates wealth. Put service first, and money takes care of itself.

One summer evening I was traveling by car through Cincinnati. It was time for a gas-up. I stopped at an ordinary-looking but surprisingly busy service station.

Four minutes later I knew why this particular service station was so popular. After filling my car with gasoline, checking under the hood, and cleaning the outside of my windshield, the attendant walked around to my side of the car and said, "Pardon me, sir. It's been a dusty day. Let me clean the inside of your windshield."

Quickly and efficiently, he did a thorough job of cleaning the inside of my windshield, something not one service station attendant in a hundred ever does.

This little special service did more than improve my night visibility (and it improved it a lot); it made me remember this station. It so happened that I made eight trips through Cincinnati during the next three months. Each time, of course, I stopped at this station. And each time I got more service than I expected to get. Interesting too was the fact that each time I stopped (once it was 4 A.M.) there were other automobiles filling up also. In all, I probably purchased about 100 gallons of gasoline from this station.

The first time I stopped the attendant could have thought to himself, "This guy is from out of state. Odds are twenty to one that he'll never be back. Why do more than give him the routine treatment? He's only a one-time customer."

But the attendants in that station didn't think that way. They put service first, and that's why they were busy pumping gasoline while other stations looked almost deserted. If the gasoline was any better than a dozen other brands, I didn't notice it. And the price was competitive.

The difference was service. And it was obvious that service was paying off in profits.

When the attendant on my first visit cleaned the inside of my windshield, he planted a money seed.

Put service first, and money takes care of itself—always.

The put-service-first attitude pays off in all situations. In one of my first jobs I worked closely with another young fellow, whom I'll call F. H.

F. H. was like many persons you know. He was preoccupied with why he needed more money instead of being preoccupied with ways to make money. Each week F. H. spent hours of company time working on his personal budget problems. His favorite topic of conversation was "I'm the most underpaid man here. Let me tell you why."

F. H. had the not uncommon attitude of "This is a big company. It's netting millions. It's paying a lot of people big salaries, so it ought to pay me more too."

F. H. had been passed over several times for pay increases. Finally one day he decided that it was high time he went in there and demanded more money. About thirty minutes later F. H. was back, all heated up. His expression made it obvious that next month's check would look exactly like this month's check.

Immediately F. H. began to let go. "Boy, am I mad! What do you suppose the old man said when I told him I wanted more money? He had the gall to ask me, 'Why do you believe you are justified in asking for an increase?'

"I gave him plenty of reasons," F. H. went on. "I told him I'd been passed over when others around here were getting pay raises. I told him my bills are getting larger and my paycheck isn't. And I told him that I do everything around here they ask me to do.

"Can you beat that? I *need* a raise, but instead of paying me more, they give out raises to other guys around here who don't need it half as much as I do.

"Why, the way he acted," F. H. continued, "you'd think I was asking for charity. All he would say is 'When your record shows that you deserve more money, you'll get more money.'

"Sure, I could do a better job if they paid me for it, but only a fool does something he isn't paid for."

F. H. is an example of the breed that is blind to the "how" of making money. His last remark sums up his mistake. In effect, F. H. wanted the company to pay him more and *then* he would produce more. But this is not how the system works. You don't get a raise on the promise of better performance; you get a raise only by demonstrating better performance. You can't harvest money unless you plant the seeds that grow money. And the seed of money is service.

Put service first, and money takes care of itself.

Consider which producers make the money from movies. The get-rich-quick producer proceeds to make a picture. Putting money ahead of entertainment (service), he cuts corners every-where. He buys a poorly written script and employs second-rate writers to adapt it. In employing actors, arranging sets, even recording sound, he puts money first. This producer thinks the moviegoer is a sucker, someone who can't tell good from bad.

But the get-rich-quick producer seldom does get rich quick. There never is a bandwagon movement to buy anything second-class, especially when it is given a first-class price.

The producer who enjoys the largest profits from pictures puts entertainment ahead of money. Rather than chisel the moviegoer, he does everything possible to give people more and better entertainment than they expect to get. The result: people like the movie. It gets talked about. It gets good reviews. And it makes money.

Again, put service first, and money takes care of itself.

The waitress who concentrates on giving the best possible service needn't worry about tips; they'll be there. But her counterpart who overlooks the empty coffee cups ("Why refill them? They don't look like tippers.") won't find any gratuities.

The secretary who resolves to make those letters look better than the boss expects will do all right on future paychecks. But the secretary who thinks, "Why worry about a few smudges? What do they expect for $65 a week?"—she is stuck at $65 a week.

The salesman who gives full service to an account need harbor no fears he'll lose the account.

Here is a simple but powerful rule that will help you to develop the put-service-first attitude: *Always give people more than they expect to get.* Each little extra something you do for others is a money seed. Volunteering to work late and get the department out of a tight spot is a money seed; giving customers *extra* service is a money seed because it brings customers back; advancing a new idea that will increase efficiency is a money seed.

Money seeds, of course, grow money. Plant service and harvest money.

Spend some time each day answering this question: "How can I give more than is expected of me?" Then apply the answers.

Put service first, and money takes care of itself.

In quick recap, grow attitudes that will carry you forward to success.

1. Grow the *"I'm activated"* attitude. Results come in proportion to the enthusiasm invested. Three things to do to activate yourself are:

Dig into it deeper. When you find yourself unin-
terested in something, dig in and learn more
about it. This sets off enthusiasm.

Life up everything about you: your smile, your
handshake, your talk, even your walk. Act
alive.

Broadcast good news. No one ever accomplished
anything positive telling bad news.

2. Grow the "You are important" attitude. People do more for
you when you make them feel important. Remember to do
these things:

Show appreciation at every opportunity. Make
people feel important.

Call people by name.

3. Grow the "Service first" attitude, and watch money take
care of itself. Make it a rule in everything you do: give
people more than they expect to get.

9

THINK RIGHT TOWARD PEOPLE

HERE IS A BASIC rule for winning success. Let's mark it in the mind and remember it. The rule is: *Success depends on the support of other people.* The only hurdle between you and what you want to be is the support of others.

Look at it this way: an executive depends on people to carry out his instructions. If they don't, the company president will fire the executive, not the employees. A salesman depends on people to buy his product. If they don't, the salesman fails. Likewise, a college dean depends on professors to carry forward his educational program; a politician depends on voters to elect him; a writer depends on people to read what he writes. A chain store magnate got to be a chain store magnate because employees accepted his leadership and consumers accepted his merchandising program.

There were times in history when a person could gain a position of authority through force and hold it with force and/or threats of force. In those days a man either cooperated with the "leader" or risked literally losing his head.

But today, remember, a person either supports you *willingly* or he doesn't support you at all.

Now it's time to ask, "Granted, I depend on others in order

to achieve the success I want, but what must I do to get these people to support me and accept my leadership?"

The answer, wrapped up in one phrase, is *think right toward people*. Think right toward people, and they will like and support you. This chapter shows how.

Thousands of times daily a scene like this takes place. A committee or group is in session. The purpose—to consider names for a promotion, a new job, a club membership, an honor—someone to be the new company president, the new supervisor, the new sales manager. A name is placed before the group. The chairman asks, "What is your feeling about so-and-so?"

Comments come forth. For some names there are positive remarks, such as "He's a good fellow. People there speak highly of him. He has a good technical background, too."

"Mr. F.? Oh, he's a personable sort of man, very human. I believe he would fit in well with our group."

Some names draw negative, lukewarm statements. "I think we should investigate that fellow carefully. He doesn't seem to get along too well with people."

"I know he has a good academic and technical background; I don't question his competence. But I am concerned about the acceptance he would receive. He doesn't command much respect from people."

Now, here is an exceptionally important observation: *In at least nine cases out of ten, the "likability" factor is the first thing mentioned. And in an overwhelmingly large number of cases, the "likability" factor is given far more weight than the technical factor.*

The above holds true even in selecting scholars for university professorships. In my own academic experience I've sat in on a considerable number of occasions when names for new faculty personnel were under question. When a name came up, the group would weigh most carefully thoughts such as "Will he fit in?" "Will students like him?" "Will he cooperate with others on the staff?"

Unfair? Unacademic? No. If the fellow isn't likable, he can't be expected to get through to his students with maximum effectiveness.

Mark this point well. A person is not *pulled up* to a higher-level job. Rather, he is *lifted up*. In this day and age nobody has time or patience to *pull* another up the job ladder, degree by painful degree. The individual is chosen whose record makes him stand higher than the rest.

We are lifted to higher levels by those who know us as likable, personable individuals. Every friend you make lifts you just one notch higher. And *being likable makes you lighter to lift*.

Successful people follow a plan for liking people. Do you? People who reach the top don't discuss much their techniques for thinking right toward people. But you would be surprised how many really big people have a clear, definite, even *written* plan for liking people.

Consider the case of President Lyndon Johnson. Long before he became president, Johnson, in the process of developing his amazing power of personal persuasion, developed his own ten-point formula for success. His rules, which even a casual observer of the president can see are practiced in everything he does, are quoted directly:

1. Learn to remember names. Inefficiency at this point may indicate that your interest is not sufficiently outgoing.

2. Be a comfortable person so there is no strain in being with you. Be an old-shoe kind of individual.

3. Acquire the quality of relaxed easy-going so that things do not ruffle you.

4. Don't be egotistical. Guard against the impression that you know it all.

5. Cultivate the quality of being interesting so people will get something of value from their association with you.

6. Study to get the "scratchy" elements out of your personality, even those of which you may be unconscious.

7. Sincerely attempt to heal, on an honest basis, every misunderstanding you have had or now have. Drain off your grievances.

8. Practice liking people until you learn to do so genuinely.

9. Never miss an opportunity to say a word of congratulation upon anyone's achievement, or express sympathy in sorrow or disappointment.

10. Give spiritual strength to people, and they will give genuine affection to you.

Living these ten simple but tremendously powerful "like people" rules makes President Johnson easier to vote for, easier to support in Congress. Living these ten rules makes President Johnson *easier to lift.*

Reread these rules again. Notice that there's no get-even philosophy here. There's no let-the-other-fellow-come-to-me-to-patch-up-differences. There's no I-know-it-all-other-people-are-stupid.

Big people, those on top in industry, the arts, sciences, and politics, are human, warm. They specialize in being likable.

But don't try to buy friendship; it's not for sale. Giving gifts is a wonderful practice if the gift is backed up with genuine sincerity, a liking to give and liking for the person to whom it is given. But without real sincerity, the gift is often regarded as nothing more than a payoff or a bribe.

Last year, just a few days before Christmas, I was in the office of the president of a medium-sized trucking firm. Just as I was about to leave, in marched a delivery man with a gift of liquid refreshment from a local tire-recapping firm. My friend was obviously provoked and, with a certain amount of chill in his voice, asked the delivery man to return the gift to its sender.

After the delivery man left, my friend hastened to explain to me: "Don't misunderstand. I like to give gifts and I like to get them."

Then he named a number of gifts he had already received from business friends that Christmas.

"But," he went on, "when the gift is just an attempt to get my business, an obvious bribe, I don't want it. I quit doing business with that firm three months ago because their work isn't what it should be and I don't like the employees. But their salesman keeps on calling.

"What burns me," he continued, "is that last week that

same d——— salesman was in here and had the gall to say, 'I sure would like to get your business back. I'm going to tell Santa to be real good to you this year.' If I hadn't sent their booze back, the first thing that so-and-so would've said to me next time he's in is 'I'll bet you enjoyed our gift, didn't you?'"

Friendship can't be bought. And when we try, we lose in two ways:

1. We waste money.

2. We create contempt.

Take the initiative in building friendships—leaders always do. It's easy and natural for us to tell ourselves, "Let him make the first move." "Let them call us." "Let her speak first."

It's easy, too, virtually to ignore other people.

Yes, it's easy and natural, but it isn't right thinking toward people. If you follow the rule of letting the other person build the foundation for friendship, you may not have many friends.

Actually, it's a mark of real leadership to take the lead in getting to know people. Next time you are in a large group, observe something very significant: *the most important person present is the one person most active in introducing himself.*

It's always a big person who walks up to you, offers his hand, and says, "Hello, I'm Jack R." Digest this observation for a moment, and you'll discover the reason the fellow is important is that he works at building friendships.

Think right toward people. As a friend of mine expresses it, "I may not be very important to him, but he's important to me. That's why I've got to get to know him."

Have you ever noticed how people freeze while waiting for elevators? Unless they are with someone they know, most folks never say anything to the person standing beside them. One day I resolved to do a little experimenting.

I resolved to say something to the stranger who was waiting as I was. I kept track of his reaction twenty-five consecutive times. And twenty-five times I got back a positive, friendly response.

Now, talking to strangers may not be very urbane, but most people like it nevertheless. And here is the big payoff:

When you make a pleasant remark to a stranger, you make him feel one degree better. This makes you feel better and helps you relax. Every time you say something pleasant to another person, you compensate yourself. It's like warming up your automobile on a cold morning.

Here are six ways to win friends by exercising just a little initiative:

1. Introduce yourself to others at every possible opportunity—at parties, meetings, on airplanes, at work, everywhere.

2. Be sure the other person gets *your* name straight.

3. Be sure you can pronounce the other person's name the way he pronounces it.

4. Write down the other person's name, and be mighty sure you have it spelled correctly; people have a fetish about

the correct spelling of their own names! If possible, get his address and phone number, also.

5. Drop a personal note or make a phone call to the new friends you feel you want to know better. This is an important point. Most successful people follow through on new friends with a letter or a phone call.

6. And last but not least, say pleasant things to strangers. It warms you up and gets you ready for the task ahead.

Putting these six rules to work is really thinking right about people. To be sure, it is not the way the average person thinks. Mr. "Average" never takes the initiative in making introductions. He waits for the other person to introduce himself first.

Take the initiative. Be like the successful. Go out of your way to meet people. And don't be timid. Don't be afraid to be unusual. Find out who the other person is, and be sure he knows who you are.

Recently an associate and I were retained to do a preliminary screening of an applicant for an industrial sales job. We found the applicant, whom we'll call Ted, to have some good qualifications. He was exceptionally intelligent, made a fine appearance, and seemed to have a lot of ambition.

But we found something that forced us to disqualify him, at least temporarily. Ted's big limitation was this: he expected perfection in other people. Ted was annoyed by many little things, like mistakes in grammar, people who were messy with cigarettes, people who had bad taste in clothes, and so on.

Ted was surprised to learn this fact about himself. But he was eager to get into higher-paying work, and he asked whether there was anything we could tell him to help overcome his weakness.

We made three suggestions:

1. *Recognize the fact that no person is perfect.* Some people are more nearly perfect than others, but no man is absolutely perfect. The most human quality about human beings is that they make mistakes, all kinds of them.

2. *Recognize the fact that the other fellow has a right to be different.* Never play God about anything. Never dislike people because their habits are different from your own or because they prefer different clothes, religion, parties, or automobiles. You don't have to approve of what another fellow does, but you must not dislike him for doing it.

3. *Don't be a reformer.* Put a little more "live and let live" into your philosophy. Most people intensely dislike being told "you're wrong." You have a right to your own opinion, but sometimes it's better to keep it to yourself.

Ted conscientiously applied these suggestions. A few months later he had a fresh outlook. He now accepts people for what they are, neither 100 percent good nor 100 percent bad.

"Besides," he says, "the things that used to annoy the heck out of me I now find amusing. It finally dawned on me what a dull world this would be if people were all alike and everybody was perfect."

THINK RIGHT TOWARD PEOPLE   201

Note this simple but key fact: No person is all good and no person is all bad. The perfect person just doesn't exist.

Now, if we let our thinking go uncontrolled, we can find much to dislike in almost anyone. By the same token, if we manage our thinking properly, if we think right toward people, we can find many qualities to like and admire in the same person.

View it this way. Your mind is a mental broadcasting station. This broadcasting system transmits messages to you on two equally powerful channels: Channel P (positive) and Channel N (negative).

Let's see how your broadcasting system works. Suppose that today your business superior (we'll call him Mr. Jacobs) called you into his office and reviewed your work with you. He complimented you on your work, but he also made some specific suggestions on how you can do it better. Tonight it's only natural for you to recall the incident and do some thinking about it.

If you tune in Channel N, the announcer will be saying something like this: "Watch out! Jacobs is out to get you. He's a crab. You don't need any of his advice. To heck with it. Remember what Joe told you about Jacobs? He was right. Jacobs wants to grind you down like he did Joe. Resist him. Next time he calls you in, fight back. Better still, don't wait. Tomorrow go in and ask him just what he really meant by his criticism . . ."

But tune in Channel P, and the announcer will say something along these lines: "You know, Mr. Jacobs is a pretty good fellow. Those suggestions he made to me seem pretty sound. If I put them to use, I can probably do a better job and position myself for an increase. The old boy did me a favor. Tomorrow I'll go in and thank him for his constructive help. Bill was right: Jacobs *is* a good man to work with . . ."

In this specific case, if you listen to Channel N, you're almost certain to make some bad, perhaps fatal, mistake in your relations with your superior. But if you are tuned to Channel P, you are definitely certain to benefit from your superior's suggestions and at the same time draw yourself closer to him. He will appreciate that visit. Try it and see.

Bear in mind that the longer you stay tuned to either Channel P or Channel N, the more interested you become and the harder it is to switch channels. This is true because one thought, positive or negative, sets off a whole chain reaction of similar thought.

You may, for example, start off with such a simple minor negative thought as a person's accent and find yourself soon thinking negatively about such unrelated topics as his political and religious beliefs, the car he drives, his personal habits, his relationship with his wife, even the way he combs his hair. And thinking this way surely won't get you where you want to go.

You own it, so manage your thought broadcasting station. When your thoughts turn to people, make Channel P your listening habit.

If Channel N cuts in, say stop. Then switch channels. To make the switch, all you must do is think of one positive quality about the individual. In true chain reaction style, this one thought will lead to another and another. And you will be glad.

When you are alone, you and only you can decide whether you will listen to Channel P or Channel N. But when you are talking with someone else, that person has a measure of control over how you think.

We must remember that most people do not understand

the concepts of thinking right toward people. So it's a very common experience for people to come rushing to you, just aching to say something negative about a person you both know: a co-worker wants to tell you about the objectionable qualities of another employee; a neighbor wants to let you know the domestic problems of another neighbor; or a customer wants to itemize the faults of his competitor, whom you will call on next.

Thoughts breed like thoughts. There is real danger that if you listen to negative comments about another person, you too will go negative toward that person. In fact, if you are not on guard, you may actually find yourself adding fuel to the fire with "Yes, and that's not all. Did you hear . . ." type of comment.

These things backfire, boomerang.

There are two ways to prevent others from switching us from Channel P to Channel N. One way is to switch topics as quickly and quietly as possible with some remark like "Pardon me, John, but while I think of it, I've been meaning to ask you . . ." A second way is to excuse yourself with a "Sorry, John, I'm late now . . ." or "I've a deadline to meet. Will you excuse me?"

Make a forceful promise to yourself. Refuse to let others prejudice your thinking. Stay tuned to Channel P.

Once you've mastered the technique of thinking only good thoughts about people, greater success is *guaranteed*. Let me tell you what an unusually successful insurance salesman told me about how thinking good thoughts about people pays off for him.

"When I first got in the insurance business," he began, "the going was tough, believe me. At first it seemed there were about as many competing agents as there were prospects. And I soon learned what all insurance men know, that nine prospects out of ten firmly believe they don't need any more insurance.

"I'm doing well. But let me tell you, it's not because I know a lot about the technical side of insurance. That's important, don't misunderstand me, but there are men trying to sell insurance who know policies and contracts better than I. In fact, I know one man who wrote a book about insurance, but he couldn't sell a policy to a man who knew he had only five days to live.

"My success," he continued, "is based on one thing. I like, *really* like the guy I'm selling. Let me say again, I really *like* him. Some of my fellow salesmen try to pretend they like the other fellow, but this won't work. You can't even fool a dog. Your mannerisms, eyes, facial expressions, all spell p-h-o-n-y when you pretend.

"Now, when I'm gathering information about a prospect, I do what every other agent does. I get his age, where he works, how much he makes, how many kids he's got, and so on.

"But I also get something else which most salesmen never search for—that is, some sound reasons why I can like the prospect. Maybe the job he's doing will supply the reason, or perhaps I can find it someplace in his past record. But I find some good reasons to like him.

"Then, whenever my attention is focused on the prospect, I review the reasons why I like him. I build a likable image of the prospect before I say one word to him about insurance.

"This little technique works. Because I like him, he sooner or later likes me. Pretty soon, instead of sitting across the table from him, I'm on the same side with him, and we're working out his insurance plan together. He trusts and believes in my judgment because I am a friend.

"Now, people don't always accept me right off the bat, but I've found that so long as I continue to like a fellow, he'll come around, and we can get down to business.

"Just last week," my friend went on, "I was making the third call on a difficult prospect. He met me at the door, and before I could even say 'Good evening,' he proceeded to give me hell. He went on and on, not even stopping for a breath until he had run down and finished with 'And don't ever come back here again.'

"After he had said that, I just stood there looking into his eyes for about five seconds, and then said softly and with genuine sincerity, because I meant it, 'But Mr. S., I'm calling tonight as your friend.'

"Yesterday he bought a $250,000 endowment policy."

Sol Polk is popularly called the appliance king of Chicago. Starting with nothing, Sol Polk now sells millions of dollars' worth of appliances in a year in metropolitan Chicago.

Sol Polk credits a lot of his success to his attitude toward shoppers. "Customers," says Mr. Polk, "should be treated like they are guests in my home."

Isn't that thinking toward people? And isn't it about the simplest success formula one can put to work? Just treat customers like guests in your home.

This technique works outside the store too. Substitute the word employees for customers so that it reads "employees should be treated like guests in my home." Give first-class treatment to your employees, and you get first-class cooperation, first-class output. Think first class about everyone around you, and you'll receive first-class results in return.

One of the reviewers of an early version of this book is a close personal friend who owns his own business management consulting firm. When he read the above illustration, he commented, "That's the positive result of liking and respecting people. Let me give you a personal experience of a friend of mine which shows what happens if you don't like and admire people."

His experience has a big point. Here it is!

"My firm obtained a contract to provide consulting services to a relatively small soft drink bottling concern. The contract was substantial. The client had little formal education. His business was in bad shape, and in recent years he had made some very costly mistakes.

"Three days after we had got the contract, an associate and I were driving out to his plant, which was about forty-five minutes from our offices. To this day I don't know how it started, but somehow we began talking about the negative qualities of our client.

"Before we realized it, we were talking about how his own stupidity had brought about the mess he was in, instead of discussing how we could best approach solving his problems.

"I remember one remark I made which I thought particularly clever—'The only thing holding up Mr. F. is fat.' My associate laughed and came up with an equally choice observation: 'And that son of his. Junior must be all of thirty-five but the only qualification he has for the job he's holding is he speaks English.'

"The whole drive out, we talked about nothing else but what a weak-minded numbskull we had as a client.

"Well, the conference that afternoon was cold. Looking back, I think our client sensed somehow the way we felt toward him. He must have thought: 'These fellows think I'm stupid or something, and all they're going to do for my money is give me some smooth-sounding talk.'

"Two days later I got a two-sentence letter from this client. It said, 'I've decided to cancel our contract for your consulting services. If there is a charge for your services to date, please bill me.'

"Printing ourselves with negative thoughts for only forty minutes cost us a contract. What made it even more painful was learning about a month later that this former client had contracted with an out-of-town firm for the professional assistance he needed.

"We would never have lost him had we concentrated on his many fine qualities. And he has them. Most people do."

Here's how you can have some fun and discover a basic success principle at the same time. For the next two days listen in on as many conversations as you can. Note two things: which person in the conversation does the most talking and which person is the more successful.

Hundreds of my own little experiments have revealed this: *The person who does the most talking and the person who is the most successful are rarely the same person.* Almost without exception, the more successful the person, the more he practices *conversation generosity,* that is, he encourages the other person to talk about himself, *his* views, *his* accomplishments, *his* family, *his* job, *his* problems.

Conversation generosity paves the way to greater success in two important ways:

1. Conversation generosity wins friends.

2. Conversation generosity helps you learn more about people.

Remember this: the average person would rather talk about himself than anything else in this world. When you give him the chance, he likes you for it. Conversation generosity is the easiest, simplest, and surest way there is to win a friend.

The second benefit of conversation generosity, learning more about other people, is important, too. As we said in Chapter 1, *people* are what we study in our success lab. The more we can learn about them, their thought processes, their strong and weak points, why they do what and as they do, the better equipped we are to influence them effectively, in the way that we want.

Let me illustrate.

A large New York advertising agency, like all advertising agencies, specializes of course in *telling* the public why it should buy the products it advertises. But this agency does something else, too. It requires its copywriters to spend one week each year behind counters so they can *listen* to what people say about the products they promote. *Listening* provides the clues these copywriters need to write better, more effective ads.

Many progressive businesses conduct so-called terminal interviews with employees who are leaving. The reason is not to sell the employees on staying with the company but to find out why he is quitting. Then the company can bring about improvements in its employee relations. Listening pays off.

Listening pays off for the salesman, too. Often people think of a good salesman as a "good talker" or a "fast talker." Sales managers, however, are not as impressed by a good talker as they are by a good listener, a fellow who can ask questions and get desired answers.

Don't be a conversation hog. Listen, win friends, and learn.

Courtesy practiced in every relationship with another person is the finest tranquilizer you can use. No commercial preparation is one tenth as effective in relaxing you as doing little things for other people. Thinking right toward people removes frustrations and stress. When you boil it all down, the big cause of stress is negative feelings toward other people. So think positive toward people and discover how wonderful, really wonderful this world is.

The real test for thinking right toward people comes when things don't go exactly the way we want. How do you think when you're passed up for a promotion? Or when you fail to win an office in a club you belong to? Or when you're criticized for the job you've done? Remember this: *how you think when you lose determines how long it will be until you win.*

The answer for thinking right toward people when things don't go exactly our way comes from Benjamin Fairless, one of the century's most outstanding persons. Mr. Fairless, who rose from very modest circumstances to become chief executive of the United States Steel Corporation, said this (quoted in *Life* magazine, October 15, 1956):

"It depends on how you look at things. For example, I never had a teacher I hated. Naturally I was disciplined just like every other pupil, but I always figured it was my fault that the discipline was necessary. I have also liked every boss I ever had. I always tried to please him and do more than he expected if I possibly could, never less.

"I have had some disappointments, times when I greatly wanted a promotion and somebody else got it. But I never figured that I was the victim of 'office politics' or prejudice or bad judgment on the boss's part. Instead of sulking or quitting in a huff, I reasoned things out. Obviously the other fellow deserved the promotion more than I did. What could I do to make myself deserving of the next opportunity? At the same time I never got angry with myself for losing and never wasted any time berating myself."

Remember Benjamin Fairless when things go wrong. Just do two things:

1. Ask yourself, "What can I do to make myself more deserving of the next opportunity?"

2. Don't waste time and energy being discouraged. Don't berate yourself. Plan to win next time.

IN A CAPSULE, PUT THESE PRINCIPLES TO WORK

1. Make yourself lighter to lift. Be likable. Practice being the kind of person people like. This wins their support and puts fuel in your success-building program.

2. Take the initiative in building friendships. Introduce yourself to others at every opportunity. Make sure you get the other person's name straight, and make certain he gets your name straight too. Drop a personal note to your new friends you want to get to know better.

3. Accept human differences and limitations. Don't expect anyone to be perfect. Remember, the other person has a right to be different. And don't be a reformer.

4. Tune in Channel P, the Good Thoughts Station. Find qualities to like and admire in a person, not things to dislike. And don't let others prejudice your thinking about a third person. Think positive thoughts towards people—and get positive results.

5. Practice conversation generosity. Be like successful people. Encourage others to talk. Let the other person talk to you about *his* views, *his* opinions, *his* accomplishments.

6. Practice courtesy *all* the time. It makes other people feel better. It makes *you* feel better too.

7. Don't blame others when you receive a setback. Remember, how you think when you lose determines how long it will be until you win.

10

GET THE ACTION HABIT

HERE'S SOMETHING LEADERS IN every field agree on: There is a shortage of top-flight, expertly qualified persons to fill key positions. There really is, as the saying goes, plenty of room at the top. As one executive explained, there are many almost-qualified people, but there is one success ingredient often missing. That is the ability to get things done, to get results.

Every big job—whether it be operating a business, high-level selling, in science, the military, or the government—requires a man who thinks action. Principal executives, looking for a key person, demand answers to questions like "Will he *do* the job?" "Will he *follow through?*" "Is he a *self-starter?*" "Can he get results, or is he just a talker?"

All these questions have one aim: to find out if the fellow is a man of action.

Excellent ideas are not enough. An only fair idea acted upon, and developed, is 100 percent better than a terrific idea that dies because it isn't followed up.

The great self-made merchant John Wanamaker often said, "Nothing comes merely by thinking about it."

Think of it. Everything we have in this world, from satellites to skyscrapers to baby food, is just *an idea acted upon*.

As you study people—both the successful and the just average—you find they fall into two classes. The successful are active; we'll call them activationists. The just average, the mediocre, the unsuccessful are passive. We'll call them passivationists.

We can discover a success principle by studying both groups. Mr. Activationist is a doer. He takes action, gets things done, follows through on ideas and plans. Mr. Passivationist is a "don'ter." He postpones doing things until he has proved he shouldn't or can't do them or until it's too late.

The difference between Mr. Activationist and Mr. Passivationist shows through in countless little ways. Mr. Activationist plans a vacation. He takes it. Mr. Passivationist plans a vacation. But he postpones it until "next" year. Mr. A. decides he should attend church regularly. He does. Mr. P thinks it's a good idea to go to church regularly too, but he finds ways to postpone acquiring this new habit. Mr. A. feels that he should drop a note to someone he knows to congratulate him on some achievement. He writes the note. Under the same circumstances, Mr. P. finds a good reason to put off writing the note and it never gets written.

The difference shows up in big things too. Mr. A. wants to go into business for himself. He does. Mr. P. also wants to go into business for himself, but he discovers just in the nick of time a "good" reason why he had better not. Mr. A., age forty, decides he wants to take up a new line of work. He does. The same idea occurs to Mr. P., but he debates himself out of doing anything about it.

The difference between Messrs. Activationist and Passivationist shows through in all forms of behavior. Mr. A. gets the things done he wants done, and as by-products he gains confidence, a feeling of inner security, self-reliance, and more income. Mr. P. doesn't get the things done he wants done because he won't act. As by-products he loses confidence in himself, destroys his self-reliance, lives in mediocrity.

Mr. Activationist *does*. Mr. Passivationist *is going to do but doesn't*.

Everyone wants to be an activationist. So let's get the action habit.

A lot of passivationists got that way because they insisted on waiting until everything was 100 percent favorable before they took action. Perfection is highly desirable. But nothing man-made or man-designed is, or can be, absolutely perfect. So to wait for the perfect set of conditions is to wait forever.

Below are three case histories that show how three persons reacted to "conditions."

CASE NO. 1: WHY G. N. HASN'T MARRIED

Mr. G. N. is now in his late thirties, is well educated, works as an accountant, and lives alone in Chicago. G. N.'s big desire is to get married. He wants love, companionship, a home, children, the works. G. N. has been close to marriage; once he was only one day away. But each time he has been near marriage, he discovers something wrong with the girl he's about to marry. ("Just in time, before I made an awful mistake.")

One instance stands out: Two years ago, G. N. thought he finally had met just the right girl. She was attractive, pleasant, intelligent. But G. N. had to be absolutely sure that marriage was the right thing. As they were discussing marriage plans one evening, the future Mrs. G. N. made a few remarks that bothered G. N.

So, to make certain he was marrying the right girl, G. N. drew up a four-page document of stipulations she was to agree to before they got married. The document, neatly typed and looking very legal, covered every segment of living G. N. could think of. There was one section on religion: what church they would go to, how often they would attend, how much they would donate. Another section covered children: how many and when.

In detail, G. N. outlined the kind of friends they would have, his future wife's employment status, where they would live, how their income would be spent. To finish the document, G. N. devoted half a page to listing specific habits the girl must break or must acquire. This covered such habits as smoking, drinking, makeup, entertainment, and so on.

When G. N.'s prospective bride reviewed his ultimatum, she did what you would expect. She sent it back with a note saying, "The usual marriage clause, 'for better or for worse,' is good enough for everyone else and it's good enough for me. The whole thing is off."

As G. N. was relating his experience to me, he said worriedly, "Now, what was so wrong in writing out this agreement? After all, marriage is a big step. You can't be too careful."

But G. N. was wrong. You *can* be too careful, too cautious, not only in planning a marriage but in planning anything in the world where things get done. The standards can be too high. G. N.'s approach to marriage was very much like his approach to his work, his savings, his friendships, everything else.

The test of a successful person is not an ability to eliminate all problems before they arise, but to meet and work out difficulties when they do arise. We must be willing to make an intelligent compromise with perfection lest we wait forever before taking action. It's still good advice to cross bridges as we come to them.

CASE NO. 2: WHY J. M. LIVES IN A NEW HOME

In every big decision, the mind battles with itself—to act or not to act, to do or not to do. Here's how one young fellow elected to act and reaped big rewards.

J. M.'s situation is similar to that of a million other young men. He is in his twenties, has a wife and child, and still has only a modest income.

Mr. and Mrs. J. M. lived in a small apartment. Both wanted a new home. They wanted the advantage of more space, cleaner surroundings, a place for the youngster to play, and a chance to build up equity in their own property.

But there was a hitch to buying a new home—the down payment. One day as J. M. was writing next month's rent check he became very disgusted with himself. He observed that the rent payment was as much as monthly payments on a new home.

J. M. called his wife and said, "How would you like to buy a new home next week?" "What's got into you?" she asked. "Why make jokes? You know we can't. We haven't even got the money for the down payment."

But J. M. was determined. "There are hundreds of thousands of couples like us who are going to buy a new home 'someday,' but only about half of them ever do. Something always comes up to stop them. We're going to buy a home. I don't know yet how we'll raise the down payment, but we will."

Well, the next week they found a house they both liked, quite unpretentious but nice, for $1,200 down. Now the obstacle was to find a way to raise $1,200. J. M. knew he couldn't borrow it through the usual channels, for this would encumber his credit so that he couldn't get a mortgage for the sale price.

Where there's a will there's always a way. Suddenly, J. M. got a brainstorm: Why not contact the builder and work out a private loan arrangement for $1,200? This J. M. did. At first, the builder was cold to the idea, but J. M. persisted. Finally, it was agreed. The builder would, in effect, advance J. M. the $1,200, to be repaid at $100 a month plus interest.

Now all J. M. had to do was to "find" $100 a month. Mr. and Mrs. J. M. sharpened their pencils and figured out a way to cut expenditures $25 a month. But that still left $75, which J. M. would have to raise each month.

Then J. M. got another idea. The next morning he went in to see his boss. He explained to his employer what he was doing. His boss was glad to learn that J. M. was going to buy a new home.

Then J. M. said, "Look, Mr. T., to work this deal out, I've got to earn at least $75 more each month. Now, I know," J. M. continued, "you'll give me a raise when you feel that I deserve it. What I want now is just a chance to earn more money. There are some things around here that could best be done on weekends. Will you make it possible for me to work then?"

The employer was impressed with J. M.'s sincerity and ambition. He proposed a way for J. M. to work ten extra hours each weekend, and Mr. and Mrs. J. M. moved into their new home.

1. The resolution to take action ignited J. M.'s mind to think of ways to accomplish his goal.

2. J. M. gained tremendously in new confidence. It will be much easier for him to take action in other major situations.

3. J. M. provided his wife and child the living standard they deserved. Had he waited, postponed buying the house until conditions were perfect, there is a real possibility they never would have owned a home of their own.

CASE NO. 3: C. D. WANTED TO START HIS OWN BUSINESS, BUT . . .

Mr. C. D. represents another case of what happens to big ideas when one waits until conditions are perfect before taking action on those ideas.

Shortly after World War II, C. D. got a job with the Customs Division of the U.S. Post Office Department. He liked his work, but after five years he became dissatisfied with the confinement, regular hours, low pay, and the seniority system with its relatively narrow chances for advancement.

Then he got an idea. He had learned a great deal about what it takes to be a successful importer. Why not set himself up in the business of importing low-cost gift items and toys? C. D. knew many successful importers who didn't have his knowledge of the ins and outs of this business.

It's been ten years now since C. D. decided he wanted to go into business for himself. But today, he's still working for the Customs Office.

Why? Well, every time C. D. was just about ready to cut loose on his own, something happened that stopped him from taking action. Lack of money, economic recession, new baby, need for temporary security, trade restrictions, and more excuses all served as reasons for waiting, for postponing.

The real truth is that C. D. let himself develop into a passivationist. He wanted conditions to be perfect before he took action. Since conditions were never perfect, C. D. never took action.

Here are two things to do to help you avoid the costly mistake of waiting until conditions are perfect before you act:

1. Expect future obstacles and difficulties. Every venture presents risks, problems, and uncertainties. Let's suppose you wanted to drive your car from Chicago to Los Angeles, but you insisted on waiting until you had absolute assurance that there would be no detours, no motor trouble, no bad weather, no drunken drivers, no risk of any kind. When would you start? *Never!* In planning your trip to Los Angeles it makes sense to map your route, check your car, in other ways to eliminate as much risk as possible before you start. But you can't eliminate all risks.

2. Meet problems and obstacles as they arise. The test of a successful person is not the ability to eliminate all problems before he takes action, but rather the ability to find solutions to difficulties when he encounters them. In business,

marriage, or in any activity, cross bridges when you come to them.

We can't buy an insurance policy against all problems.

Make up your mind to do something about your ideas. Five or six years ago a very capable professor told me of his plans for writing a book, a biography of a controversial personality of a few decades ago. His ideas were more than interesting; they were alive, fascinating. The professor knew what he wanted to say, and he had the skill and energy to say it. The project was destined to reward him with much inner satisfaction, prestige, and money.

Last spring I saw my friend again, and I innocently asked him whether the book was about finished. (This was a blunder; it opened up an old wound.)

No, he hadn't written the book. He struggled with himself for a moment as if he were debating with himself whether to explain why. Finally he explained that he had been too busy, he had more "responsibilities" and just couldn't get to it.

In reality, what the professor had done was to bury the idea deep in his mental graveyard. He let his mind grow negative thoughts. He visualized the tremendous work and sacrifices that would be involved. He saw all sorts of reasons why the project would fail.

Ideas are important. Let's make no mistake about that. We *must* have ideas to create and improve anything. Success shuns the man who lacks ideas.

But let's make no mistakes about this point either. Ideas in themselves are not enough. That idea for getting more business, for simplifying work procedures, is of value only when it is acted upon.

Every day thousands of people bury good ideas because they are afraid to act on them.

And afterward, the ghosts of those ideas come back to haunt them.

Put these two thoughts deep in your mind. First, give your ideas value by acting on them. Regardless of how good the idea, unless you do something with it, you gain nothing.

Second, act on your ideas and gain mind tranquillity. Someone once said that the saddest words of tongue or pen are these: it might have been. Every day you hear someone saying something like "Had I gone into business seven years ago, I'd sure be sitting pretty now." Or "I had a hunch it would work out like that. I wish I had done something about it." A good idea if not acted upon produces terrible psychological pain. But a good idea acted upon brings enormous mental satisfaction.

Got a good idea? Then do something about it.

Use action to cure fear and gain confidence. Here's something to remember. Action feeds and strengthens confidence; inaction in all forms feeds fear. To fight fear, *act*. To increase fear—wait, put off, postpone.

Once I heard a young paratrooper instructor explain, "The jump really isn't so bad. It's the waiting to jump that gets a fellow. On the trip to the jump site I always try to make the time pass quickly for the men. It's happened more than once that a trainee thought too much about what may happen and panicked. If we can't get him to jump the next trip, he's through as a paratrooper. Instead of gaining confidence, the longer he postpones the jump, the more scared he gets."

Waiting even makes the experts nervous. *Time* magazine reported that Edward R. Murrow, the nation's top newscaster, perspires and is on edge just before he telecasts. But once he's in action, fear disappears. Many veteran actors experience the same sensation. They agree that the only cure for stage fright is action. Getting right out there before the audience is the cure for dread, worry, fear.

Action cures fear. One evening we were visiting in a friend's home when their five-year-old boy, who had been put to bed thirty minutes before, cried out. The youngster had been over-stimulated by a science fiction film and was afraid the little green monsters were going to enter his room and kidnap him. I was intrigued by the way the boy's father relieved the lad's worry. He didn't say, "Don't worry, son, nothing is going to get you. Go back to sleep." Instead he took positive action. He made quite a show for the boy by inspecting the windows to be sure they were tight. Then he picked up one of the boy's plastic guns and put it on a table beside his bed and said, "Billy, here's a gun for you just in case." The little fellow had a look of complete relief. Four minutes later he was fast asleep.

Many physicians give neutral, harmless "medication" to people who insist they've got to have something to make them sleep. To lots of folks the act of swallowing a pill, even though (unknown to them) the pill has no medication, makes them feel better.

It's perfectly natural to experience fear in one of many forms. But the usual methods of combating it simply don't work. I've been with many salesmen who tried to cure fear, which creeps up on even the most experienced of them at times, by going around the block a few times or drinking extra coffee. But these things don't get results. The way to combat that kind of fear—yes, any kind of fear—yes, *any* kind of fear—is *action*.

Dread making a certain phone call? Make it, and dread disappears. Put it off, and it will get harder and harder to make.

Dread going to a doctor for a checkup? Go, and your worry vanishes. Chances are nothing serious is wrong with you, and if there is, you know where you stand. Put off that checkup, and you feed your fear until it may grow so strong that you actually are sick.

Dread discussing a problem with your superior? Discuss it, and discover how those worries are conquered.

Build *confidence*. Destroy *fear* through *action*.

START YOUR MENTAL ENGINE—MECHANICALLY

An aspiring young writer who wasn't experiencing success made this confession: "My trouble is, whole days and weeks pass that I can't get a thing written.

"You see," he remarked, "writing is creative. You've got to be inspired. Your spirit must move you."

True, writing is creative, but here's how another creative man, also a writer, explained his "secret" for producing quantities of successful material.

"I use a 'mind force' technique," he began. "I've got deadlines to meet, and I can't wait for my spirit to move me. I've got to move my spirit. Here's how my method works. I make myself sit down at my desk. Then I pick up a pencil and go through mechanical motions of writing. I put down anything. I doodle. I get my fingers and arm in motion, and sooner or later, without my being conscious of it, my mind gets on the right track.

"Sometimes, of course, I get ideas out of the blue when I'm not trying to write," he went on, "but these are just bonuses. Most of the good ideas come from just getting to work."

Action must precede action. That's a law of nature. Nothing starts itself, not even the dozens of mechanical gadgets we use daily.

Your home is heated automatically, but you must select (take action) the temperature you want. Your car shifts gears automatically only after you have set the right lever. The same principle applies to mind action. You get your mind in gear to make it produce for you.

A young branch sales manager for a door-to-door sales organization explained how he trained his sales force the "mechanical way" to start each day earlier and more successfully.

"There's a tremendous resistance to the door-to-door salesman, as any one who has ever sold house to house knows," he commented. "And it's hard, even for the veteran salesman, to make that first call in the morning. He knows the odds are pretty good that he'll get some pretty rough treatment before the day is over. So it's natural for him to put off getting started in the morning. He'll drink a couple of extra cups of coffee, maybe cruise around the neighborhood awhile or do a dozen little things to postpone that first call.

"I train each new man this way. I explain to him that the only way to start is to start. Don't deliberate. Don't postpone getting started. Do this: Just park your car. Get your sample case. Walk to the door. Ring the bell. Smile. Say 'Good morning,' and make your presentation, all mechanically, without a lot of conscious thought. Start making calls this way and you break the ice. By the second or third call, your mind is sharp and your presentations become effective."

A humorist once said the most difficult problem in life was getting out of a warm bed into a cold room. And he had a point.

The longer you lie there and think how unpleasant it will be to get up, the more difficult it becomes. Even in such a simple operation as this, mechanical action, just throwing off the covers and putting your feet on the floor, defeats dread.

The point is clear. People who get things done in this world don't wait for the spirit to move them; they move the spirit.

Try these two exercises:

1. Use the mechanical way to accomplish simple but sometimes unpleasant business and household chores. Rather than think about the unpleasant features of the task, jump right in and get going without a lot of deliberation.

   Perhaps the most unpleasant household task to most women is washing dishes. My mother is no exception. But she has mastered a mechanical approach to dispensing with this task quickly, so she can return to things she likes to do.

   As she leaves the table, she always mechanically picks up several dishes and, without thinking about the task ahead, just gets started. In just a few minutes she is through. Doesn't this beat stacking dishes and dreading the unpleasant inevitable?

   Do this today: Pick the one thing you like to do least. Then, without letting yourself deliberate on or dread the task, *do* it. That's the most efficient way to handle chores.

2. Next, use the mechanical way to create ideas, map out plans, solve problems, and do other work that requires top mental performance. Rather than wait for the spirit to move you, sit down and move your spirit.

Here's a special technique guaranteed to help you: *Use a pencil and paper.* A simple pencil is the greatest concentration tool money can buy. If I had to choose between an ultrafancy, deeply carpeted, beautifully decorated, soundproof office and a pencil and paper, I'd choose the pencil and paper every time. With a pencil and paper you can tie your mind to a problem.

When you write a thought on paper, your full attention is automatically focused on that thought. That's because the mind is not designed to think one thought and write another at the same time. And when you write on paper, you "write" on your mind, too. Tests prove conclusively that you remember something much longer and much more exactly if you write the thought on paper.

And once you master the pencil-and-paper technique for concentration, you can think in noisy or other distracting situations. When you want to think, start writing or doodling or diagramming. It's an excellent way to move your spirit.

Now is the magic word of success. *Tomorrow, next week, later, sometime, someday* often as not are synonyms for the failure word, *never.* Lots of good dreams never come true because we say, "I'll start someday," when we should say, "I'll start now, *right* now."

Take one example, saving money. Just about everybody agrees that saving money is a good idea. But just because it's a good idea doesn't mean many folks follow an organized savings and investment program. Many people have intentions to save, but only relatively few *act* on these intentions.

Here's how one young couple got into gear with a regular wealth accumulation program. Bill's take-home income was

$1,000 a month, but he and his wife, Janet, spent $1,000 each month too. Both wanted to save, but there were always reasons why they felt they couldn't begin. For years they had promised themselves, "We'll start when we get a raise," "When we've caught up with our installments," "When we're over the hump," "next month," "next year."

Finally Janet got disgusted with their failure to save. She said to Bill, "Look, do we want to save or don't we?" He replied, "Of course we do, but you know as well as I we can't put aside anything now."

But for once Janet was in a do-or-die mood. "We've been telling ourselves for years we're going to start a savings program. We don't save because we think we can't. Now let's start thinking we *can*. I saw an ad today that shows if we'd save just $100 a month, in fifteen years, we'd have $18,000 plus $6,600 accumulated interest. The ad also said it's easier to spend what's left over after savings than it is to save what's left over after spending. If you're game, let's start with 10 percent of your pay and let's save off the top. We may eat crackers and milk before the month's up, but if we have to, we will."

Bill and Janet were cramped for a few months, but soon they were adjusted to their new budget. Now they feel it's just as much fun to "spend" money on savings as it is to spend it on something else.

Want to write a note to a friend? Do it now. Got an idea you think would help your business? Present it now. Live the advice of Benjamin Franklin: "Don't put off until tomorrow what you can do today."

Remember, thinking in terms of *now* gets things accomplished. But thinking in terms of *someday* or *sometime* usually means failure.

One day I stopped in to see an old business friend. She had just returned from a conference with several of her executives. The moment I looked at her, I could tell there was something she wanted to get off her chest. She had the look of a woman who had suffered real disappointment.

"You know," she said, "I called that conference this morning because I wanted some help on a proposed policy change. But what kind of help did I get? I had six men in there, and only one of them had anything to contribute. Two others talked, but what they said was just an echo of what I had said. It was like talking with a bunch of vegetables. I confess it's hard for me to find out what those fellows think.

"Really," she went on, "you'd think those fellows would speak up and let me know what they think. After all, it directly affects each of them."

My friend didn't get help in the conference. But had you roamed the hall after the meeting broke up, you'd have heard her junior associates making remarks like "I felt like saying . . . ," "Why didn't someone suggest . . . ," "I don't think . . . ," "We ought to go ahead . . ."

So often the vegetables, those who have nothing to say in the conference room, are full of talk after the meeting, when what they've got to say won't make any difference. They're suddenly full of life when it's too late.

Business executives want comment. The fellow who hides his light under a bushel hurts himself.

Get the "speak up" habit. Each time you speak up, you

strengthen yourself. Come forward with your constructive ideas.

We all know how many college students prepare their assignments. With fine intentions, Joe College sets aside a whole evening for some concentrated study. Here is a general pattern of how, too often, the evening is spent.

Joe's ready to begin studying at 7 P.M., but his dinner seems just a bit heavy, so he decides to get in a little TV. A little turns out to be an hour's worth since the program was pretty good. At 8 P.M. he sits down at his desk but gets right back up because he just remembered he promised to call his girl. This shoots another forty minutes (he hadn't talked to her all day). An incoming call takes another twenty minutes. On his way back to his desk Joe is drawn into a Ping-Pong game. Another hour gone. The Ping-Pong makes him feel sweaty, so he takes a shower. Next he needs a snack. The combined effect of the Ping-Pong and the shower have made him hungry.

And so the evening planned with good intentions drifts away. Finally, at 1 A.M., he opens the book, but he's too sleepy to absorb the subject. Finally he surrenders completely. Next morning he tells the professor, "I hope you give me a break. I studied till 2 A.M. for this exam."

Joe College didn't get into action because he spent too much time getting ready to get into action. And Joe College isn't alone in being a victim of "overpreparedness." Joe Salesman, Joe Executive, Joe Professional Worker, Josephine Housewife—they all often try to build strength and get ready with office chats, coffee breaks, sharpening pencils, reading, personal business, getting the desk cleared off, TV, and dozens of other little escape devices.

But there's a way to break this habit. Tell yourself, "I'm in condition *right now* to begin. I can't gain a thing by putting it off. I'll use the 'get ready' time and energy to get going instead."

"What we want more than anything else in our business," an executive in a machine tool company said in an address to a group of sales executives, "is more people who get sound ideas and then push them through. There's not one job in our production and marketing setup that can't be done better, a lot better. I don't want to infer that we're not doing a good job now. We are. But like all progressive companies, we need new products, new markets, new and more efficient ways of doing things. We depend on people with initiative. They're the ball carriers on our team."

Initiative is a special kind of action. It's doing something worthwhile without being told to do it. The person with initiative has a standing invitation to join the high income brackets in every business and profession.

The director of marketing research in a medium-sized drug manufacturing firm told me how he got to be a director of marketing research. It's a good lesson in the power of initiative.

"Five years ago I got an idea," he told me. "I was working then as a sort of missionary salesman, calling on wholesalers. I discovered that one thing we lacked was facts about the consumers we wanted to buy our drug line. I talked about the need for market research to everyone here. At first I got only deaf ears because management couldn't see the need for it.

"I was pretty much obsessed with the idea of marketing research in our company, so I sort of took the bull by the horns. I asked and got permission to prepare a monthly report on 'Facts of Drug Marketing.' I collected information from every source I could find. I kept on with this, and pretty soon management, and the other salesmen, found themselves really interested in what I was doing. Just one year after I started crusading for research, I was relieved of my regular duties and asked to concentrate on developing my ideas.

"The rest," he continued, "was just natural development. Now I've got two assistants, a secretary, and about three times the yearly income I had five years ago."

Here are two special exercises for developing the initiative habit:

1. Be a crusader. When you see something that you believe ought to be done, pick up the ball and run.

A new subdivision not far from where I live was about two-thirds built when expansion came almost to a standstill. A few families with a don't-care attitude had moved in. This prompted several of the finest families in the area to sell their homes (at a loss) and move on. As so often happens, the do-care families caught the don't-care attitude from their don't-care neighbors—everyone, that is, except Harry L. Harry did care, and he decided to crusade for a fine neighborhood.

Harry began by calling together some friends. He pointed out that this subdivision had tremendous potential but that something must be done now or the area would soon be a strictly second-class neighborhood. Harry's enthusiasm and initiative quickly won support. Soon there were clean-up-the-vacant-lots projects. Garden clubs were organized, a massive tree-planting project was started. A playground was built for the youngsters. A community swimming pool was constructed. The don't-care families became eager supporters. The whole subdivision took on new life and new sparkle. It's really a pleasure now to drive through that community. It shows what a crusader can do.

Do you feel your business should develop a new department, make a new product, or in some other way expand? Well, then, crusade for it. Feel your church needs a new building? Crusade for it. Would you like your children's school to have better equipment? Crusade and get it for them.

And you can bank on this: while crusades may start out as one-man crusades, if the idea behind the enterprise is good, soon you'll have lots of support.

Be an activationist and crusade.

2. Be a volunteer. Each of us has been in situations in which we wanted to volunteer for some activity but didn't. Why? Because of fear. Not fear that we couldn't accomplish the task, but rather fear of what our associates would say. The fear of being laughed at, of being called an eager beaver, of being accused of bucking for a raise holds many people back.

It's natural to want to belong, to be accepted, to have group approval. But ask yourself, "Which group do I want to have accept me: the group that laughs because it is secretly jealous or the group that is making progress by doing things?" The right choice is obvious.

The volunteer stands out. He receives special attention. Most important of all, he gives himself an opportunity to show he has special ability and ambition by volunteering. By all means, volunteer for those special assignments.

Think about the leaders you know in business, the military, your community. Do they fit the description of activationist or would you say they are passivationists?

Ten times out of ten they're activationists, people who do things. The fellow who stands on the sidelines, who holds off, who is passive, does not lead. But the doer, the fellow who thinks action, finds others want to follow him.

People place confidence in the fellow who acts. They naturally assume he knows what he is doing.

I've never heard anyone complimented and praised because "he doesn't disturb anyone," "he doesn't take action," or "he waits until he's told what to do."

Have you?

GROW THE ACTION HABIT

Practice these key points:

1. Be an activationist. Be someone who does things. Be a doer, not a don't-er.

2. Don't wait until conditions are perfect. They never will be. Expect future obstacles and difficulties and solve them as they arise.

3. Remember, ideas alone won't bring success. Ideas have value only when you act upon them.

4. Use action to cure fear and gain confidence. Do what you fear, and fear disappears. Just try it and see.

5. Start your mental engine mechanically. Don't wait for the spirit to move you. *Take action,* dig in, and you move the spirit.

6. Think in terms of *now. Tomorrow, next week, later,* and similar words often are synonymous with the failure word, *never.* Be an "I'm starting right now" kind of person.

7. Get down to business—*pronto.* Don't waste time getting ready to act. Start acting instead.

8. Seize the initiative. Be a crusader. Pick up the ball and run. Be a volunteer. Show that you have the ability and ambition to *do.*

Get in gear and go!

11

HOW TO TURN DEFEAT INTO VICTORY

SOCIAL WORKERS AND OTHERS who work on skid row find many differences in age, religious faith, education, and background among the tragic souls who have dropped into America's gutters. Some of these citizens are surprisingly young. Others are old. A sprinkling are college graduates; a few have essentially no formal education. Some are married; others are not. But the people on skid row do have something in common: each one is defeated, whipped, beaten. Each one has encountered situations that conquered him. Each is eager, even anxious, to tell you about the situation that wrecked him, about his own private Waterloo.

These situations cover the waterfront of human experience from "My wife ran out on me" to "I lost everything I had and had no place else to go" to "I did a couple of things that made me a social outcast, so I came down here."

When we move up from skid row into the dominion of Mr. and Mrs. Average American, we see obvious differences in living habits. But again we discover that Mr. Mediocre gives essentially the same reasons to explain his mediocrity as Mr. Skid Row gave to explain his complete collapse. Inside, Mr. Mediocre feels defeated. He has unhealed wounds suffered in situations that beat him. Now he is supercautious. He plods along, ducking the thrill of living victoriously, discontented with himself. He feels beaten but tries hard to endure the sentence of mediocrity that "fate" has handed him.

He, too, has surrendered to defeat, but in a reasonably clean, socially "accepted" way.

Now, when we climb upstairs into the uncrowded world of success, we again discover people from every possible background. Corporate executives, leading ministers, government officials, top men in every field, we discover, come from poor homes, rich homes, broken homes, cotton patches, cornfields, and slums. These people, who lead every branch of our society, have experienced every tough situation you can describe.

It is possible to match every Mr. Skid Row with a Mr. Mediocre and a Mr. Success on every score—age, intelligence, background, nationality, you name it—with one exception. The one thing you can't match them on is their response to defeat.

When the fellow we call Mr. Skid Row got knocked down, he failed to get up again. He just lay there, splattered out. Mr. Mediocre got up to his knees, but he crawled away, and when out of sight, ran in the opposite direction so he'd be sure never to take a beating again.

But Mr. Success reacted differently when he got knocked down. He bounced up, learned a lesson, forgot the beating, and moved upward.

One of my closest friends is an exceptionally successful management consultant. When you walk into his office, you feel that you are really "uptown." The fine furniture, the carpeting, the busy people, the important clients, all tell you his company is prosperous.

A cynic might say, "It must have taken a real con man to put across an operation like this." But the cynic would be wrong. It didn't take a con man. And it didn't take a brilliant man or a wealthy man or a lucky man. All (and I hesitate to use the word *all* because all means so much sometimes) *all it took was a persistent man who never thought he was defeated.*

Behind this prosperous and respected company is the story of a man fighting, battling his way upward: losing ten years' savings in his first six months in business, living in his office several months because he lacked money to pay rent on an apartment, turning down numerous "good" jobs because he wanted more to stay with his idea and make it work, hearing prospects for his service say no a hundred times as often as they said yes . . .

During the seven unbelievably hard years it took him to succeed, I never heard my friend complain once. He'd explain, "Dave, I'm learning. This is competitive business, and because it's intangible, it's hard to sell. But I'm learning how."

And he did.

Once I told my friend that this experience must be taking a lot out of him. But he replied, "No, it's not taking something out of me; it's putting something into me instead."

Check the lives of the people in *Who's Who in America,* and you'll find that those who have succeeded in a major way have been pounded by losing situations. Each person in this elite corps of successful men has encountered opposition, discouragement, setbacks, personal misfortune.

Read the biographies and autobiographies of great people, and again you discover that each of these people could have surrendered to setbacks many times.

Or do this. Learn the background of the president of your company or the mayor of your city, or select any person you consider a real success. When you probe, you'll discover the individual has overcome big, real obstacles.

It is *not* possible to win high-level success without meeting opposition, hardship, and setback. But it *is* possible to use setbacks to propel you forward. Let's see how.

I saw some commercial airline statistics recently showing that there is only one fatality per 10 billion miles flown. Air travel is a magnificently safe way to go these days. Unfortunately, air accidents still occur. But when they do, the Civil Aviation Administration is on the scene quickly to find out what caused the crash. Fragments of metal are picked up from miles around and pieced together. A variety of experts reconstruct what probably happened. Witnesses and survivors are interviewed. The investigation goes on for weeks, months, until the question "What caused this crash?" is answered.

Once the CAA has the answer, immediate steps are taken to prevent a similar accident from happening again. If the crash was caused by a structural defect, other planes of that type must have that defect corrected. Or if certain instruments are found faulty, corrections must be made. Literally hundreds of safety devices on modern aircraft have resulted from CAA investigations.

The CAA studies setbacks to pave the way to safer air travel. And it's obvious that their efforts pay off.

Doctors use setbacks to pave the way to better health and

longer life. Often when a patient dies for an uncertain reason, doctors perform a postmortem to find out why. In this way they learn more about the functioning of the human body, and lives of other people are saved.

A sales executive friend of mine devotes one entire sales meeting a month to helping his salesmen discover why they lost important sales. The lost sale is reconstructed and carefully examined. In this way, the salesman learns how to avoid losing similar sales in the future.

The football coach who wins more games than he loses goes over the details of each game with his team to point out their mistakes. Some coaches have movies made of each game so the team can literally see its bad moves. The purpose: to play the next game better.

CAA officials, successful sales executives, physicians, football coaches, and professionals in every field follow this success principle: *salvage something from every setback.*

When a setback hits us personally, our first impulse is often to become so emotionally upset that we fail to learn the lesson.

Professors know that a student's reaction to a failing grade provides a clue to his success potential. When I was a professor at Wayne State University in Detroit some years ago, I had no choice but to turn in a failing grade for a graduating senior. This was a real blow to the student. He had already made graduation plans, and canceling was embarrassing. He was left with two alternatives: retake and pass the course and receive his degree at a later graduation, or quit school without earning a degree.

I expected that the student would be disappointed, perhaps even somewhat belligerent, when he learned of his setback. I was right. After I explained that his work was far below passing standards, the student admitted that he hadn't put forth a serious effort in the course.

"But," he continued, "my past record is at least average. Can't you consider that?"

I pointed out that I could not, because we measure performance one course at a time. I added that rigid academic codes prohibited changing grades for any reason other than an honest mistake on the part of the professor.

Then the student, realizing that all avenues toward a grade change were closed, became quite angry. "Professor," he said, "I could name fifty people in this city who've succeeded in a big way without taking this course or even knowing about it. What's so blasted important about this course? Why should a few bad marks in one course keep me from getting my degree?

"Thank God," he added, "they don't look at things on the 'outside' like you professors do."

After that remark I paused for about forty-five seconds. (I've learned that when you've been sniped at, one fine way to prevent a war of words is to take a long pause before answering.)

Then I said to my student friend, "Much of what you say is true. There are many, many highly successful people who know absolutely nothing about the subject matter in this course. And it is possible for you to win success without this knowledge. In the total scheme of life, this course content won't make or break you. But your attitude toward this course may."

"What do you mean by that?" he asked.

"Just this," I answered. "Outside they grade you just as we grade you. What counts there just as what counts here is doing the job. Outside they won't promote you or pay you more for doing second-class work."

I paused again to make certain the point got through.

Then I said, "May I make a suggestion? You're highly disappointed now. I can appreciate how you feel. And I don't think any less of you if you're a little sore at me. But look at this experience positively. There's a tremendously important lesson here: if you don't produce, you don't get where you want to go. Learn this lesson, and five years from now you'll regard it as one of the most profitable lessons you learned in all the time you invested here."

I was glad when I learned a few days later that this student had reenrolled for the course. This time he passed with flying colors. Afterward, he made a special call to see me to let me know how much he had appreciated our earlier discussion.

"I learned something from flunking your course the first time," he said. "It may sound odd, but you know, Professor, now I'm glad I did not pass the first time."

We can turn setbacks into victories. Find the lesson, apply it, and then look back on defeat and smile.

Moviegoers will never forget the great Lionel Barrymore. In 1936 Mr. Barrymore broke his hip. The fracture never healed. Most people thought Mr. Barrymore was finished. But not Mr. Barrymore. He used the setback to pave the way to even greater acting success. For the next eighteen years, despite pain that never abated, he played dozens of successful roles in a wheelchair.

On March 15, 1945, W. Colvin Williams was walking behind a tank in France. The tank hit a mine, exploded, and permanently blinded Mr. Williams.

But this didn't stop Mr. Williams from pursuing his goal to be a minister and counselor. When he was graduated from college (and with honors too), Mr. Williams said he thought his blindness "will actually be an asset in my career. I can never judge by appearances. Therefore, I can always give a person a second chance. My blindness keeps me from cutting myself off from a person because of the way he looks. I want to be the kind of person to whom anyone can come and feel secure, to express himself."

Isn't that a magnificent living example of cruel, bitter defeat being turned into victory?

Defeat is *only* a state of mind, and nothing more.

One of my friends, who is a substantial and successful investor in the stock market, carefully appraises each investment decision in the light of his past experiences. One time he told me, "When I first started investing fifteen years ago, I really got singed a few times. Like most amateurs, I wanted to get rich quick. Instead I got broke quick. But that didn't stop me. I knew the basic strengths of the economy and that, over the long pull, well-selected stocks are about the best investment anybody can make.

"So I just regarded those first bad investments as part of the cost of my education," he laughed.

On the other hand, I know a number of people who, having made an unwise investment or two, are strictly "antisecurities." Rather than analyze their mistakes and join in a good thing, they reach the completely false conclusion that investing in common stocks is just a form of gambling and sooner or later everybody loses.

Decide right now to salvage something from every set-back. Next time things seem to go wrong on the job or at home, calm down and find out what caused the trouble. This is the way to avoid making the same error twice.

Being licked is valuable if we learn from it.

We human beings are curious creatures. We're quick to accept full credit for our victories. When we win, we want the world to know about it. It's natural to want others to look at you and say, "There goes the fellow who did such and such."

But human beings are equally quick to blame someone else for each setback. It's natural for salesmen to blame customers when sales are lost. It's natural for executives to blame employees or other executives when things get out of gear. It's natural for husbands to blame wives and wives to blame husbands for quarrels and family problems.

It is true that in this complex world others may trip us. But it is also true that more often than not we trip ourselves. We lose because of personal inadequacy, some personal mistake.

Condition yourself for success this way. Remind yourself that you want to be as nearly perfect as is humanly possible. Be objective. Put yourself in a glass tube and look at yourself as a disinterested third party would look at the situation. See if you have a weakness that you've never noticed before. If you have, take action to correct it. Many people become so accustomed to themselves that they fail to see ways for improvement.

The great Metropolitan Opera star Risë Stevens said in *Reader's Digest* (July 1955) that at the unhappiest moment of her life she received the best advice she's ever had.

Early in her career, Miss Stevens lost the Metropolitan Opera "Auditions of the Air." After losing, Miss Stevens was bitter. "I longed to hear," she said, "that my voice was really better than the other girl's, that the verdict was grossly unfair, that I had just lacked the right connections to win."

But Miss Stevens's teacher didn't coddle her. Instead she said to Miss Stevens, "My dear, have the courage to face your faults."

"Much as I wanted to fall back on self-pity," continued Miss Stevens, "they [those words] kept coming back to me. That night they woke me. I couldn't sleep until I faced my shortcomings. Lying there in the dark, I asked myself, 'Why did I fail?' 'How can I win next time?' and I admitted to myself that my voice range was not as good as it had to be, that I had to perfect my languages, that I must learn more roles."

Miss Stevens went on to say how facing her faults not only helped her to succeed on stage but also helped her win more friends and develop a more pleasing personality.

Being self-critical is constructive. It helps you to build the personal strength and efficiency needed for success. Blaming others is destructive. You gain absolutely nothing from "proving" that someone else is wrong.

Be constructively self-critical. Don't run away from inadequacies. Be like the real professionals. They seek out their faults and weaknesses, then correct them. That's what makes them professionals.

Don't, of course, try to find your faults so you can say to yourself, "Here's another reason I'm a loser."

Instead view your mistakes as "Here's another way to make me a bigger winner."

The great Orville Hubbard once said, "A failure is a man who has blundered but is not able to cash in on the experience."

Often we blame luck for our setbacks. We say, "Well, that's the way the ball bounces," and let it go at that. But stop and think. Balls don't bounce in certain ways for uncertain reasons. The bounce of a ball is determined by three things: the ball, the way it is thrown, and the surface it strikes. Definite physical laws explain the bounce of a ball, not luck.

Suppose the CAA were to issue a report saying, "We're sorry the crash occurred, but folks, that's just the way the ball bounces."

You'd say it's time to get a new CAA. Or suppose a doctor explained to a relative, "I'm awfully sorry. I don't know what happened. It's just one of those things."

You'd switch doctors when you or another relative became ill.

The that's-the-way-the-ball-bounces approach teaches us nothing. We're no better prepared to avoid a duplication of the mistake the next time we face a similar situation. The football coach who takes Saturday's loss with "Well, boys, that's the way the ball bounces" isn't helping his team avoid the same mistakes the next Saturday.

Orville Hubbard, mayor of Dearborn, Michigan, for seventeen consecutive years, is one of the nation's most colorful and respected urban administrators.

For ten years prior to becoming mayor of Dearborn, Mr. Hubbard could have used the "bad luck" excuse and stepped out of politics.

Before becoming a perennial winner, Orville Hubbard was "unlucky" three times in trying to get the nomination for mayor.

Three times he tried to get the nomination for state senator, but failed. Once he was beaten in a race for a congressional nomination.

But Orville Hubbard studied these setbacks. He regarded them as part of his political education. And today he is one of the sharpest, most unbeatable politicians in local government.

Instead of blaming luck, research those setbacks, If you lose, learn. Lots of folks go through life explaining their mediocrity with "hard luck," "tough luck," "sour luck," "bad luck." These people are still like children, immature, searching for sympathy. Without realizing it, they fail to see opportunities to grow bigger, stronger, more self-reliant.

Stop blaming luck. Blaming luck never got anyone where he wanted to go.

A friend who is a literary consultant, writer, and critic chatted with me recently about what it takes to be a successful writer.

"A lot of would-be writers," he explained, "simply aren't serious about wanting to write. They try for a little while but give it up when they discover there is real work involved. I haven't much patience with these people because they're looking for a shortcut and there just isn't one.

"But," he went on, "I don't want to imply that pure persistence is enough. The plain truth is, often it isn't.

"Just now I'm working with a fellow who's written sixty-two short fiction pieces but hasn't sold one. Obviously, he is persistent in his goal to become a writer. But this fellow's problem is that he uses the same basic approach in everything he writes. He's developed a hard format for his stories. He has never experimented with his material—his plots and characters, and perhaps even style. What I'm trying to do now is to get this client to try some new approaches and some new techniques. He has ability, and if he'll do some experimenting, I'm sure he'll sell much of what he writes. But until he does, he'll just go on receiving one rejection slip after another."

The advice of the literary consultant is good. We must have persistence. But persistence is only one of the ingredients of victory. We can try and try, and try and try and try again, and still fail, unless we combine persistence with experimentation.

Edison is credited with being one of America's most persistent scientists. It's reported that he conducted thousands of experiments before he invented the electric lightbulb. But note: Edison conducted *experiments*. He persisted in his goal to develop a lightbulb. But he made that persistence pay off by blending it with experimentation.

Persisting in one way is not a guarantee of victory. But persistence blended with experimentation does guarantee success.

Recently I noticed an article about the continuous search for oil. It said that oil companies study the rock formations carefully before they drill a well. Yet, despite their scientific analysis, seven out of eight wells drilled turn out to be dry holes. Oil companies are persistent in their search for oil, not by digging one hole to ridiculous depths but rather by experimenting with a new well when good judgment says the first well won't produce.

Many ambitious people go through life with admirable persistence and show of ambition, but they fail to succeed because they don't experiment with new approaches. Stay with your goal. Don't waver an inch from it. But don't beat your head against a wall. If you aren't getting results, try a new approach.

People who have bulldog persistence, who can grab something and not let go, have an essential success quality. Here are two suggestions for developing greater power to experiment, the ingredient, that, when blended with persistence, gets results.

1. *Tell yourself,* *"There IS a way."* All thoughts are magnetic. As soon as you tell yourself, "I'm beaten. There's no way to conquer this problem," negative thoughts are attracted, and each of these helps convince you that you are right, that you are whipped.

Believe instead, "There *is* a way to solve this problem," and positive thoughts rush into your mind to help you find a solution.

It's believing there is a way that is important.

Marriage counselors report no success in saving marriages until one and preferably both partners see that it *is* possible to win back happiness.

Psychologists and social workers say an alcoholic is doomed to alcoholism until *he* believes he can beat his thirst.

This year thousands of new businesses are being formed. Five years from now only a small portion will be still in operation. Most of those who fail will say, "Competition was just too much. We had no choice but to quit." The real problem is that when most people hit the *TAR* (things are rough) barrier, they think only defeat and so they are defeated.

When you believe *there is a way* you automatically convert negative energy (let's quit, let's go back) into positive energy (let's keep going, let's move ahead).

A problem, a difficulty, becomes unsolvable only when you think it is unsolvable. Attract solutions by believing solutions are possible. Refuse, simply refuse, to even let yourself say or think that it's impossible.

2. *Back off and start afresh.* Often we stay so close to a problem for so long that we can't see new solutions or new approaches.

An engineer friend was retained a few weeks ago to design a distinctly new aluminum structure; in fact, nothing even resembling it had even been developed, or designed, before. I saw him just a few days ago, and I asked him how his new building was coming along.

"Not too well," he replied. "I guess I haven't spent enough time with my garden this summer. When I live with tough design problems for a long stretch, I've got to get away and let some new ideas soak in.

"You'd be surprised," he continued, "to know how many engineering ideas come to me when I'm just sitting beside a tree holding a water hose on the grass."

President Eisenhower once was asked at a news conference why he took so many weekend vacations. His answer is good advice for everybody who wants to maximize his creative ability. Mr. Eisenhower said, "I do not believe that any individual, whether he is running General Motors or the United States of America, can do the best job just by sitting at a desk and putting his face in a bunch of papers. Actually, the president ought to be trying to keep his mind free of inconsequential details and doing his own thinking on the basic principles and factors . . . so that he can make clear and better judgments."

A former business associate of mine takes a seventy-two-hour out-of-town vacation with his wife once each month. He found this backing off and starting afresh increased his mental efficiency, thereby making him more valuable to his clients.

When you hit a snag, don't throw up the whole project.

Instead, back off, get mentally refreshed. Try something as simple as playing some music or taking a walk or a short nap. Then, when you tackle it again, the solution often comes almost before you know it.

Seeing the good side pays off in big situations, too. A young man told me how he concentrated on seeing the good side when he lost his job. He explained it this way: "I was working for a large credit reporting company. One day I was given short notice to leave. There was an economy wave on, and they dismissed the employees who were 'least valuable' to the company.

"The job didn't pay too well, but by the standards I grew up with, it was pretty good. I really felt terrible for a few hours, but then I decided to look at being bounced as a blessing in disguise. I really didn't like the job much, and had I stayed there, I'd never have gone far. Now I had a chance to find something I really liked to do. It wasn't long until I found a job that I liked a lot better that paid more money, too. Being fired from that credit company was the best thing that ever happened to me."

Remember, you see in any situation what you expect to see. See the good side and conquer defeat. All things *do* work together for good if you'll just develop clear vision.

IN QUICK REVIEW

The difference between success and failure is found in one's attitudes toward setbacks, handicaps, discouragements, and other disappointing situations.

Five guideposts to help you turn defeat into victory are:

1. Study setbacks to pave your way to success. When you lose, learn, and then go on to win next time.

2. Have the courage to be your own constructive critic. Seek out your faults and weaknesses and then correct them. This makes you a professional.

3. Stop blaming luck. Research each setback. Find out what went wrong. Remember, blaming luck never got anyone where he wanted to go.

4. Blend persistence with experimentation. Stay with your goal but don't beat your head against a stone wall. Try new approaches. Experiment.

5. Remember, there *is* a good side in every situation. Find it. See the good side and whip discouragement.

12

USE GOALS TO HELP YOU GROW

EVERY BIT OF HUMAN progress—our inventions big and little, our medical discoveries, our engineering triumphs, our business successes—were first visualized before they became realities. Baby moons circle the earth not because of accidental discoveries but because scientists set "conquer space" as a goal.

A goal is an objective, a purpose. A goal is more than a dream; it's a dream being acted upon. A goal is more than a hazy "Oh, I wish I could." A goal is a clear "This is what I'm working toward."

Nothing happens, no forward steps are taken, until a goal is established. Without goals individuals just wander through life. They stumble along, never knowing where they are going, so they never get anywhere.

Goals are as essential to success as air is to life. No one ever stumbles into success without a goal. No one ever lives without air. Get a clear fix on where you want to go.

Dave Mahoney rose from a low-paying job in the mail room of an advertising agency to an agency vice president at twenty-seven, and president of the Good Humor Company at thirty-three. This is what he says about goals: "The important thing is not where you were or where you are but where you want to get."

The important thing is not where you were or where you are but where you want to get.

The progressive corporation plans company goals ten to fifteen years ahead. Executives who manage leading businesses must ask, "Where do we want our company to be ten years from now?" Then they gauge their efforts accordingly. New plant capacity is built not for today's needs but rather for needs five to ten years in the future. Research is undertaken to develop products that won't appear for a decade or longer.

The modern corporation does not leave its future to chance. Should you?

Each of us can learn a precious lesson from the forward-looking business. We can and should plan at least ten years ahead. You must form an image *now* of the person you want to be ten years from now if you are to become that image. This is a critical thought. Just as the business that neglects to plan ahead will be just another business (if it even survives), the individual who fails to set long-range goals will most certainly be just another person lost in life's shuffle. Without goals we cannot grow.

Let me share with you an example of why we must have long-run goals to achieve real success. Just last week a young man (let me call him F. B.) came to me with a career problem. F. B. looked well mannered and intelligent. He was single and had finished college four years ago.

We talked for a while about what he was doing now, his education, his aptitudes, and general background. Then I said to him, "You came to see me for help on making a job change. What kind of job are you looking for?"

"Well," he said, "that's what I came to see you about. I don't know what I want to do."

His problem, of course, was a very common one. But I realized that just to arrange for the young man to have interviews with several possible employers would not help him. Trial and error is a pretty poor way to select a career. With dozens of career possibilities, the odds of stumbling into the right choice are several dozen to one. I knew I had to help F. B. see that before he starts going some place careerwise, he's got to know where that someplace is.

So I said, "Let's look at your career plan from this angle. Will you describe for me your image of yourself ten years from now?"

F. B., obviously studying the question, finally said, "Well, I guess I want what just about everyone else wants: a good job that pays well and a nice home. Really, though," he continued, "I haven't given it too much thought."

This, I assured him, was quite natural. I went on to explain that his approach to selecting a career was like going to an airline ticket counter and saying "Give me a ticket." The people selling the tickets just can't help you unless you give them a destination. So I said, "And I can't help you find a job until I know what your destination is, and only you can tell me that."

This jarred F. B. into thinking. We spent the next two hours not talking about the merits of different kinds of jobs, but rather discussing how to set goals. F. B. learned, I believe, the most important lesson in career planning: *Before you start out, know where you want to go.*

Like the progressive corporation, plan ahead. You are in a sense a business unit. Your talent, skills, and abilities are your "products." You want to develop your products so they command the highest possible price. Forward planning will do it.

Here are two steps that will help:

First, visualize your future in terms of three departments: work, home, and social. Dividing your life this way keeps you from becoming confused, prevents conflicts, helps you look at the whole picture.

Second, demand of yourself clear, precise answers to these questions: What do I want to accomplish with my life? What do I want to be? and What does it take to satisfy me?

Use the planning guide below to help.

AN IMAGE OF ME, 10 YEARS FROM NOW:
10 YEARS' PLANNING GUIDE

A. *Work Department:* 10 years from now:
1. What income level do I want to attain?
2. What level of responsibility do I seek?
3. How much authority do I want to command?
4. What prestige do I expect to gain from my work?

B. *Home Department:* 10 years from now:
1. What kind of standard of living do I want to provide for my family and myself?
2. What kind of house do I want to live in?
3. What kind of vacations do I want to take?
4. What financial support do I want to give my children in their early adult years?

C. *Social Department:* 10 years from now:
1. What kinds of friends do I want to have?
2. What social groups do I want to join?
3. What community leadership positions would I like to hold?
4. What worthwhile causes do I want to champion?

A few years ago, my young son insisted the two of us build a doghouse for Peanut, an intelligent pup of dubious pedigree and my son's pride and joy. His persistence and enthusiasm won, so we proceeded to build a home Peanut could call her own. Our combined carpentry talent equaled zero, and the end product clearly reflected that fact.

Shortly afterward a good friend stopped by and upon seeing what we had done asked, "What's that you've stuck up there among the trees? That's not a doghouse, is it?" I replied that it was. Then he pointed out just a few of our mistakes and summed it all up with "Why didn't you get a plan? Nobody these days builds a doghouse without a blueprint."

And, please, as you visualize your future, don't be afraid to be blue sky. People these days are measured by the size of their dreams. No one accomplishes more than he sets out to accomplish. So visualize a big future.

Below is a word-for-word excerpt from the life plan of one of my former trainees. Read it. Note how well this fellow visualized his "home" future. As he wrote this, it is obvious he really saw himself in the future.

"My home goal is to own a country estate. The house will be of the typical Southern-manor type, two stories, white columns and all. We will have the grounds fenced in, and probably will have a fishpond or two on the place as my wife and I both enjoy fishing. We will keep our Doberman kennels back of the house somewhere. The thing I have always wanted is a long winding driveway with trees lining each side.

"*But* a house is not necessarily a home. I am going to do everything I can to make our house more than just a place to eat and sleep. Of course, we do not intend to leave God out of our plans and throughout the years we will spend a certain amount of time in church activities.

"Ten years from now I want to be in a position to take a family cruise around the world. I would like very much to do this before the family gets scattered all over the world by marriages, etc. If we can't find time to make the cruise all at once, we will put it into four or five separate vacations and visit a different part of the world each year. Naturally, all these plans in 'home department' depend on how well things go in my 'work department,' so I'll have to keep on the ball if I'm to accomplish all this."

This plan was written five years ago. The trainee then owned two small dimestores. Now he owns five. And he has purchased seventeen acres for his country estate. He's thinking and progressing right along toward his goal.

The three departments of your life are closely interrelated. Each depends on the others to some extent. But the one department that has the most influence over the other departments is your work. Thousands of years ago the caveman who had the happiest home life and was most respected by his cavemates was the fellow who was most successful as a hunter. As a generalization, the same point holds true today. The standard of living we provide our families and the social and community respect we attain depends largely on our success in the work department.

Not long ago the McKinsey Foundation for Management Research conducted a large-scale study to determine what it takes to become an executive. Leaders in business, government, science, and religion were questioned. Over and over again in different ways these researchers kept getting one answer: the most important qualification for an executive is the *sheer desire to get ahead.*

Remember this advice of John Wanamaker: "A man is not doing much until the cause he works for possesses all there is of him."

Desire, when harnessed, is *power*. Failure to follow desire, to do what you want to do most, paves the way to mediocrity.

I recall a conversation with a very promising young writer on a college newspaper. This fellow had ability. If anyone showed promise for a career in journalism, it was he. Shortly before his graduation I asked him, "Well, Dan, what are you going to do, get into some form of journalism?" Dan looked at me and said, "Heck, no! I like writing and reporting very much, and I've had a lot of fun working on the college paper. But journalists are a dime a dozen, and I don't want to starve."

I didn't see or hear from Dan for five years. Then one evening I chanced to meet him in New Orleans. Dan was working as an assistant personnel director for an electronics company. And he was quick to let me know that he was quite dissatisfied with his work. "Oh, I'm reasonably well paid. I'm with a wonderful company, and I've got reasonable security, but you know, my heart isn't in it. I wish now I'd gone with a publisher or newspaper when I finished school."

Dan's attitude reflected boredom, uninterest. He was cynical about many things. He will never achieve maximum success until he quits his present job and gets into journalism. Success requires heart-and-soul effort, and you can put your heart and soul only into something you really desire.

Had Dan followed his desire, he could have risen to the very top in some phase of communication. And over the long pull he would have made much more money and achieved far more personal satisfaction than he will find in his present kind of work.

Switching from what you don't like to do to what you do like to do is like putting a five-hundred-horsepower motor in a ten-year-old car.

All of us have desires. All of us dream of what we really want to do. But few of us actually surrender to desire. Instead of surrendering to desire, we murder it. Five weapons are used to commit success suicide. Destroy them. They're dangerous.

1. *Self-depreciation.* You have heard dozens of people say, "I would like to be a doctor (or an executive or a commercial artist or in business for myself) but I can't do it." "I lack brains." "I'd fail if I tried." "I lack the education and/or experience." Many young folks destroy desire with the old negative self-depreciation.

2. *"Security-itis."* Persons who say, "I've got security where I am" use the security weapons to murder their dreams.

3. *Competition.* "The field is already overcrowded," "People in that field are standing on top of each other" are remarks which kill desire fast.

4. *Parental dictation.* I've heard hundreds of young people explain their career choice with "I'd really like to prepare for something else, but my parents want me to do this so I must." Most parents, I believe, do not intentionally dictate to their children what they must do. What all intelligent parents want is to see their children live successfully. If the young person will patiently explain why he or she prefers a different career, and if the parent will listen, there will be

no friction. The objectives of both the parent and the young person for the young person's career are identical: success.

5. *Family responsibility.* The attitude of "It would have been wise for me to change over five years ago, but now I've got a family and I can't change," illustrates this kind of desire murder weapon.

Throw away those murder weapons! Remember, the only way to get full power, to develop full go force, is to do what you want to do. Surrender to desire and gain energy, enthusiasm, mental zip, and even better health.

And it's never too late to let desire take over.

The overwhelming majority of really successful people work much longer than forty hours a week. And you don't hear them complain of overwork. Successful people have their eyes focused on a goal, and this provides energy.

The point is this: energy increases, multiplies, when you set a desired goal and resolve to work toward that goal. Many people, millions of them, can find new energy by selecting a goal and giving all they've got to accomplish that goal. Goals cure boredom. Goals even cure many chronic ailments.

Let's probe a little deeper into the power of goals. When you surrender yourself to your desires, when you let yourself become obsessed with a goal, you receive the physical power, energy, and enthusiasm needed to accomplish your goal. But you receive something else, something equally valuable. You receive the "automatic instrumentation" needed to keep you going straight to your objective.

The most amazing thing about a deeply entrenched goal is

that it keeps you on course to reach your target. This isn't double-talk. What happens is this. When you surrender to your goal, the goal works itself into your subconscious mind. Your subconscious mind is always in balance. Your conscious mind is not, unless it is in tune with what your subconscious mind is thinking. Without full cooperation from the subconscious mind, a person is hesitant, confused, indecisive. Now, with your goal absorbed into your subconscious mind you react the right way automatically. The conscious mind is free for clear, straight thinking.

Let's illustrate this with two hypothetical persons. As you read on you'll recognize these characters among the real people you know. We'll call them Tom and Jack. These fellows are comparable in all respects except one: Tom has a firmly entrenched goal; Jack does not. Tom has a crystal-clear image of what he wants to be. He pictures himself as a corporation vice president ten years hence.

Because Tom has surrendered to his goal, his goal through his subconscious mind signals to him saying "do this" or "don't do that; it won't help get you where you want to go." The goal constantly speaks, "I am the image you want to make real. Here is what you must do to make me real."

Tom's goal does not pilot him in vague generalities. It gives him specific directions in all his activities. When Tom buys a suit, the goal speaks and shows Tom the wise choice. The goal helps to show Tom what steps to take to move up to the next job, what to say in the business conference, what to do when conflict develops, what to read, what stand to take. Should Tom drift a little off course, his automatic instrumentation, housed securely in his subconscious mind, alerts him and tells him what to do to get back on course.

Tom's goal has made him supersensitive to all the many forces at work that affect him.

Jack, on the other hand, lacking a goal, also lacks the automatic instrumentation to guide him. He is easily confused. His actions reflect no personal policy. Jack wavers, shifts, guesses at what to do. Lacking consistency of purpose, Jack flounders on the rutty road to mediocrity.

May I suggest you reread the above section, right now. Let this concept soak in. Then look around you. Study the very top echelon of successful persons. Note how they, without exception, are totally devoted to their objective. Observe how the life of a highly successful person is integrated around a purpose.

Surrender to that goal. Really surrender. Let it obsess you and give you the automatic instrumentation you need to reach that goal.

On occasion all of us have waked up on Saturday morning with no plans, no agenda either mental or written that spells out what we're going to do. On days like that we accomplish next to nothing. We aimlessly drift through the day, glad when it's finally over. But when we face the day with a plan, we get things done.

This common experience provides an important lesson: to accomplish something, we must plan to accomplish something.

Before World War II our scientists saw the potential power locked in the atom. But relatively little was known about how to split the atom and unleash that tremendous power. When the United States entered the war, forward-looking scientists saw the potential power of an atomic bomb. A crash program was developed to accomplish just one goal: build an atomic bomb. The result is history. In just a few years the concentrated effort paid off. The bombs were dropped, and the war was ended. But without that crash program to accomplish a goal, splitting the atom would have been delayed perhaps a decade, maybe longer.

Set goals to get things done.

Our great production system would be hopelessly bogged down if production executives did not establish and adhere to target dates and production schedules. Sales executives know salesmen sell more when they are given a carefully defined quota to sell. Professors know students get term papers written on time when a deadline is set.

Now, as you press forward to success, set goals: deadlines, target dates, self-imposed quotas. You will accomplish only what you plan to accomplish.

According to Dr. George E. Burch of the Tulane University School of Medicine, an expert in the study of human longevity, many things determine how long you will live: weight, heredity, diet, psychic tension, personal habits. But Dr. Burch says, "The quickest way to the end is to retire and do nothing. Every human being must keep an interest in life just to keep living."

Each of us has a choice. Retirement can be the beginning or the end. The "do nothing but eat, sleep, and rock" attitude is the poison-yourself-fast form of retirement. Most folks who regard retirement as the end of purposeful living soon find retirement is the end of life itself. With nothing to live for, no goals, people waste away fast.

The other extreme, the sensible way to retire, is the "I'm going to pitch right in and start fast" method. One of my finest friends, Lew Gordon, has chosen this way to retire. Lew's retirement several years ago as a vice president of Atlanta's biggest bank was really Commencement Day for him. He established himself as a business consultant. And his pace is amazing.

Now in his sixties, he serves numerous clients and is in national demand as a speaker. One of his special projects is helping to build Pi Sigma Epsilon, a young but fast-growing fraternity for professional salesmen and sales executives. Every time I see Lew he seems younger. He's a young thirty in spirit. Few people I know of any age are reaping more from life than this senior citizen who resolved not to go out to pasture.

And the Lew Gordons aren't the boring old grumps feeling sorry for themselves because they're old.

Goals, intense goals, can keep a person alive when nothing else will. Mrs. D., the mother of a college friend of mine, contracted cancer when her son was only two. To darken matters, her husband had died only three months before her illness was diagnosed. Her physicians offered little hope. But Mrs. D. would not give up. She was determined that she would see her two-year-old son through college by operating a small retail store left her by her husband. There were numerous surgical operations. Each time the doctors would say, "Just a few more months."

The cancer was never cured. But those "few more months" stretched into twenty years. She saw her son graduated from college. Six weeks later she was gone.

A goal, a burning desire, was powerful enough to stave off sure death for two decades.

Use goals to live longer. No medicine in the world—and

your physician will bear this out—is as powerful in bringing about long life as is *the desire to do something.*

The person determined to achieve maximum success learns the principle that *progress is made one step at a time.* A house is built a brick at a time. Football games are won a play at a time. A department store grows bigger one new customer at a time. Every big accomplishment is a series of little accomplishments.

Eric Sevareid, the well-known author and correspondent, reported in *Reader's Digest* (April 1957) that the best advice he ever received was the principle of the "next mile." Here's part of what he said:

"During World War II, I and several others had to parachute from a crippled Army transport plane into the mountainous jungle on the Burma-India border. It was several weeks before an armed relief expedition could reach us, and then we began a painful, plodding march 'out' to civilized India. We were faced by a 140-mile trek, over mountains, in August heat and monsoon rains.

"In the first hour of the march I rammed a boot nail deep into one foot; by evening I had bleeding blisters the size of a 50-cent piece on both feet. Could I hobble 140 miles? Could the others, some in worse shape than I, complete such a distance? We were convinced we could not. But we *could* hobble to that ridge, we *could* make the next friendly village for the night. And that, of course, was all we had to do. . . .

"When I relinquished my job and income to undertake a book of a quarter of a million words, I could not bear to let my mind dwell on the whole scope of the project. I would surely

have abandoned what has become my deepest source of professional pride. I tried to think only of the next paragraph, not the
next page and certainly not the next chapter. Thus, for six solid
months, I never did anything but set down one paragraph after
another. The book 'wrote itself.'

"Years ago, I took on a daily writing and broadcasting chore
that has totaled, now, more than 2000 scripts. Had I been asked
at the time to sign a contract 'to write 2000 scripts' I would have
refused in despair at the enormousness of such an undertaking.
But I was only asked to write one, the next one, and that is all I
have ever done."

The principle of the "next mile" works for Eric Sevareid,
and it will work for you.

The step-by-step method is the only intelligent way to
attain any objective. The best formula I have heard for quitting
smoking, the one that has worked for more of my friends than
any other, I call the hour-by-hour method. Instead of trying to
reach the ultimate goal—freedom from the habit—just by resolv-
ing never to smoke again, the person resolves not to smoke for
another hour. When the hour is up, the smoker simply renews
his resolution not to smoke for *another* hour. Later, as desire
diminishes, the period is extended to two hours, later to a day.
Eventually, the goal is won. The person who wants freedom
from the habit *all at once* fails because the psychological pain is
more than he can stand. An hour is easy; forever is difficult.

Winning any objective requires a step-by-step method. To
the junior executive, each assignment, however insignificant it
may appear, should be viewed as an opportunity to take one step
forward. A salesman qualifies for management responsibilities
one sale at a time.

To the minister each sermon, to the professor each lecture, to the scientist each experiment, to the business executive each conference is an opportunity to take one step forward toward the large goal.

Sometimes it appears that someone achieves success all at once. But if you check the past histories of people who seemed to arrive at the top suddenly, you'll discover a lot of solid groundwork was previously laid. And those "successful" people who lose fame as fast as they found it simply were phonies who had not built a solid foundation.

Just as a beautiful building is created from pieces of stone, each of which in itself appears insignificant, in like manner the successful life is constructed.

Do this: Start marching toward your ultimate goal by making the next task you perform, regardless of how unimportant it may seem, a step in the right direction. Commit this question to memory and use it to evaluate everything you do: *"Will this help take me where I want to go?"* If the answer is no, back off; if yes, press ahead.

It's clear. We do not make one big jump to success. We get there one step at a time. An excellent plan is to set monthly quotas for accomplishment.

Examine yourself. Decide what specific things you should do to make yourself more effective. Use the form below as a guide. Under each of the major headings make notes of the things you will do in the next thirty days. Then, when the thirty-day period is up, check your progress and build a new thirty-day goal. Always keep working on the "little" things to get you in shape for the big things.

THIRTY-DAY IMPROVEMENT GUIDE
Between now and _____ I will

A. Break these habits: (suggestions)
   1. Putting off things.
   2. Negative language.
   3. Watching TV more than 60 minutes per day.
   4. Gossip.

B. Acquire these habits: (suggestions)
   1. A rigid morning examination of my appearance.
   2. Plan each day's work the night before.
   3. Compliment people at every possible opportunity.

C. Increase my value to my employer in these ways: (suggestions)
   1. Do a better job of developing my subordinates.
   2. Learn more about my company, what it does, and the customers it serves.
   3. Make three specific suggestions to help my company become more efficient.

D. Increase my value to my home in these ways: (suggestions)
   1. Show more appreciation for the little things my wife does that I've been taking for granted.
   2. Once each week, do something special with my whole family.
   3. Give one hour each day of my undivided attention to my family.

E. Sharpen my mind in these ways: (suggestions)
1. Invest two hours each week in reading professional magazines in my field.
2. Read one self-help book.
3. Make four new friends.
4. Spend 30 minutes daily in quiet, undisturbed thinking.

Next time you see a particularly well-poised, well-groomed, clear-thinking, effective person, remind yourself that he wasn't born that way. Lots of conscious effort, invested day by day, made the person what he is. Building new positive habits and destroying old negative habits is a day-by-day process.

Create your first thirty-day improvement guide right now.

Often, when I discuss setting goals, someone comments along these lines, "I see that working toward a purpose is important, but so often things happen that upset my plans."

It's true that many factors outside your control do affect your destination. There may be serious illness or death in your family, the job you're gunning for may be dissolved, you may meet with an accident.

So here is a point we must fix firmly in mind: *prepare to take detours in stride.* If you are driving down a road and you come to a "road closed" situation, you wouldn't camp there, nor would you go back home. The road closed simply means you can't go where you want to go on this road. You'd simply find another road to take you where you want to go.

Observe what military leaders do. When they develop a master plan to take an objective, they also map out alternative plans. If something unforeseen happens that rules out plan A, they switch to plan B. You rest easy in an airplane even though the airport where you planned to land is closed in, because you know the fellow up there driving the plane has alternative landing fields and a reserve fuel supply.

It's a rare person who has achieved high-level success who has not had to take detours—many of them.

When we detour, we don't have to change our goals. We just travel a different route.

You've probably heard many persons say something like "Oh, how I wish I had bought XX stock back in 19—. I'd have a pile of money today."

Normally, people think of investing in terms of stocks or bonds, real estate, or some other type of property. But the biggest and most rewarding kind of investment is *self-investment*, purchasing things that build mental power and proficiency.

The progressive business knows that how strong it will be five years from now depends not on what it does five years in the future but rather on what it does, invests, this year. Profit comes from only one source: investment.

There's a lesson for each of us. To profit, to get the extra reward above a "normal" income in the years ahead, we must invest in ourselves. We must invest to achieve our goals.

Here are two sound self-investments that will pay handsome profits in the years ahead:

1. *Invest in education.* True education is the soundest investment you can make in yourself. But let's be sure we understand what education really is. Some folks measure education by the number of years spent in school or the number of diplomas, certificates, and degrees earned. But this quantitative approach to

education doesn't necessarily produce a successful person. Ralph J. Cordiner, chairman of General Electric, expressed the attitude of top business management toward education this way: "Two of our most outstanding presidents, Mr. Wilson and Mr. Coffin, never had an opportunity to attend college. Although some of our present officers have doctor's degrees, twelve out of forty-one have no college degrees. We are interested in competency, not diplomas." A diploma or degree may help you get a job, but it will not guarantee your progress on the job. "Business is interested in competency, not diplomas."

To others, education means the quantity of information a person has stashed away in his brain. But the soak-up-facts method of education won't get you where you want to go. More and more we depend on books, files, and machines to warehouse information. If we can do only what a machine can do, we're in a real fix.

Real education, the kind worth investing in, is that which develops and cultivates your mind. How well educated a person is, is measured by how well his mind is developed—in brief, by how well he thinks.

Anything that improves thinking ability is education. And you can obtain education in many ways. But the most efficient sources of education for most people are nearby colleges and universities. Education is their business.

If you haven't been to college lately, you're in for some wonderful surprises. You'll be pleased at the wide course offerings available. You'll be even more pleased to discover who goes to school after work. Not the phonies, but rather really promising persons, many of whom already hold very responsible positions.

In one evening class of twenty-five persons I conducted recently, there were an owner of a retail chain of twelve stores, two buyers for a national food chain, four graduate engineers, an Air Force colonel, and several others of similar status.

Many people earn degrees in evening programs these days, but the degree, which in the final analysis is only a piece of paper, is not their primary motivation. They are going to school to build their minds, which is a sure way to invest in a better future.

And make no mistake about this. Education is a real bargain. A moderate investment will keep you in school one night each week for a full year. Compute the cost as a percentage of your gross income and then ask yourself, "Isn't my future worth this small investment?"

Why not make an investment decision right now? Call it *School: One Night a Week for Life.* It will keep you progressive, young, alert. It will keep you abreast of your areas of interest. And it will surround you with other people who also are going places.

2. *Invest in idea starters.* Education helps you mold your mind, stretch it, train it to meet new situations and solve problems. Idea starters serve a related purpose. They feed your mind, give you constructive material to think about.

Where are the best sources of idea starters? There are many, but to get a steady supply of high-quality idea material, why not do this: resolve to purchase at least one stimulating book each month and subscribe to two magazines or journals that stress ideas. For only a minor sum and a minimum of time, you can be tuned in to some of the best thinkers available anywhere.

At a luncheon one day I overheard one fellow say, "But it costs too much. I can't afford to take *The Wall Street Journal.*"

His companion, obviously a much more success-minded person, replied, "Well, I've found that I can't afford not to take it."

Again, take your cue from the successful people. Invest in yourself.

LET'S TAKE ACTION

Now in a quick recap, put these success-building principles to work:

1. Get a clear fix on where you want to go. Create an image of yourself ten years from now.

2. Write out your ten-year plan. Your life is too important to be left to chance. Put down on paper what you want to accomplish in your work, your home, and your social departments.

3. Surrender yourself to your desires. Set goals to get more energy. Set goals to get things done. Set goals and discover the real enjoyment of living.

4. Let your major goal be your automatic pilot. When you let your goal absorb you, you'll find yourself making the right decisions to reach your goal.

5. Achieve your goal one step at a time. Regard each task you perform, regardless of how small it may seem, as a step toward your goal.

6. Build thirty-day goals. Day-by-day effort pays off.

7. Take detours in stride. A detour simply means another route. It should never mean surrendering the goal.

8. Invest in yourself. Purchase those things that build mental power and efficiency. Invest in education. Invest in idea starters.

13

HOW TO THINK LIKE A LEADER

REMIND YOURSELF ONCE AGAIN that you are not pulled to high levels of success. Rather, you are *lifted* there by those working beside and below you.

Achieving high-level success requires the support and the cooperation of others. And gaining this support and cooperation of others requires leadership ability. Success and the ability to lead others—that is, getting them to do things they wouldn't do if they were not led—go hand in hand.

The success-producing principles explained in the previous chapters are valuable equipment in helping you develop your leadership capacity. At this point we want to master four special leadership rules or principles that can cause others to do things for us in the executive suite, in business, in social clubs, in the home, anywhere we find people.

These four leadership rules or principles are:

1. Trade minds with the people you want to influence.

2. Think: What is the human way to handle this?

3. Think progress, believe in progress, push for progress.

4. Take time out to confer with yourself and develop your supreme thinking power.

Practicing these rules produces results. Putting them to use in everyday situations takes the mystery out of that gold-plated word, *leadership*.

Let's see how.

LEADERSHIP RULE NUMBER 1: TRADE MINDS WITH THE PEOPLE YOU WANT TO INFLUENCE.

Trading minds with the people you want to influence is a magic way to get others—friends, associates, customers, employees—to act the way you want them to act. Study these two case histories and see why.

Ted B. worked as a television copywriter and director for a large advertising agency. When the agency obtained a new account, a children's shoe manufacturer, Ted was assigned responsibility for developing several TV commercials.

A month or so after the campaign had been launched, it became clear that the advertising was doing little or nothing to increase "product movement" in retail outlets. Attention was focused on the TV commercials, because in most cities only television advertising was used.

Through research of television viewers, they found that about 4 percent of the people thought it was simply a great commercial, "one of the best," these 4 percent said.

The remaining 96 percent were either indifferent to the commercials or, in plain language, thought they "smelled."

Hundreds of comments like these were volunteered: "It's wacky. The rhythm sounds like a New Orleans band at 3 A.M." "My kids like to watch most TV commercials, but when that shoe thing comes on they go to the bathroom or refrigerator." "I think it's too uppity up." "Seems to me someone's trying to be too clever."

Something especially interesting turned up when all the interviews were put together and analyzed. The 4 percent who liked the commercial were people pretty much like Ted in terms of income, education, sophistication, and interests. The remaining 96 percent were definitely in a different socioeconomic class.

Ted's commercials, which cost a lot of money, flopped because Ted thought only of his own interests. He had prepared the commercials thinking of the way he buys shoes, not the way the great majority buys shoes. He developed commercials that pleased him *personally,* not commercials that pleased the great bulk of the people.

The results would have been much different had Ted projected himself into the minds of the masses of ordinary people and asked himself two questions: "If I were a parent, what kind of a commercial would make me want to buy those shoes?" "If I were a child, what kind of a commercial would make me go tell my Mom or Dad that I want those shoes?"

Why Joan failed in retailing

Joan is an intelligent, well-educated, attractive girl of twenty-four. Fresh from college, Joan got a job as an assistant buyer in ready-to-wear goods at a low-to-medium-priced department store. She came highly recommended. "Joan has ambition, talent, and enthusiasm," one letter said. "She is certain to succeed in a big way."

But Joan did not succeed in a "big way." Joan lasted only eight months and then quit retailing for other work.

I knew her buyer well, and one day I asked him what happened.

"Joan is a fine girl, and she has many fine qualities," he said. "But she had one major limitation."

"What was that?" I asked.

"Well, Joan was forever buying merchandise that she liked but most of our customers didn't. She selected styles, colors, materials, and prices she liked without putting herself in the shoes of the people who shop here. When I'd suggest to her that maybe a certain line wasn't right for us, she'd say, 'Oh, they'll love this. I do. I think this will move fast.'

"Joan had been brought up in a well-to-do home. She had been educated to want quality. Price was not important to her. Joan just couldn't see clothing through the eyes of low-to-middle-income people. So the merchandise she bought just wasn't suitable."

The point is this: To get others to do what you want them to do, you must see things through their eyes. When you trade minds, the secret of how to influence other people effectively shows up. A very successful salesman friend told me he spends a lot of time anticipating how prospects will react to his presentation before he gives it. Trading minds with the audience helps the speaker design a more interesting, harder-hitting talk. Trading minds with employees helps the supervisor provide more effective, better received instructions.

A young credit executive explained to me how this technique worked for him.

"When I was brought into this store [a medium-sized clothing store] as assistant credit manager, I was assigned the job of handling all collection correspondence. The collection letters the store had been using greatly disappointed me. They were strong, insulting, and threatening. I read them and thought, 'Brother, I'd be mad as hell if somebody sent me letters like these. I never would pay.' So I just got to work and started writing the kind of letter that would move me to pay an overdue bill if I received it. It worked. By putting myself in the shoes of the overdue customer, so to speak, collections climbed to a record high."

Numerous political candidates lose elections because they fail to look at themselves through the minds of the typical voters. One political candidate for a national office, apparently fully as qualified as his opponent, lost by a tremendous margin for one single reason. He used a vocabulary that only a small percentage of the voters could understand.

His opponent, on the other hand, thought in terms of the voters' interests. When he talked to farmers, he used their language. When he spoke to factory workers, he used words they were easily familiar with. When he spoke on TV, he addressed himself to Mr. Typical Voter, not to Dr. College Professor.

Keep this question in mind: "What would I think of this if I exchanged places with the other person?" It paves the way to more successful action.

Thinking of the interests of the people we want to influence is an excellent thought rule in every situation. A few years ago a small electronics manufacturer developed a fuse that would never blow out. The manufacturer priced the product to sell for $1.25 and then retained an advertising agency to promote it.

The account executive placed in charge of the advertising immediately became intensely enthusiastic. His plan was to blanket the country with mass advertising on TV, radio, and newspapers. "This is it," he said. "We'll sell ten million the first year." His advisers tried to caution him, explaining that fuses are not a popular item, they have no romantic appeal, and people want to get by as cheaply as possible when they buy fuses. "Why not," the advisors said, "use selected magazines and sell it to the high income levels?"

They were overruled, and the mass campaign was under way, only to be called off in six weeks because of "disappointing results."

The trouble was this: the advertising executive looked at the high-priced fuses with his eyes, the eyes of a high-income person. He failed to see the product through the eyes of the mass market income levels. Had he put himself in their position, he would have seen the wisdom of directing the promotion toward the upper income groups and the account would have been saved.

Develop your power to trade minds with the people you want to influence. The exercises below will help.

PRACTICE TRADING MINDS EXERCISES

SITUATION	FOR BEST RESULTS, ASK YOURSELF
1. Giving someone work instructions	"Looking at this from the viewpoint of someone who is new to this, have I made myself clear?"

SITUATION	FOR BEST RESULTS, ASK YOURSELF
2. Writing an advertisement	"If I were a typical prospective buyer, how would I react to this ad?"
3. Telephone manners	"If I were the other person, what would I think of my telephone voice and manners?"
4. Gift	"Is this gift something I would like, or is it something he will like?" (often there is an enormous difference)
5. The way I give orders	"Would I like to carry out orders if they were given to me the way I give them to others?"
6. Child discipline	"If I were the child—considering his age, experience, and emotions—how would I react to this discipline?"
7. My appearance	"What would I think of my superior if he were dressed like me?"
8. Preparing a speech	"Considering the background and interests of the audience, what would I think of this remark?"
9. Entertainment	"If I were my guests, what kinds of food, music, and entertainment would I like best?"

Put the trading minds principle to work for you

1. Consider the other person's situation. Put yourself in his shoes, so to speak. Remember, his interests, income, intelligence, and background may differ considerably from yours.

2. Now ask yourself, "If I were in his situation, how would I react to this?" (Whatever it is you want him to do.)

3. Then take the action that would move you if you were the other person.

LEADERSHIP RULE NUMBER 2: THINK: WHAT IS THE HUMAN WAY TO HANDLE THIS?

People use different approaches to leadership situations. One approach is to assume the position of a dictator. The dictator makes all decisions without consulting those affected. He refuses to hear his subordinates' side of a question because, down deep perhaps, he's afraid the subordinate might be right and this would cause him to lose face.

Dictators don't last long. Employees may fake loyalty for a while, but unrest soon develops. Some of the best employees leave, and those remaining get together and plot against the tyrant. The result is that the organization ceases to function smoothly. This puts the dictator in a bad light with *his* superior.

A second leadership technique is the cold, mechanical, I'm-a-rule-book-operator approach. The fellow using this approach handles everything exactly according to the book. He doesn't recognize that every rule or policy or plan is only a guide for the *usual* cases. This would-be leader treats human beings as machines. And of all things people don't like, perhaps the most disliked is being treated like a machine. The cold, impersonal efficiency expert is not an ideal. The "machines" that work for him develop only part of their energy.

Persons who rise to tremendous leadership heights use a third approach that we call "Being Human."

Several years ago I worked closely with John S., who is an executive in the engineering development section of a large aluminum manufacturer. John had mastered the "be-human" approach and was enjoying its rewards. In dozens of little ways John made his actions say, "You are a human being. I respect you. I'm here to help you in every way I can."

When an individual from another city joined his department, John went to considerable personal inconvenience to help him find suitable housing.

Working through his secretary and two other women employees, he set up office birthday parties for each member of the staff. The thirty minutes or so required for this was not a cost; rather, it was an investment in getting loyalty and output.

When he learned that one of his staff members belonged to a minority faith, John called him in and explained that he would arrange for him to observe his religious holidays that don't coincide with the more common holidays.

When an employee or someone in the employee's family was ill, John remembered. He took time to compliment his staff individually for their off-the-job accomplishments.

But the largest evidence of John's be-human philosophy showed up in the way he handled a dismissal problem. One of the employees who had been hired by John's predecessor simply lacked the aptitude and interest for the work involved.

John handled the problem magnificently. He did not use the conventional procedure of calling the employee into his office and giving him, first, the bad news and then, second, fifteen or thirty days to move out.

Instead, he did two unusual things. First, he explained why it would be to the employee's personal advantage to find a new situation where his aptitudes and interests would be more useful. He worked with the employee and put him in touch with a reputable vocational guidance consultant. Next, he did something else above and beyond the call of duty. He helped the employee find a new job by setting up interviews with executives in other companies where the employee's skills were needed. In just eighteen days after the "dismissal" conference the employee was relocated in a very promising situation.

This dismissal procedure intrigued me, so I asked John to explain his thinking behind it. He explained it this way: "There's an old maxim I've formed and held in my mind," he began. "Whoever is under a man's power is under his protection, too. We never should have hired this man in the first place because he's not cut out for this kind of work. But since we did, the least I could do was help him to relocate.

"Anybody," John continued, "can hire a man. But the test of leadership is how one handles the dismissal. By helping that employee relocate before he left us built up a feeling of job security in everyone in my department. I let them know by example that no one gets dumped on the street as long as I'm here."

Make no mistake. John's be-human brand of leadership paid off. There were no secret gossip sessions about John. He received unquestioned loyalty and support. He had maximum job security because he gave maximum job security to his subordinates.

For about fifteen years I've been close to a fellow I'll call Bob W. Bob is in his late fifties. He came up the hard way. With a hit-or-miss education and no money, Bob found himself out of work in 1931. But he's always been a scrambler. Not one to be idle, Bob started an upholstery shop in his garage. Thanks to his untiring efforts, the business grew, and today it's a modern furniture manufacturing plant with over three hundred employees.

Today Bob is a millionaire. Money and material things have ceased to be a concern. But Bob is rich in other ways too. He's a millionaire in friends, contentment, and satisfaction.

Of Bob's many fine qualities, his tremendous desire to help other people stands out. Bob is *human* and he's a specialist in treating others the way human beings want to be treated.

One day Bob and I were discussing the matter of criticizing people. Bob's human way of doing it is a master formula. Here's the way he put it. "I don't think you could find anybody who would say I'm a softie or a weakling. I run a business. When something isn't going right, I fix it. But it's the way I fix it—that's important. If employees are doing something wrong or are making a mistake, I am doubly careful not to hurt their feelings and make them feel small or embarrassed. I just use four simple steps:

"First, I talk to them privately.

"Second, I praise them for what they are doing well.

"Third, I point out the one thing at the moment that they could do better and I help them find the way.

"Fourth, I praise them again on their good points.

"And this four-step formula works. When I do it this way, people thank me because I've found that's exactly the way they like it. When they walk out of this office, they have been reminded that they are not only pretty good, they can be even better.

"I've been betting on people all my life," Bob says. "And the better I treat them, the more good things happen to me. I honestly don't plan it that way. That's just the way it works out.

"Let me give you an example. Back about, oh, five or six years ago, one of the production men came to work drunk. Pretty soon there was a commotion in the plant. It seems this fellow had taken a five-gallon can of lacquer and was splashing it all over the place. Well, the other workmen took the lacquer away from him, and the plant superintendent escorted him out.

"I walked outside and found him sitting against the building in a kind of stupor. I helped him up, put him in my car, and took him to his home. His wife was frantic. I tried to reassure her that everything would be all right. 'Oh, but you don't understand,' she said. 'Mr. W. [me] doesn't stand for anyone being drunk on the job. Jim's lost his job, and now what will we do?' I told her Jim wouldn't be dismissed. She asked how I knew. The reason, I explained, is because I'm Mr. W.

"She almost fainted. I told her I'd do all I could to help Jim at the plant and I hoped she'd do all she could at home; and just have him on the job in the morning.

"When I got back to the plant, I went down to Jim's department and spoke to Jim's co-workers. I told them, 'You've seen something unpleasant here today, but I want you to forget it. Jim will be back tomorrow. Be kind to him. He's been a good worker for a long time, and we owe it to him to give him another chance.'

"Jim got back on the ball, and his drinking was never again a problem. I soon forgot about the incident. But Jim didn't. Two years ago the headquarters of the local union sent some men here to negotiate the contract for the local. They had some staggering, simply unrealistic demands. Jim—quiet, meek Jim—

suddenly became a leader. He got busy and reminded the fellows in the plant that they'd always gotten a fair deal from Mr. W. and we didn't need outsiders coming to tell us how to run our affairs.

"The outsiders left, and as usual we negotiated our contract like friends, thanks to Jim."

Here are two ways to use the be-human approach to make you a better leader. First, each time you face a difficult matter involving people, ask yourself, *"What is the human way to handle this?"*

Ponder over this question when there is a disagreement among your subordinates or when an employee creates a problem.

Remember Bob W.'s formula for helping others correct their mistakes. Avoid sarcasm. Avoid being cynical. Avoid taking people down a peg or two. Avoid putting others in their place.

Ask, "What is the human way to deal with people?" It always pays—sometimes sooner, sometimes later, but it always pays.

A second way to profit from the be-human rule is to *let your action show you put people first*. Show interest in your subordinates' off-the-job accomplishments. Treat everyone with dignity. Remind yourself that the primary purpose in life is to enjoy it. As a general rule, the more interest you show in a person, the more he will produce for you. And his production is what carries you forward to greater and greater success.

Praise your subordinates to your supervisor by putting in plugs for them at every opportunity. It's an old American custom to admire the fellow who's on the side of the little man. Your subordinates will appreciate your plugs, and their loyalty to you will grow. And do not fear that this will lower your own importance in the eyes of your supervisor. Rather, a man big enough to be humble appears more confident than the insecure man who feels compelled to call attention to his accomplishments. A little modesty goes a long way.

Praise your subordinates personally at every opportunity. Praise them for their cooperation. Praise them for every extra effort they put forth. Praise is the greatest single incentive you can give people, and it costs you nothing. Besides, a write-in vote has often overthrown a powerful, known candidate. You never know when your subordinates can do you a turn by coming to your defense.

Practice praising people.

Rub people the *right* way. Be human.

LEADERSHIP RULE NUMBER 3: THINK PROGRESS, BELIEVE IN PROGRESS, PUSH FOR PROGRESS.

One of the most complimentary things anyone can say about you is "He stands for progress. He's the man for the job."

Promotions in all fields go to individuals who believe in—and push for—progress. Leaders, real leaders, are in short supply. Status-quo-ers (the everything's-all-right-let's-don't-upset-the-apple-cart folks) far outnumber the progressives (the there's-lots-of-room-for-improvement-let's-get-to-work-and-do-it-better people). Join the leadership elite. Develop a forward look.

There are two special things you can do to develop your progressive outlook:

1. Think improvement in everything you do.
2. Think high standards in everything you do.

Several months ago the president of a medium-sized company asked me to help him make an important decision. This executive had built the business by himself and had been functioning as sales manager. Now, with seven salesmen employed, he decided his next step was to promote one of his salesmen to the job of sales manager. He narrowed the choice down to three, all of whom were about equal in experience and sales performance.

My assignment was to spend one day in the field with each man and then report my views on which fellow seemed to be best qualified to lead the group. Each man was told that a consultant would visit him to discuss the overall marketing program. For obvious reasons, they were not told the specific purpose of my visit.

Two of the men reacted pretty much the same way. Both were uncomfortable with me. They seemed to sense that I was there to "change things." Each of these men was a real defender of the status quo. Both approved of the way everything was being done. I raised questions about how the territories were laid out, the compensation program, the sales promotional material—every facet of the marketing effort. But on all points, the response was always "Everything is okay." On specific points these two men explained why the present way couldn't and shouldn't be changed. Summed up, both men wanted the status quo to remain the status quo. One of them said to me as he dropped me by my hotel, "I don't know exactly why you spent the day with me, but tell Mr. M. for me that everything is okay as is. Don't go refiguring anything."

The third man was wonderfully different. He was pleased with the company and proud of its growth. But he was not wholly content. He wanted improvements. All day this third salesman gave me his ideas for getting new business, providing better service to customers, reducing wasted time, revising the compensation plan to give more incentive, all so that he—and the company—would make more. He had mapped out a new advertising campaign he had been thinking about. When I left him, his parting remark was "I sure appreciate the chance to tell someone about some of my ideas. We've got a good outfit, but I believe we can make it better."

My recommendation, of course, was for the third man. It was a recommendation that coincided perfectly with the feelings of the company president. Believe in expansion, efficiency, new products, new processes, better schools, increased prosperity.

Believe in—and push for—progress; and you'll be a leader!

As a youngster, I had an opportunity to see how the different thinking of two leaders can make an amazing difference in the performance of followers.

I attended a country elementary school: eight grades, one teacher, and forty children all jammed together inside four brick walls. A new teacher was always a big deal. Led by the *big* boys—the seventh- and eighth-graders—the pupils set out to see how much they could get away with.

One year there was little more than chaos. Every day there were dozens of the usual school pranks, "wars" of spitballs, and paper airplanes. Then there were the major incidents such as locking the teacher outside the school for half a day at a time, or on another occasion the opposite, barricading her within the building for hours. Another day each boy in the upper grades brought his dog into the schoolroom.

Let me add that these children were not delinquents. Stealing, physical violence, and deliberate harm were not their objectives. They were healthy kids conditioned by vigorous rural living and needing an outlet for their tremendous pent-up energies and ingenuities.

Well, the teacher somehow managed to stay with the school until the end of that year. To no one's surprise, there was a new teacher the following September.

The new teacher extracted strikingly different performance from the children. She appealed to their personal pride and sense of respect. She encouraged them to develop judgment. Each child was assigned a specific responsibility like washing blackboards or cleaning erasers, or practicing paper grading for the younger grades. The new teacher found creative ways to use the energy that had been so misdirected a few months before. Her educational program was centered on building character.

Why did the children act like young devils one year and like young angels the next? The difference was the leader, their teacher. In all honesty, we cannot blame the kids for playing pranks an entire school year. In each instance the teacher set the pace.

The first teacher, deep down, didn't care whether the children made progress. She set no goals for the children. She didn't encourage them. She couldn't control her temper. She didn't like teaching, so the pupils didn't like learning.

But the second teacher had high, positive standards. She sincerely liked the children and wanted them to accomplish much. She considered each one as an individual. She obtained discipline easily because in everything she did, *she* was well disciplined.

And in each case, the pupils adjusted their conduct to fit the examples set by the teachers.

We find this same form of adjustment taking place every day in adult groups. During World War II military chiefs continually observed that the highest morale was not found in units where commanders were "easy," "relaxed," and "lackadaisical." Crack units were led by officers with high standards who enforced military regulations fairly and properly. Military personnel simply do not respect and admire officers with low standards.

College students, too, take their cue from the examples set by the professors. Students under one professor cut classes, copy term papers, and connive in various ways to pass without serious study. But the same students under another professor willingly work extra hard to master the subject.

In business situations we again find individuals patterning their thinking after that of the superior. Study a group of employees closely. Observe their habits, mannerisms, attitudes toward the company, ethics, self-control. Then compare what you find with the behavior of their superior, and you discover amazing similarities.

Every year many corporations that have grown sluggish and are headed downward are rebuilt. And how? By changing a handful of executives at the *top*. Companies (and colleges and churches and clubs and unions and all other types of organizations) are successfully rebuilt from the top down, not from the bottom up. Change the thinking at the top, and you automatically change the thinking at the bottom.

Remember this: when you take over the leadership of a group, the persons in that group immediately begin to adjust themselves to the standards you set. This is most noticeable during the first few weeks. Their big concern is to clue you in, zero you in, find out what you expect of them. They watch every move you make. They think, how much rope will he give me? How does he want it done? What does it take to please him? What will he say if I do this or that?

Once they know, they act accordingly.

Check the example you set. Use this old but ever-accurate quatrain as a guide:

> *What kind of world*
> *would this world be,*
> *If everyone in it*
> *were just like me?*

To add meaning to this self-imposed test, substitute the word *company* for *world* so it reads:

> *What kind of company*
> *would this company be,*
> *If everyone in it*
> *were just like me?*

In similar fashion, ask yourself what kind of club, community, school, church would it be if everyone in it acted like you.

Think, talk, act, live the way you want your subordinates to think, talk, act, live—and they will.

Over a period of time, subordinates tend to become carbon copies of their chief. The simplest way to get high-level performance is to be sure the master copy is worth duplicating.

Am I a Progressive Thinker? Checklist

A. *Do I Think Progressively Toward My Work?*

1. Do I appraise my work with the "how can we do it better?" attitude?
2. Do I praise my company, the people in it, and the products it sells at every possible opportunity?

3. Are my personal standards with reference to the quantity and quality of my output higher now than three or six months ago?

4. Am I setting an excellent example for my subordinates, associates, and others I work with?

B. *Do I Think Progressively Toward My Family?*

1. Is my family happier today than it was three or six months ago?

2. Am I following a plan to improve my family's standard of living?

3. Does my family have an ample variety of stimulating activities outside the home?

4. Do I set an example of "a progressive," a supporter of progress, for my children?

C. *Do I Think Progressively Toward Myself?*

1. Can I honestly say I am a more valuable person today than three or six months ago?

2. Am I following an organized self-improvement program to increase my value to others?

3. Do I have forward-looking goals for at least five years in the future?

4. Am I a booster in every organization or group to which I belong?

D. *Do I Think Progressively Toward My Community?*

1. Have I done anything in the past six months that I honestly feel has improved my community (neighborhood, churches, schools, etc.)?

2. Do I boost worthwhile community projects rather than object, criticize, or complain?
3. Have I ever taken the lead in bringing about some worthwhile improvement in my community?
4. Do I speak well of my neighbors and fellow citizens?

LEADERSHIP RULE NUMBER 4: TAKE TIME OUT TO CONFER WITH YOURSELF AND TAP YOUR SUPREME THINKING POWER.

We usually picture leaders as exceptionally busy people. And they are. Leadership requires being in the thick of things. But while it's usually overlooked, it is noteworthy that leaders spend considerable time alone, alone with nothing but their own thinking apparatus.

Check the lives of the great religious leaders, and you'll find each of them spent considerable time alone. Moses frequently was alone, often for long periods of time. So were Jesus, Buddha, Confucius, Mohammed, Gandhi—every outstanding religious leader in history spent much time in solitude, away from the distractions of life.

Political leaders, too, those who made lasting names in history for good or bad, gained insight through solitude. It is an interesting question whether Franklin D. Roosevelt could have developed his unusual leadership capacities had he not spent much time alone while recovering from his polio attack. Harry Truman spent much time as a boy and as an adult alone on a Missouri farm.

Quite possibly Hitler would never have achieved power had he not spent months in jail alone, where he had time to construct *Mein Kampf,* that brilliantly wicked plan for world conquest that sold the Germans in a blind moment.

Many of the leaders of communism who proved to be so diplomatically skillful—Lenin, Stalin, Marx, and many others—spent time in jail, where they could, without distraction, plan their future moves.

Leading universities require professors to lecture as few as five hours per week so that the professor has time to think.

Many outstanding business executives are surrounded all day by assistants, secretaries, telephones, and reports. But follow them around for 168 hours a week and 720 hours a month, and you discover they spent a surprising amount of time in uninterrupted thought.

The point is this: the successful person in any field takes time out to confer with himself or herself. Leaders use solitude to put the pieces of a problem together, to work out solutions, to plan, and, in one phrase, to do their superthinking.

Many people fail to tap their creative leadership power because they confer with everybody and everything else but themselves. You know this kind of person well. He's the fellow who goes to great lengths *not* to be alone. He goes to extremes to surround himself with people. He can't stand being alone in his office, so he goes prowling to see other people. Seldom does he spend evenings alone. He feels a compelling need to talk with others every waking moment. He devours a huge diet of small talk and gossip.

When this person is forced by circumstances to be physically alone, he finds ways to keep from being mentally alone. At times like these he resorts to television, newspapers, radio, telephone, anything that will take over his thinking process for him. In effect he says, "Here, Mr. TV, Mr. Newspaper, occupy my mind for me. I'm afraid to occupy it with my own thoughts."

Mr. I-can't-stand-to-be-alone shuns independent thought.

He keeps his own mind blacked out. He is, psychologically, scared of his own thoughts. As time goes by, Mr. I-can't-stand-to-be-alone grows increasingly shallow. He makes many ill-considered moves. He fails to develop firmness of purpose, personal stability. He is, unfortunately, ignorant of the superpower lying unused just behind his forehead.

Don't be a Mr. I-can't-stand-to-be-alone. Successful leaders tap their superpower through being alone. You can, too.

Let's see how.

As part of a professional development program I asked thirteen trainees to closet themselves for one hour each day for two weeks. The trainees were asked to shut themselves off from all distractions and think constructively about anything that came to mind.

At the end of two weeks each trainee, without exception, reported the experience proved amazingly practical and worthwhile. One fellow stated that before the managed solitude experiment he was on the verge of a sharp break with another company executive, but through clear thinking he found the source of the problem and the way to correct it. Others reported that they solved problems relating to such varied things as changing jobs, marriage difficulties, buying a home, and selecting a college for a teenage child.

Each trainee enthusiastically reported that he had gained a much better understanding of himself—his strengths and weaknesses—than he had ever had before.

The trainees also discovered something else that is tremendously significant. *They discovered that decisions and observations made alone in managed solitude have an uncanny way of being 100 percent right!* The trainees discovered that when the fog is lifted, the right choice becomes crystal clear.

Managed solitude pays off.

One day recently an associate of mine reversed her stand completely on a troublesome issue. I was curious to know why she had switched her thinking, since the problem was very basic. Her answer went like this. "Well, I haven't been at all clear in my mind as to what we should do. So I got up at 3:30 this morning, fixed a cup of coffee, and just sat on the sofa and thought until 7 A.M. I see the whole matter a lot clearer now. So the only thing for me to do is reverse my stand."

And her new stand proved completely correct.

Resolve now to set aside some time each day (at least thirty minutes) to be completely by yourself.

Perhaps early in the morning before anyone else is stirring about would be best for you. Or perhaps late in the evening would be a better time. The important thing is to select a time when your mind is fresh and when you can be free from distractions.

You can use this time to do two types of thinking: directed and undirected. To do directed thinking, review the major problem facing you. In solitude your mind will study the problem objectively and lead you to the right answer.

To do undirected thinking, just let your mind select what it wishes to think about. In moments like these your subconscious mind taps your memory bank, which in turn feeds your conscious mind. Undirected thinking is very helpful in doing self-evaluation. It helps you get down to the very basic matters like "How can I do better? What should be my next move?"

Remember, the main job of the leader is thinking. And the best preparation for leadership is thinking. Spend some time in managed solitude every day and think yourself to success.

SUMMARY

To be a more effective leader, put these four leader-ship principles to work

1. Trade minds with the people you want to influence. It's easy to get others to do what you want them to do if you'll see things through their eyes. Ask yourself this question before you act: "What would I think of this if I exchanged places with the other person?"

2. Apply the "Be-Human" rule in your dealings with others. Ask, "What is the human way to handle this?" In everything you do, show that you put other people first. Just give other people the kind of treatment you like to receive. You'll be rewarded.

3. Think progress, believe in progress, push for progress. Think improvement in everything you do. Think high standards in everything you do. Over a period of time subordinates tend to become carbon copies of their chief. Be sure the master copy is worth duplicating. Make this a personal resolution: "At home, at work, in community life, if it's progress I'm for it."

4. Take time out to confer with yourself and tap your supreme thinking power. Managed solitude pays off. Use it to release your creative power. Use it to find solutions to personal and business problems. So spend some time alone every day just for thinking. Use the thinking technique all great leaders use: confer with yourself.

HOW TO USE THE MAGIC OF THINKING BIG IN LIFE'S MOST CRUCIAL SITUATIONS

There is magic in thinking big. But it is so easy to forget. When you hit some rough spots, there is danger that your thinking will shrink in size. And when it does, you lose.

Below are some brief guides for staying big when you're tempted to use the small approach.

Perhaps you'll want to put these guides on small cards for even handier reference.

A. When Little People Try to Drive You Down, THINK BIG

To be sure, there are some people who want you to lose, to experience misfortune, to be reprimanded. But these people can't hurt you if you'll remember three things:

1. You win when you refuse to fight petty people. Fighting little people reduces you to their size. Stay big.
2. Expect to be sniped at. It's proof you're growing.
3. Remind yourself that snipers are psychologically sick. Be Big. Feel sorry for them.

Think Big Enough to be immune to the attacks of petty people.

B. When That "I-Haven't-Got-What-It-Takes" Feeling Creeps Up on You, THINK BIG

Remember: if you think you are weak, you are. If you think you're inadequate, you are. If you think you're second-class, you are.

Whip that natural tendency to sell yourself short with these tools:

1. Look important. It helps you think important. How you

look on the outside has a lot to do with how you feel on
the inside.

2. Concentrate on your assets. Build a sell-yourself-to-
yourself commercial *and use it.* Learn to supercharge
yourself. Know your *positive* self.

3. Put other people in proper perspective. The other person
is just another human being, so why be afraid of him?

Think Big Enough to see how good you really are!

C. When an Argument or Quarrel Seems Inevitable, THINK BIG.

Successfully resist the temptation to argue and quarrel by:

1. Asking yourself, "Honestly now, is this thing really
important enough to argue about?"

2. Reminding yourself, you never gain anything from an
argument but you always lose something.

Think Big Enough to see that quarrels, arguments, feuds,
and fusses will never help you get where you want to go.

D. When You Feel Defeated, THINK BIG.

It is not possible to achieve large success without hardships and
setbacks. But it *is* possible to live the rest of your life without
defeat. Big thinkers react to setbacks this way:

1. Regard the setback as a lesson. Learn from it. Research
it. Use it to propel you forward. Salvage something from
every setback.

2. Blend persistence with experimentation. Back off and
start afresh with a new approach.

Think Big Enough to see that defeat is a state of mind, nothing more.

E. When Romance Starts to Slip, THINK BIG

Negative, petty, "She's-(He's)-unfair-to-me-so-I'll-get-even" type of thinking slaughters romance, destroys the affection that can be yours. Do this when things aren't going right in the love department:

1. Concentrate on the biggest qualities in the person you want to love you. Put little things where they belong—in second place.
2. Do something special for your mate—and do it often.

Think Big Enough to find the secret to marital joys.

F. When You Feel Your Progress on the Job Is Slowing Down, THINK BIG

No matter what you do and regardless of your occupation, higher status, higher pay come from one thing: increasing the quality and quantity of your output. Do this:

Think, "I can do better." The best is not unattainable. There is room for doing everything better. Nothing in this world is being done as well as it could be. And when you think, "I can do better," ways to do better will appear. Thinking "I can do better" switches on your creative power.

Think Big Enough to see that if you put service first, money takes care of itself.

In the words of Publilius Syrus:

A wise man will be master of his mind,
A fool will be its slave.

INDEX